The Old Road to Endon

Take the old road
To Endon
With new eyes
Re-appraise the view,
How little we knew.

EDITED BY
ROBERT SPEAKE, MLitt, AdvDipEd

Published by the Department of Adult Education, The University, Keele, Staffs., ST5 5BG

1974

PREFACE

This is the fifth in a series of local histories published by the Department of Adult Education at Keele University. The others deal with Eccleshall, Barlaston, Madeley and Audley. They all spring from the work of university adult education courses, and their excellence is a tribute to the qualities of the part-time adult students and of the tutor.

Perhaps partly because the present is less than enchanting, many people are beginning to take an increased interest in the past, particularly the history of their own localities. We hope that like the others in our series this history will be widely read, and we can promise further local studies in the near future.

Professor ROY SHAW
Director of Adult Education
Keele University

Members of the Endon Local History Course 1971-73 : C Bellamy, E S Bellamy, F Berrisford, T W Cook, M J Goulding, A Hook, D M Hook, H Mear (Mrs), H Mear (Mr), D Myatt, C G Perkin, A Pointon, F R Stubbs, I E Williamson.

FOREWORD TO THE 1994 FACSIMILE EDITION

This book was first published in 1974 as a result of the work of members of the Endon Local History Course arranged by Keele University in 1971-73. Their names are recorded beneath the original preface.

Twenty years later, it is republished in facsimile form by Churnet Valley Books in collaboration with the Endonian Society and with the permission of the Department of Adult and Continuing Education, Keele University.

The year 1994 marks the 150th anniversary of Endon's traditional well-dressing ceremony, and it is appropriate that this history of the village should be re-published to celebrate the event.

Since the original edition was published a number of small errors have been noted, in the light of subsequent research, and these have been included on a page of addenda, or corrected in the text where possible.

The Endonian Society exists to promote an interest in the village and its history, and is always pleased to receive records, photographs or other memorabilia relating to the area.

F.Williamson (President, Endonian Society)
C.G.Perkin (Chairman, Endon Well Dressing Committee)

This fascimile reprint published by
Churnet Valley Books 1994

ISBN   1 897949 06 5

CONTENTS

Chapter   *Page*

   I   Endon: Its setting from the earliest times to the Domesday Survey - - - - - - 5

  II   The Middle Ages - - - - - - 13

 III   Endon from the end of The Middle Ages to 1700 - 27

 IV   Ecclesiastical Developments - - - - - 35

  V   Endon in the Eighteenth Century - - - - 87

 VI   The Tanyard, The Mill, The Houses, The People and the Parish Registers - - - - - - 93

 VII   The Population of Endon - - - - - 117

VIII   Agriculture in Endon - - - - - - 133

 IX   Roads, Railway and Canal - - - - - 143

  X   Endon a century ago - - - - - - 163

 XI   Education - - - - - - - 191

 XII   Well-dressing - - - - - - - 205

XIII   Endon and its neighbour, Brown Edge - - - 215

ACKNOWLEDGEMENTS

We would like to thank the following people who have given valuable assistance or have made records available to those working on the production of this book.

The staffs of the County Record Office, Stafford, the Joint Record Office, Lichfield, The Reference Library, Hanley, and the Leek Public Library; Mr F B Stitt, BA, BLitt, County Archivist; Rev A J Alban, Vicar of Endon; Rev P D S Blake, MA, Vicar of Leek; Rev S J Ramsey and Rev W H Jones, BD; Mr and Mrs W James, Mr and Mrs G Knot, Mr N P Bowcock, MA for help with records of local Methodism, Mr J Charlesworth for help on the Free Mission Brown Edge; the editor of "The Post and Times", Leek; Hill Brothers (Leek) Ltd., for permission to research files; Mr Alan W Jeffery for assistance with material about the canal and for permission to reproduce his diagram and to many scores of people who have openly offered help in a variety of ways.

PARISH OF ENDON WITH STANLEY

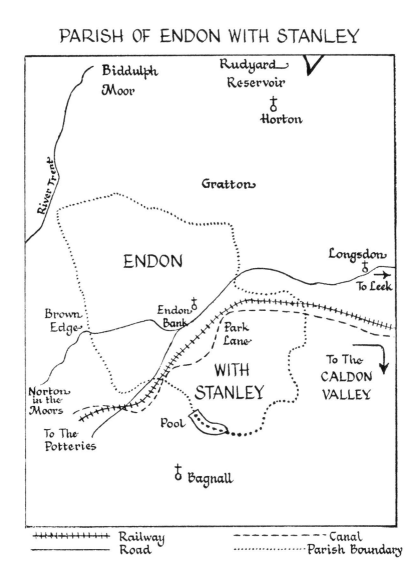

4

Chapter I

ENDON: ITS SETTING FROM THE EARLIEST TIMES TO THE DOMESDAY SURVEY

'... a pleasant scattered village'

S taffordshire is a county of variety where

'... scenery ranges from the untamed grandeur of the northern hills to the industrial squalor of the Potteries and the Black Country, from the barren waste of Cannock Chase to the verdant luxuriance of the dairying country in the Vale of the Dove.'[1]

Endon lies to the extreme north of this county within a few miles of the Derbyshire and Cheshire borders in an area which is the extension of the Pennine Chain and is composed of Carboniferous rocks containing the coal bearing strata which forms the 'Potteries'. This region consists of a series of elongated plateaux running in a south-easterly direction. To the west of the Potteries is a ridge that has made communication in that direction more difficult than those to the south and east; such a feature greatly influencing the turnpike development of later years.

Geologically, this area cannot really be classed as the Midlands, the great Midland Plain being much more uniform in character. Here there are noticeable scenery changes within a few miles, not in the physical features of the landscape, but in, for example, farming methods and building materials. The comparatively high ground of Staffordshire formed a partial barrier to the ice penetration of the Irish Sea ice-sheets which covered the nearby Cheshire Plain. This meant that glacial deposits tend to be discontinuous and thin. Several outliers of Triassic rocks have been found within the area, the largest being to the north and south of Leek. Endon is situated on an area, about a quarter of a mile in diameter, of new red sandstone in the midst of a stratum of millstone grit, responsible for the high ridge running through Brown Edge, Lask Edge to the Cloud. In fact, throughout the whole length of their outcrop the grits can be recognised at a glance by the distinctive features to which they give rise in the Roaches, Axe Edge, Ladderedge, Brown Edge and Congleton Edge.

5

Rocks and soil particularly determine man's way of life in an area, for example, many houses in this area are made of millstone grit, a local stone. It is a non-porous rock causing water to remain on the surface. The whole question of man's vital water-supply is bound up with the nature of rocks, the way in which they affect the circulation of ground water, the formation of natural springs, the sinking of wells to reach the water-holding strata, the amount of surface water run off in the form of rivers (in millstone grit areas the rivers are fast flowing and in the past were vital for the driving of mills, which in turn provided the occupation of building mills and making millstones), and the prospects of natural or artificial storage reservoirs. The rocks of the floor of a hollow to be used as a reservoir should be such that leakage due to permeability is not possible. Within a short walking distance of Endon are three reservoirs: Knypersley, Stanley and Rudyard, built as feeders for the Trent-Mersey Canal; all of which are now local beauty spots.

In the neighbourhood of Endon a considerable area of land is low lying and affords very poor natural drainage facilities. After a period of heavy rain some areas resemble a large lake. The area lies on the watershed forming the natural boundary between Cheshire and Staffordshire; north-west is the Dane flowing across Cheshire to join the Weaver, which in its turn flows west to join the Mersey system, and the Trent which rises on Biddulph Moor one thousand feet above sea level and flows south across moorland country, before it reaches the Midland plain on its way to the East coast.

> 'The English landscape as we know it today is almost entirely a product of the last fifteen hundred years, beginning with the early Anglo-Saxon villages . . . the direct pre-historic contribution is small.'[2]

The thickly wooded landscape through to the Middle Ages caused early man to follow the open ridgeways which rose above the ice sheets. These local ridgeways provided a slight but important link with Knutsford and Macclesfield, a route for the earliest migrations of man from the Mersey Estuary to the Trent Valley. Man by this time was a hunter, fisher and a farmer in a very general sense and the southern Pennines saw the early farming methods in the form of 'summer pastures'. Invaders from the west caused the inhabitants of Britain to seek refuge in the least accessible spots, among which the rugged slopes of the southern Pennine Chain were ideal for this purpose. Early settlers occupied the land in folk groups and gradual developments in their way of life, for example the development of flints, many of which have been found at Alderley Edge, caused these people to become the foundation stock racially and culturally of the area they occupied. They built up places in which they could live. The earliest evidence of human settlement in North Staffordshire comes from the Manifold Valley. Three caves: Thor's cave, Ossum's cave and Thor's fissure have yielded flint instruments which are believed to be of old or middle Stone Age or Iron Age.

From the East, the discovery of bronze smelting crossed Europe and reached Britain in the period 2,000 to 1800 BC. A Bronze Age axe head, said to be dated at approximately 2,000 BC, has been discovered at Moor Hall Farm, Tomkin, near Bagnall and in 1916 an axe head was discovered at Henridding Farm, Endon, both are now in Hanley Museum.[3]

About this period was also the Beaker Age. People from Europe infiltrated into Britain along the river valleys, bringing with them the distinctively decorated beakers. Associated with these Beaker Folk were semi-nomadic traders who placed food vessels in the grave with the dead, as found on the hills near Wetton and Caldon.

Another tribe of people were more ambitious and left behind such megaliths as the Bridestones near Biddulph and the Devil's Ring and Finger near Mucklestone to remind us of their culture.[4] The Bridestones were built about two thousand seven hundred and fifty years ago, at a height of eight hundred and twenty feet above sea level, near to a pass through the western foothills of the Pennines to and from the Mersey to the Trent Valley in the location described thus:

> 'The spot lies between Leek and Congleton within one hundred yards north of the Turnpike Road, three miles from Congleton and seven miles from Leek, on the back of a hill called Cloud, which frowns over the Cheshire Plain and seems a well-chosen seat from which the Arch Druid might survey a large portion of his Cornavian domains.'[5]

Thus we seem to have proof in the surrounding area of Druidical occupation. Possibly they were altars for the celebration of marriage rites and were eventually called by their present name by the Saxons who knew, by tradition, the purposes for which they had been used. A more likely supposition is that they were altars of sacrifice and probably tombs of chief Druids. The stones are placed in a position that runs in a line due east to west, an ancient custom of burial before Christianity. There are accounts of tumuli of loose stones being carried away when the neighbouring turnpike was built.

7

The Roman contribution to the landscape was hardly any more substantial than contributions made in pre-Roman years.

The network of major Roman roads is well-known and a large system of secondary roads gradually came into existence to serve local needs. The Roman road systems, both the main roads and the local roads were very important in the history of the English landscape, not only do many still survive as trunk roads, for example Watling Street, or as useful secondary roads between villages, but they opened up, in their time, whole tracts of countryside on a scale hitherto unknown. Even the lesser local roads pushed through the forested clay lands in all directions and crossed the high moorlands. Among these roads is a Roman road traced from Derby to Stoke, which then disappears to reappear again at Wolstanton en route for the Roman site at Chesterton, a distance of just over thirty miles. There is also the Buxton to Leek road which probably continued to Longton where it would connect with the road from Derby.[6] It follows the Axe Edge-Oliver Hill route and then on to Leek. The present road follows the same route except for a sharp bend at Oliver Hill. Buxton was an important Roman centre, built as a result of their desire to part-take of the properties of the waters. The centre was mainly used for the military. Thus the nearest that Endon lies to the Roman road system of this area is five to five and a half miles, though Sleigh writing in his history of Leek states that 'the only traceable Roman road in the neighbourhood is that from Buxton via Laidman Lowe, Axe Edge, Flash, Bramcote, Upper Tittesworth and Leek to Medialanum, i.e. Chesterton. But the trail of the Roman has often been struck hereabout.'[7]

To the north of this area, in Lancashire and Yorkshire, lived the famous Brigantes a tribe whose presence and activities generally caused the Romans to regard the area as a military zone and possibly used Chesterton as a training and resting base for soldiers from the north. The Roman forts were generally twenty miles apart, an easy distance for marching soldiers to return to safety at nightfall. Another Roman site has been discovered at Holditch, a few miles to the west of Endon, but it appears to have been more of a settlement, in the evidence supplied by the traces of coal-fired pottery kilns, than the more conventional fort and training camp of Chesterton.

A further invasion of these islands began in 449 AD with the arrival of the Angles and Saxons at Pegwell Bay. In twenty years they conquered Kent and began to settle in Sussex, Wessex, Essex and Anglia as families in small groups. In 613 AD the battle of Chester finally fixed the western limits, the Welsh were beaten and the first boundary of Mercia, land of the Middle Angles, was fixed between the Anglo-Saxons and the Celts. Nothing is known of local government in Staffordshire under the Romans, but through the inheritance of, for example, place-names, we can begin to build up a picture of life at this time. The Anglo-Saxons established an orderly society in England and created 'Hundreds'; thereby the head of the family or the family name began to prefix 'Ley', 'Ham', or 'Ton' in place-names, as in Heakley and Baddeley. The 'Hundreds' were established for adminis-trative purposes. The basic unit of government under the Saxons was the Vill headed by the Reeve, elected or approved by the Lord of the Manor. The Vill managed its own affairs through the Moot. Its duties included the payment of taxes, the maintenance of roads and bridges, and service in the national militia. For taxation each Vill was assessed on the basis of Hides, the amount of land sufficient to support a peasant household. In 1086 most of the Vills in Staffordshire were rated at less than five hides, while the whole county was assessed at 513 hides. These Vills were grouped into the 'Hundred'. There were only five such groupings in Staffordshire: Seisdon, Cuttlestone, Offlow, Pirehill and Totmanslow. A large tract was often needed to support one family because of the varying nature of the land. This gave rise to a seemingly irregular boundary pattern, the land either being barren or thickly wooded. Nevertheless the boundaries were still of great importance and each Hundred took its name from some object which strangers could easily find. Thus Totmanslow, of which Endon is a part, took its name from the burial place of Totman. About 2,000 BC a race of primitive farmers lived in wild uplands. The largest settlement of such people seems to have been in Wiltshire at a place called Windmill Hill, but the settlements were widespread and remains of their burial places are plentiful in North Staffordshire. The burial places were called 'Lows'—hence Totmanslow, the burial place of Totman.

Anglo-Saxon names began to arrive in this area about 624 AD:

Set dwellers or settlers
Leah or Ley clearing or pasture in a wooded glade
Tun fenced enclosure around a homestead
Toft homestead

Halh or *Halg*	spinney or clearing by a river
Stead, Steed	
or Stock	a place
Ham	an earlier 'clearing' word
Hey or *Hay*	deer hays or buck stalls where animals were kept for winter venison

Endon is seen as a place name for the first time in 1006 and in the Domesday Book of 1086.[8] It is possibly a derivation of Enandon' or 'Eanandon', meaning a high hill or down. Neighbouring Stanley is also mentioned in the Domesday Book as 'Stan Leah' or 'Stoney Ley', a stoney hill or clearing.[9]

The Domesday Book was a land utilisation survey made by William in an attempt to discover as much as possible about the country he had conquered. It shows that the most densely populated areas were to the south and east of the country. There were fewer people in the north, indicative of the barren nature of the land much of which was waste and probably made so at the hands of William, whose armies marched through the country and laid waste to many settlements in an effort to quell uprisings amongst the people. In the local survey about thirty lordships are mentioned including Biddulph, Norton, Endon, Bucknall, Shelton and Cheadle.

Endon is described as follows:

Endon was held by Dunning. 'There is land for one or two ploughs. It is waste.' Endon was probably laid waste when the Normans put down the Staffordshire rising in 1069. It was recorded as one of the King's possessions though it was of small importance.

Some comparisons with other local entries:

Leek	(1 Hide) with its appendages was held by Earl Alfgar. There is land for 12 ploughs. The 15 villeins and 13 borders have 6 ploughs. There are 3 acres of meadow and woodland 4 leagues long and 4 leagues wide and is valued at 100s.
Biddulph	(1 Hide) with appendages was held by Grifin. There is land for 3 ploughs. It is waste.
Rownall	(Nr. Cheddleton) was held by Wlmar. There is land for 1 plough. It is waste.
Rudyard	was held by Wlmar. There is land for 1 or 2 ploughs. It is waste.

Ruston	(Nr. Leek) was held by Uluiet. There is land for 1 or 2 ploughs. It is waste.
Cheddleton	is held under the Earl Roger by William. It was held by Godwin. There is land for 4 ploughs. The desmense is ½ plough. The 3 villeins and 1 border have ½ plough. The woodland is ½ league long and 3 furlongs wide.
Basford	(¼ Hide) is part of above manor. The 4 villeins and 1 border there have 1 plough. There is 1 acre of meadow and woodland, 2 leagues long and 1½ leagues wide. The whole is valued at 15s.
Norton	Robert de Stafford holds 2 hides in Nortone, and in its appendages. Godric and Ulviet who were free held it. There is land for 4 ploughs. There are 6 villeins and 3 bordars with 3 ploughs. Wood 3 leagues in length and 2 in breadth. It is worth 40s.

References

[1] Drabble, Phil.: 'Staffordshire'.

[2] Hoskins, W. G.: 'Making of the English Landscape'.

[3] Found in 1916 by Fred Stubbs (Henrhydding) now in Hanley Museum, Reference No. HANL. SJ 91553 (NSFC lxi 143; lxvi 190; lxxxviii 105).

[4] *V.C.H.*, Vol. 1, p. 365.

[5] Ward, J. W.: 'The History of the Borough of Stoke-on-Trent' 1843.

[6] Report on Excavations No. 1, Stoke-on-Trent Archaelogical Society. 1965, p. 10.

[7] Sleigh, J.: 'A History of the Ancient Parish of Leek'.

[8] First documentary reference to Endon 1006, see Oxford Dictionary of Placenames.

[9] Duignan, W. H.: 'Notes on Staffordshire Placenames' (Ref. Endon, Stanley), London 1902. Also see Oxford Dictionary of Placenames and others.

Chapter II

THE MIDDLE AGES

I n the Middle Ages Endon was a place of considerable importance within the context of a Staffordshire which was generally regarded as poor, made up of only five Hundreds. It was the site of a manor belonging to the Audley family who were among the foremost landowners in Staffordshire and the recipients of the infamous 'heriot', a tax placed on the estates of tenants of the manor.[1] The manor comprised of the two Longsdons and Bagnall though the names do not appear until many years after the Domesday Survey of 1086. The Assize of tenants in 1307[2] and the subsidy roll of 1327[3] provide lists of tenants and the placenames connected with their habitations which have persisted down through the centuries and some appear in 1775, on Yates map and on the Ordnance Survey of 1836 and are commonly known today. The medieval placenames are as follows.

Stonylow—(Stanlow) also appears in Plot's map.[4]
Crowborough (Crowebarn)
Fernyhough.
Mosshouse
Chaterley (manor of Tunstall)
Bond House (manor of Horton)
Gretton (Gratton)
Blackwood
Bradshaw
Longedon (Londgsdon)
Bagyn Holt (Bagnall)

Leek, Endon, Rudyard, Cheddleton, Tunstall and Bucknall are all mentioned in the Poll Tax of 1377.[5]

Among the names in the post mortem inquisition of the Audley tenants are, Lyme and Smith. Lime House and Smithy House also appear on Yates Map.[6] On the manor lands of the Audleys, and still persisting, are, Norton, Heakley, Baddeley, Snead, Tunstall, Burslem, Rushton James, Rushton Grange, Abbey Hilton and Carmount. In the

13

fourteenth century Dunwode, Haracles, Horton and Stanley were local placenames which are mentioned frequently in connection with tenancies.

Some idea of the contrasting nature of the area around Endon can be gleaned from Erdeswick who, writing in the seventeenth century said that, 'being a large and goodly manor it lieth in so barren a country.'[7] It is safe to say that this description would be apt throughout the Middle Ages. About 1160 Adam de Aldithlegh's name appears as witness to an agreement between Bertram de Verdon and Hugoni de Draycote. He was then a principal tenant of Bertram de Verdon holding, under him, Audley, Heighley, Talke, Endon, Longsdon and one of the Rushtons, a large area of land which in those days had some common shape and system of communication. Today it is crossed and broken up by more recent boundary changes and divisions of the land, notably the industrial development of the potteries which has cut the western end from the eastern end of this tract of land. About this time the Audleys established themselves as lords of the manor. According to documents in the Harleian collection the manorial seat in 1227 was 'in the way between Endon and Park Lane,'[8] but there are no remains except perhaps evidence of a moat. The area of the manor site can be seen on the right hand side of Park Lane and the undulations in the field would suggest that this was the early site and the beginnings of Norman settlement in Endon. It was a moated manor house with a park. In 1273 and 1276 an inquest on the Staffordshire estates of the Audleys states, 'At Endon there is a messuage, garden and the Oldparke.'[9] The Horton court held since Domesday replaced, later on, the jurisdiction of the old vills of Endon, Stanley and Rushton James. In 1272/3 the rent of assize year was 23/6d—the pannage and herbage of the park 10 marks—meadow yearly 100s.

Herbage of Foreign Wood 3s.

Messuage with garden 10s.

Two thirds of one mill 52/-

There were other items making a grand total of £16.15.2d.

Pannage was the amount paid to the Lord of the Manor for the privilege of feeding beasts in the woods near to the settlement.

By 1278 the amounts were different but reference is still made to the rents of assizes, ⅔ of the water mill and Over and Nether Longisdon. The fishery at Dunnismoor was worth 5s. and the issues of Dunwode worth 20s. Cowscot was valued at 20s. every third year.

Cowscot[10] was an ancient customary payment sometimes called 'kylgh' to which tenants, freeholders, copyholders or serfs seem to have been liable at intervals of three years, a custom attached only to old thane-lands held under soccage tenure.

The rents paid by individuals were:

William de Loversete	$1\frac{1}{2}$ bovates	4s.
Jordan de Couhale	3 acres	18d.
Adam de Enedon	$2\frac{1}{2}$ acres	16d.
William Fernihalg	6 acres	22d.
Richard de Enedon	$1\frac{1}{2}$ acres	6d.
William de Stanlowe	6 acres	2s.
John de Stanlowe	2 acres	8d.
Richard de Couhale	3 acres	18d.
Brian le Smith	3 acres	17d.
Robert Wylimot	4 acres	$22\frac{1}{2}$d.
Robert Lyme	1 croft	12d.
Roger de Schawe	2 acres	8d.
Adam Coly	$\frac{1}{2}$ acre	3d.
Stephen Turne(r)	$\frac{1}{4}$ acre	$1\frac{1}{2}$d.
Ranulph Ball	$1\frac{1}{4}$ acres	5d.
Richard Walewyn—as easement of fire and water		6d.

Because of the transfer of the authority to Horton Manor the pleas and perquisites of the court were said to be worthless.

Surrounding the site of the manor and stretching along the valley was a deer park, one of several in North Staffordshire. Within the deerpark were deerheys or buckstalls. These were earthwork enclosures made to house the rounded up deer and designed to facilitate the sorting of the animals presumably for venison and for breeding. However, the location of these heys gave several placenames an added interest.[11]

To begin with we have Little Hart Hill near to Jackhey, then comes Bryan Hey, Stonehey Wood (Stoney Lane), Parkhey, Hollin Hey, Deephey and Reynold's Hey.

The park in 1288 was some 300 to 400 acres in size. In 1278 William of Audley sued Lucy widow of Henry Audley for 'waste and destruction of houses and woods in the park at Endon, Dunwood and Haracheles,' which she held in dower. Lucy did not appear at the hearing and the Sheriff was ordered to distrain and produce her on the morrow of the Purification. Having already had a royal prohibition against her causing waste and destruction she persisted and pulled down two houses worth £10 and had sold 60 oaks by which William's estate had been damaged to the extent of £20.[12] However, Lucy was represented by Attorney, denied the charges and appealed to the jury. The Sheriff was commanded to go 'in his own person to the said lands and summon a jury and return their verdict into the court on the Octaves of St. John the Baptist.' Lucy re-married later and her husband William of Ryther became involved in Lucy's quarrels with the Audleys. In 1303 Thomas of Audley sued William of Ryther and Lucy his wife for causing waste and destruction of houses and woods in Endon. William of Ryther was away on King's service in Scotland and held letters of protection in respect of all his properties, making it impossible for the court to act on behalf of Thomas of Audley.

By 1312 Lucy, once more a widow had been busy again. Holding as dower two-thirds of the Manor of Endon she had pulled down a grange, a stable and an oxstall, each worth 20 marks, cut down and sold 200 oak trees and 40 ash trees. For this destruction and for destruction in Cold Norton, Nicholas de Audley sued Lucy claiming £1,000 damages. Lucy's attorney referring to an agreement made by Nicholas's father with Lucy in 1297 concerning her 'dower-land', said that Nicholas had no right to claim damages of Lucy for waste and destruction in the 'wood of Dunwode, nor in the wood of Harachils, nor in the Park of Henedon nor in any other place she held in dower.'[13] Nicholas acknowledged the agreement but produced proof of waste and destruction since the date of the agreement and he appealed to a jury.

In 1282 another incident concerning the park involved William of Rye who appeared against Ralph de Alleshache, William, his son, Richard son of Nicholas of Alleshache, John the groom of Edmund of Stafford and eight others accusing them of breaking into his Park at Endon and taking from it wild animals viz. a certain eyry of hawks. The accused were to answer the charges at the Octaves of St. Martin.[14]

Among the property inherited by Nicholas de Audley in 1307 was a third part of Enedon in the King's hands, a park called Oldepark with a yearly profit of £8, a third part of a certain water mill 14s. and two serfs, one holding, one bovate of land (approx. 10 to 18 acres), with waste, for 6/11, the other holding the same but valued at 3/-. The serfs were to render 'scuth' every third year. Some of the tenants named in the inquisition were,

Bronze Axe Head found at Henridding in 1916, now in Hanley Museum.

An aerial view of Endon, showing the road, railway and canal of modern times. The medieval manor site can be clearly seen between the road and railway on the extreme left of the picture. Ministry of Defence (Air Force Department) Photograph. Crown Copyright Reserved.

Thomas of Fernyhalg
Richard Borgy
Thomas Coye
Adam son of Richard
Richard son of John
Richard Coker
Alice wife of Roger de Coupere
William de Knoll
Margaret la Lavendere
Henry Fimar

By 1293 Nicholas de Audithlegh claimed free warren in the manors of Endon and Horton and he claimed to have, in Endon, view of frankpledge, assizes of bread and beer, wayf and infangenthef on the ground that they had been held by his ancestors for time out of memory. The jury supported his claim.

The 'view of Frankpledge' was a court held periodically for the protection of the members of a company of ten householders commonly called a tithing. Under frank pledge every member of a 'tithing' was answerable for the good conduct of or damage done by any one of the other members. Assize of bread and beer was a statutory right granted to settle the price of bread and beer; a Free Warren applied to hunting rights; wayf or strayed cattle and other unclaimed goods became after the 'Hue and Cry' properties of the lord of the manor. Infangenthef granted jurisdiction over a thief apprehended within the lord's manor.

In 1350 a case at the Manor court concerned the wardship of Matthew of Chetelton. It was brought by James de Audilege and is interesting because some claims were made on account of military service due, others were claiming that it was held by homage and fealty and scutage of the King. This involved doing suit at the court of James at Endon every three weeks, and 'for the service of accompanying the said James for 9 days at his own costs with a man at arms, two hobelars and two archers in Wales whenever war should happen between the King and the Welsh.' John de Arderne defending denied that Matthew had held his lands of James by military service and appealed to a jury.[24]

Each manor had a court of jurisdiction. The Audleys in order to secure their position and enforce their right to heriot were prepared to fight duels. On one occasion Henry de Audley resorted to such action against Hervey Bagot, Baron of Stafford.

In 1227 Henry de Audley sued Hervey Bagot (Baron of Stafford) for the Manor of Horton. Henry de Audley claimed the Manor. His mother, Emma, had inherited an estate which included the Manor of Horton. Hervey Bagot disagreed and offered to defend his right to the Manor by the body of his freeman, Richard de Newenham. Henry de Audley offered to prove his right by the body of his freeman Gilbert of Anant. A duel should be waged on the Monday after the Octaves of St. Martin . . . . [15]

No harm could befall the freeman of the rightful owner of the manor . . . 'Hervey de Stafford gives 5 marks for licence of concord with Henry de Audley in respect of the Manor of Horton regarding which a duel was waged between them' . . . Were both freemen mortally wounded? . . . 'Hervey acknowledges the Manor to be the right of Henry and gave it to him for a rent of 10 shillings a year. For this acknowledgement Henry de Audley gave him land in Norton worth £10 a year and if the librates cannot be made up there, then in a fitting place in the vicinity of his land in Endon.' In addition he gave Hervey Bagot 50 marks. [16]

The doling out of justice did not finish with the fighting of duels even if the duellists were 'free-men' prepared to fight to the death for their lords. References have been found which suggest that Endon had its Gallows. In 1293 in the reign of Edward I, Edmund the king's brother claimed to have gallows and assize of bread and beer in his manors at Leyk and Endon. [17]

Abduction in Endon 1361 A.D.

'The Hundred of Totmonslowe presented that William son of Roger of Greeneweye had feloniously entered the house of Wm. del Mosse the elder at Endon in 34 Ed III and had carried off the wife of the said Wm and goods and chattels of Wm to the value of 40 shillings.'

In 1327 the Subsidy Roll for Endon contained the names of local people and amounts of money paid in tax on moveable possessions (i.e. sheep).

Will' o de Stanlow
Adam de Fernihaleugh
Rog'o de Greneway
Will O' de Mos

Richs de Cuh
Joh'e de Crowebarn
Will O' Chaterleye
Will O' Rugge
Adam de Longedon
Hug(h) le bonde ('le Bond' indicative of Serfdom)
Hug(h) de Gretton
Henri de Cliffe
Johne de Blackwode
Thoma de Bagynholt
Will o' de Bradeshawe
Thoma de Kockyleye
Rico le Serjaunt ('le Serjaunt' or bailiff, 'mouthpiece' of the lord
of the manor. The bailiff usually lived in the
manor house).[18]

Military service was performed by Staffordshire tenants under Richard II in 1380. Included in the retinue of Hugh de Calveleys, which was mustered at Clary sur Somme in support of Thomas, Earl of Bukyngham, were people bearing names which appeared in the Endon rolls and tenant lists.

Amongst the esquires were, William Stanlegh, and William de Egerton. In the retinue of the Earl of Stafford were Gilbert de Colchyecle (Colclough), Thomas Greneway, Robert Balle, all were shown as archers.

Wages per day were, a knight 2 shillings, an esquire 1 shilling, an archer 6 pence.[19]

However, in the muster rolls there is no definite indication of the area from which the listed men were drawn.

Hulton (Hilton) Abbey the last monastic settlement in North Staffordshire housed an abbot and 8 monks of the Cistercian Order. It was endowed in 1223 by Henry de Audley who, among other things, was Lord of the Manor of Endon. Included in Henry's donations to the Abbey were,

'The town of Hilton, ye wood called Sneyd, the hey of Kenvermunt, ye town of Rushton and all his lands in Normancote, Middlescliffe, Bockenhall, ye villages and tenements of Mixne and Bradenhop, pasture of Morrudge and Whiteward-wood, Bucklegh Meadow and a pension of 10s out of ye Church at Audley.'[20]

19

The Abbey was situated in a sheltered picturesque valley to the east of the meandering river Trent. The site was ideal for religious contemplation and provided limited material support for the inmates.

An extract from an Ecclesiastical Survey lists the properties owned by the Abbot and Monks of Hulton in 1291.

A grange at the Abbey of 2 carucates (240 acres)

The grange of Rushton 3 carucates

The grange of Normacote 4 carucates

A farm or grange of 1 curate with pasturage at Mixon.

In addition at Hulton, Normacote and Mixon there was farming stock, which together with farm rents, manorial dues, two water-mills and a tannery must have provided a considerable income.[21]

A large endowment was received from the Lady Elizabeth, widow of Nicholas the 5th Baron Audley. By her will dated the last day of September A.D. 1400 she also bequeathed her body to be buried in the choir of Hulton Abbey in her husband's tomb.

As an abbey worth less than £200 Hulton should have been suppressed under the Act of 1536 but in 1537 the crown granted an exemption for a fine of £66.13s.4d. but eventually on the 18th September 1538 the Abbot and eight monks surrendered Hulton to the crown and the land was disposed of. None of the property went to the Audleys, in spite of their early connection with the foundation of an Abbey.[22]

Dieulacres was a Cistercian Abbey, founded in 1214, possibly on the site of a former hermitage by Ranulph, Earl of Chester. His wife was instrumental in the Abbey being named 'Dieulacres'. On hearing of her husband's intention to found an abbey she exclaimed Deux encres! (may God grant it increase). It is recorded that Ranulph laid the foundation stone of the great church naming the place where the Abbey was erected 'Dieul l'encres' later known as Dieulacres. The Abbey church was about 160 feet long, of medium size, a typical cistercian construction though probably without transepts.[23]

In 1246 and 1270 the Audleys figure as witnesses to agreements made in respect of the Abbey.

A quarrel with the Abbot and monks of Hulton Abbey ended in 1252 in an agreement setting out the rights of the two Abbeys, mainly in connection with pasture and tithes at Mixon, Bradnop and Morridge and in Leek Parish generally.

In 1254 Henry III conferred the title Earl of Chester upon his eldest son Edward. From that date until the dissolution of the monasteries the patron of the Abbey was either the heir to the throne or the King himself.

The monks of Dieulacres commenced a large scale programme of land reclamation in the Churnet Valley altering the course of the river and laying on an intricate system of land drainage.

In 1291 the Abbey's several estates were valued. The Staffordshire estates were worth £27.13.8d., Cheshire estates valued at £29.15s. and those at Rossall £61.10.5d. The churches at Leek and Sandbach were worth £28 and £22.13.4d respectively. At this time Dieulacres was engaged in the wool trade and the Black Prince bought wool from there in 1347, visiting the Abbey himself in 1351 and donating over £300 towards the cost of a new Abbey Church. In the mid 13th century the abbey possessed numerous granges in the Leek, Cheshire and Rossall districts, but by 1538 there were only seven or eight granges mostly in the Leek area.[24]

The size of the Abbey community dropped during the fourteenth century. In 1351 it was stated that 'only a small number of monks were serving God there' and in 1377 the number including the abbot was seven but it had risen to eleven in 1381. The abbey housed a community of thirteen monks at the dissolution.[25]

Some of the land in Endon was in the possession of the Abbey and in 1371, a monk who was also the vicar of Leek, by name one Thomas of Rydyard, figured in a land dispute.

The Abbey's gross income in 1535 was £243.3s.6d. including £68 10s. 4d. from spiritualities, most of the latter was from Leek parish. Under the Act of 1536 it was, unlike Hulton, classed as one of the greater monasteries and on the 20th October 1538 the Royal Commission arrived from Stafford to take possession in the name of the King.

Lords of the Manor.

Liulf de Aldidele murdered Gamel Fitz Griffin, thane of Betley, before 1130 A.D. His three sons Adam de Aldithele, Roger de Aldithele and Liulf brother of Adam were named in documents of the latter half of the twelfth and early thirteenth centuries.

The Draycotte Charters record the name of Adam de Aldithlegh. He was first witness to a deed of about 1160 A.D. and styled 'Principal

Tenant' of Bertram de Verdon, Baron of Alton, holding under him several manors including Endon.[26] In 1188 during the minority of Ranulp, Earl of Chester, he became keeper of Cheshire and from 1199-1203 gave jury service as a Knight. He married Emma, daughter and heiress of Ralph Fitz Orme, granddaughter of a wealthy and powerful King's thane, Orme le Gulden (Orme of Darlaston). By this marriage he took possession of extensive lands in North Staffordshire. Adam and Emma's eldest son Adam, died, his brother Henry then inherited his father's estates.

This Henry of Audley, was held in great esteem by the now grown-up Earl of Chester who gave him many estates in Cheshire and Staffordshire. Henry purchased the Castle of Newhall, he held Norton-under Cavermont, and lands at Heakley, Baddeley and Milton from Peter of Norton, and Cheddleton from Hugh de Lacy. 'He erected the Castle of Heighley for his security on earth and built and endowed the Abbey of Hulton to propitiate the favour of heaven towards his soul and the souls of all his ancestors—Henry possessed not only great property but great power in an equal degree.'[27]

He began his career as Constable to Hugh de Lacy. Served as Sheriff of Shropshire and Staffordshire 1216-1221 and again 1223-1232. King Henry III entrusted him with positions of command appointing him governor of the Castles of Carmarthen and Cardigan, and a Baron Marcher, a body commissioned to defend England against the Welsh. In 1227 he was appointed Constable of the Castles of Shrewsbury and Bridgnorth and in 1233 Governor of Shrewsbury Castle. Later he was made Governor of the Castles of Beeston, Chester and Newcastle-under-Lyme. The King gave Henry several tokens of his respect, allowing him to build a castle in Shropshire known as Redcastle, deriving its name from the colour of the rock on which it was erected, granting him a Charter for a weekly market and a fair at Betley and making him a grant of the Manors of Egmundson, Newport, and Forde in the County of Shropshire.

Henry died in 1246 and was succeeded by his son James who married Ela daughter of William Longspee, Earl of Salisbury. James was appointed Constable of Newcastle in 1250. One of the Baron Marchers he was a formidable attacker of the marauding Welsh. In 1253 A.D. 'free warren was granted by King Henry III to James de Aditheley in all his lands of his manors of Aditheley, Belteley, Cestreton, Bradwell, Bicnou?, Talk, Chadderley, Tunstall, Buewardeslime, Chell Thursefield, Whitfield, Bemersley, Enedon, Horton, Gretton, Longsdon, Alstonfield and Norton in Com. Stafford.[28] James also became Sheriff of Staffordshire and Shropshire and was appointed Judge of Chester in 1266. Whilst holding the office of Chief Justiciary in Ireland he sustained an accident, falling from his horse, and died in Ireland in 1272. Ela in search of a dowry sued the estate and was granted, 'a third of the vills of Endon, Gratton, Horton, Bagnall, Stanley and Longsden.' The title passed in succession to her son, James, who died in 1273. His brother Henry 'holds Enedone by the service of a knights fee.' This Henry married Lucy who on his death in 1275 received a widow's share, for life, of her husband's estate. William Ryther (Rye, Rycher) became her second husband. The dower possessions involved Lucy and William in several law suits with the Barons Audley.

William brother of Henry became the next Lord Audley and on his death in 1282 Nicholas succeeded to the whole inheritance. This Nicholas was created Baron Audley in 1296. He was the one who was with Edward I in his wars in Scotland and France. On his death in 1298 the estates and title passed on to his son Thomas who died a minor.

Nicholas the 3rd Baron married Joan, widow of Henry Lacey, Earl of Lincoln. He died in 1316 when his son and heir, James, was only three years old. James inherited great estates which had received considerable additions from the lines of both his mother and grandmother. This James, 4th Baron Audley also fought in Scotland in 1336 and subsequently became Governor of Berwick-upon-Tweed. He was with Edward III and his sons in their wars in France fighting at Crecy and Calais. This war veteran enjoyed his honourable title and estates for many long years. He died in 1385 more than 70 years old and by his will 'desired his body to be buried at Hulton Abbey.' His son and heir Nicholas married Elizabeth daughter of Lord Beaumont. He died leaving no heir. John Ward in his 'History of the Borough of Stoke upon Trent' claims that 'Nicholas the 5th Baron Audley was buried in the choir of Hulton Abbey.'[29]

The title passed to Sir John Touchet of Buglawton son of Joan, Nephew of Nicholas, 5th Baron Audley. He also was a distinguished warrior being with King Henry IV both in France and Wales. His son James became the 7th Baron Audley fighting with Henry V in France and supporting the Lancastrian cause throughout the Wars

23

of the Roses. He finally commanded an army of 10,000 men at the Battle of Blore Heath, near Market Drayton in Shropshire, in an endeavour to halt the progress of the Earl of Salisbury, a Yorkist, in his march from Ludlow. James Touchet, 7th Baron Audley was defeated and died on the battle field. 'A stone set upon Blore Heath, slain just in that place in the quarrel of Henry VI valiantly fighting for his sovereign.'[30] Local legend maintains that his defeat was watched by Queen Margaret, wife of Henry VI from the Tower of Mucklestone Church. His son and heir John also supported the Lancastrian cause. He accompanied the Duke of Somerset, fighting in France, where he was taken prisoner by the Yorkists. During his captivity the Yorkists treated him so well that he changed his allegiance and accepted an appointment under Edward IV, a Yorkist, who in 1461 made him steward of all the Crown lands in County Dorset, Warden of all his Forests and Parks in that County and of the Castle of Wardore in Wiltshire, he died in 1491.

James 9th Baron Audley became a Knight of the Order of the Bath. He 'was summoned to Parliament but taking offence at a subsidy granted he joined the Cornishmen in their insurrection.' Taken prisoner at the Battle of Blackheath he was 'drawn from Newgate to Tower Hill in his own coat of arms, painted on paper but reversed and torn, and there beheaded on June 28th, 1497.'[31] The titles were then forfeited. His son John received royal favour and the Audley titles were restored. The Audley status and fortune began to decline in North Staffordshire and though engaged in royal service the family never regained the prestige and affluence enjoyed by their medieval ancestors. George the 13th Baron Audley was severely wounded at the Battle of Kinsale in Ireland on the 24 December 1601. This was the Baron Audley who according to Erdeswick, 'sold his portion of the manor of Tunstall, the Castle of Helegh, the manor of Audley and all his other lands in Staffordshire to every man a parcel.'[32]

Thus Endon entered modern times under the Manorial lordship of the Edges of Horton.

The other great family with connections in the district were the Earls of Derby whose lineage according to Burke's Peerage started with: Adam de Audley, brother of Liulf who had three sons.

William, his heir, Adam and Thomas.

William (de Stanley) was granted Stanley and half of Balterley by his first cousin Adam de Audley son of Liulf.

In 1298 Walter de Stanley held Stanley. In 1380 William Stanlegh fought in France for Richard II. By 1397 a William de Stanley who was the forrester of Wirral held Stanley. He came into the title of heiretary forrester of Wirral because he married Joan the daughter of the previous title holder. Thus he 'became possessed of manor and bailswick and assumed the manorial bearings' of that office and established a line away from the area of the family's origins. The last mention of the Stanley's connection with the district is in 1660 when William Stanley of Hootton and others sold the manor to Thomas Fernyhough for £900.

References

[1] Hilton, R. H.: 'Lord and Peasant in Staffordshire in the Middle Ages', *N.S.J.F.S.*, Vol. 10, 1970, p. 1.

[2] *H.C.S.*, Vol. XI, New Series.

[3] *H.C.S.*, Vol. VII.

[4] Plot, Robert: 'The Natural History of Staffordshire', 1686.

[5] *H.C.S.*, Vol. IV, 4th Series.

[6] *H.C.S.*, Vol. XI, New Series.

[7] Erdswick, Sampson: 'Survey of Staffordshire'.

[8] British Museum. Harl. Ms. No. 2062. fo. 2.

[9] *H.C.S.*, Vol. XI, New Series.

[10] *H.C.S.*, Vol. XI, New Series, p. 235.

[11] Horton Inclosures 1813, and Ordnance Survey Map 1836.

[12] *H.C.S.*, Vol. VI, Part 1.

[13] *H.C.S.*, Vol. IX.

[14] *H.C.S.*, Vol. VI, Part 1.

[15] *H.C.S.*, Vol. IV, p. 50

[16] *H.C.S.*, Vol. IV, p. 67.

[17] *H.C.S.*, Vol. VI, Part 1.

[18] *H.C.S.*, Vol. VII.

[19] *H.C.S.*, Vol. XIV, pp. 228 and 232.

[20] *H.C.S.*, Vol. XII, New Series.

[21] Ward, John: 'History of the Borough of Stoke-on-Trent', 1843.

[22] *V.C.H.*, Vol. III.

[23] Bayliss, Mary: 'Dieulacres Abbey, *N.S.J.F.S.*, Vol. 2, 1962, p. 78.

[24] *V.C.H.*, Vol. III.

[25] *V.C.H.*, Vol. III.

[26] *H.C.S.*, Vol. III, Part 1.

[27] Ward, John: 'History of the Borough of Stoke-on-Trent' 1843.

[28] Ward, John: 'History of the Borough of Stoke-on-Trent' 1843, see Appendix.

[29] Ward, John: 'History of the Borough of Stoke-on-Trent', 1843, see Appendix.

[30] Plot, Robert: 'Natural History of Staffordshire' 1686, Chapter X.

[31] Burke's Peerage, Baronetage and Knightage.

[32] Ward, John: 'History of the Borough of Stoke-on-Trent', 1843, p. 144.

Chapter III

ENDON FROM THE END OF THE MIDDLE AGES TO 1700

P erhaps one of the most significant documents to come out of
the period before 1500 is the one of 1288 which sets out the
tithes due to Leek and to the Abbot of Dieulacres. It reads:
Wax candle offering at Purification

Tithe—hemp and flax	8s	4d.
Tithe—geese	20s.	od.
Pigs and eggs	6s.	od.
Tithe—fruit and hay in garden and crofts and others with Endon tithe hay	10s.	od.
Total paid by Endon	£3 9s.	8d.
Longsdon	£1 15s.	10d.
Ipstones	£4 15s.	2d.

The two points to be noted are (a) the size of Endon compared with
the other two places named, twice the size of Longsdon and about
two-thirds the size of Ipstones. (b) the wax candle offered, as a token
of loyalty, at the Purification, a practice which was discontinued at the
Reformation.

The relative size of Endon is difficult to establish since most of its
records are included in over-all totals for Leek. However, from wills
and inventories, we do now know that several large properties were in
existence and the community was essentially a scattered one, made up
of low-ranking gentry who lived fairly comfortably on holdings which
were not large. One such person was John Wedgwood whose estate
in 1590 suggests a large hall at Harracles and a position of some
authority in the district[2] Another important Staffordshire document
was the muster roll of 1539. This is a list of ninety-five men who could
be called to arms to help suppress a rising in the reign of Henry VIII.
Most are shown as able-bodied but some nine men are not described
as 'able' and could possibly be veterans who still possessed arms. The
armour had been acquired for use in the French wars and some of it
may have been handed down. The arms described would be at the
height of fashion for footmen about the year 1480. One or two men

27

are shown as possessing a horse. In the following list a Jack is a leather jerkin, with pieces of iron sewn on for protection. Some men had bows and arrows.[3]

Muster Roll of Staffordshire, A.D. 1539

All these above wrytton be archers redy furnysshed with horse and harnesse.

Thomas Stanlow hath a bowe

Roger Fernyhalge a jesterne, a bow and a sheff aroes

John Sherat a bowe

John Fernyhalge junior a jacke

John Bradshaw a jacke

John Malkyn a bow and arows

William Malkyn a bowe and sheff of arows

John Benteley a bowe and arows

In 1547 Richard Sutton, a husbandman of Endon, though not wealthy left in his will some sixteen pounds worth of goods and chattels. He decreed that he should be buried at 'Saint Edwards church yarde of Leke', and he declared, 'I will that Jane my wife and my child son shall have all my lands during the space of three years jointly together, and then to be at his rule and order. I will that my said wife shall have after the third year the third part of my goods and the other two parts be divided amongst my children equally.'[4]

The following inventory made at the death of the same Richard Sutton illustrated the type and assortment of goods possessed by a man who was described in 1547 as a husbandman. He had a wide range of animals and fowl, corn for food for the animals, some equipment to carry out his work and a quantity of personal goods such as brass and pewter ware. Some idea of the value of animals at the time can be gained from a closer look (i.e. swine, 1s. each; colt 5s. each; a mare £1).

Imprimis	2 horses	...	...	...	...	43	4
Item	a cow with a calf and a heifer				...	30	0
„	a filly	...	...	...	...	10	0
„	4 young swine	...	...	...	4	0
„	all the husbandrye stuff		...	...	3	0
„	a mare	...	...	...	...	20	0
„	2 colts	...	...	...	...	10	0
„	2 stirks	...	...	...	...	10	0

28

„	in brass	...	...	...	...	5	0
„	in pewter	...	...	...	...	2	0
„	in bedding		...	...	...	13	4
„	his raiment		...	...	...	6	8
„	in all man's treen ware		...	...	5	0
„	the corne	...	...	...	...	6	8
„	in nappery ware		...	...	...	2	0
„	geese and hens		...	...	...		12[1]

Staffordshire Muster of A.D. 1640

This is 'A booke containing the names of all the Trayned Souldiers to be ready for that service the first day of July next at Utoxiter.'[5]

Before the outbreak of the Civil War in England, some concern was shown at the rising of the Covenanters in Scotland. They were opposed to the impositions made upon the Scottish Church by the Stuart king. In 1640, three hundred Staffordshire men were impressed for the occasion and were to assemble at Uttoxeter, ready for service in Scotland on July 1st. They were to be paid eightpence per day. Their leaders were to be   Sir Harvey Bagot
                 Walter Wrottesely and
                 Thomas Crompton

The men were divided into two groups. (a) The Trayned Band, and (b) The Impressed Band. Of local names mentioned, the following have been selected as an example, though we do not know which of them would have been Endon men. Endon is not mentioned. If there were any Endon people trained or impressed, it is likely that they would be included in the Horton Manor lists.

The Trayned Band	The Impressed Band
William Morrice	John Hartley
Peter Halmarke	William Walker
John Hulme	a rioter
Thomas Lawton	Richard Jones

Horton:	Traine	Presse
	Raphe Mills	William Pedley
	John Simson	John Dyasse
	Thomas Biddral	Thomas Marine
	Charles Lowe	
	John Mallet	

Chedulton: **Traine**
Richard Bruerton
John Edge
John Bagnall
Lyonell Boote

Presse
David Jones
William Burnett
William Fletcher

During the Civil War, the moorlanders tended to be Parliamentarian and the yeomen stock similar to that found in Endon tended to be sympathisers, though it is difficult to isolate the general attitudes found in Endon from those of the main parish of Leek. It is at the local level that Staffordshire became involved with most of the larger land-owners such as the Sneyds and the Leveson Gowers supporting the royalists. The two principal events were the skirmish on Hopton Heath and the seige of Lichfield. The county also had connections with the ultimate outcome of the royal succession because it was at Boscobel, near Shifnal in Shropshire that Charles II took refuge after the battle of Worcester in 1651. The Restoration in 1660 and the later Glorious Revolution of 1688 gave rise to royalist feelings again. A special day, May 29th, was kept aside to mark Oak Apple Day, and Thomas Jodrell gave six shillings and eightpence per annum to the incumbent of Endon for the preaching of a sermon on that day. In Stafford and some other parts of the county, the date was acknow-ledged with celebration down to the early nineteenth century. It does not need much imagination to lead one to suppose that the early decorations at the well and the celebrations associated with the occasion were a continuation of a special event which involved a church service, the preaching of a sermon and a thanksgiving on 29th May annually. That is Oak Apple Day. The day is the same, but since 1845 the reason for the commemoration has changed.

Hearth Tax Returns

The hearth tax, or chimney tax as it was sometimes called, was a payment made to the King on every hearth. It was paid by all houses paying to the church and the poor, requiring the owners to pay two shillings per hearth. The tax was levied between 1662 and 1689 and lists, by townships, the names of the persons who paid, and the number of hearths assessed for each person. In this respect it is a useful indicator of the relative wealth of an area, and since people who did not pay a rent of 20s. or more per year, or owned less than £10 of real or personal estate, were excused, it is possible to estimate the amount of relative poverty in the distirct.

In Endon in 1666,[6] forty people paid tax on seventy-three hearths. It is likely that all those excused were single hearth cottages and the larger and presumably wealthier houses had more than one hearth. The Endon returns are included in the Horton Constablewicke figures, forming twenty per cent. of the total. The other areas in the return are:

				Households	Hearths
Horton	...	...	...	67	99
Rushton James		...	...	28	38
Gratton	...	...	...	6	7
Longsdon	...	...	...	25	62
Stanley	...	...	...	7	12
Bagnall	...	...	...	19	30
Wall-grange	...	...	...	2	13
				154	261
Endon	...	...	...	40	73
				194	334

However the returns also show that some eighty-five households were excused paying the tax. This would put the total number of households in the Constablewicke at 279 and the total hearths at 419. Thus some 30 per cent. of the people in the area were excused the payment of tax, indicating that about one third of the people would be living in considerable poverty. Because those who were excused payment are listed for the whole Constablewicke, it is difficult to determine which particular area they came from, but assuming the poverty was spread fairly evenly, and since Endon has 20 per cent. of the total households it is reasonable to suppose that Endon had 20 per cent. of those excused. This would suggest seventeen households were excused payment and together with the forty paying the tax, this would indicate a total of fifty-seven households in Endon.

Those paying tax were:

Samuel Malkin	One	Roger Tomkinson, son	Three
Ann Miller	Two	William Tomkinson	One
John Goodwin	One	William Malkin	One
Frances Tomkisson	One	Laurance Finney	One

Widdow Chalner	One	John Hordern	Two
Francis Chalner	One	William Tayler	Two
Edward Mare	One	Richard Heath	One
Simon Fernihough	One	William Smyth	One
Joseph Wilkinson	Six	John Bolton	Three
Charles Malkin,		John Ball	Three
gentleman	Three	Francis Smith	One
William Sutton	Two	Adam Meare	Two
Raph Tomkinson	One	Raphe Benteley	One
Thomas Sutton	Three	William Forde	Two
Nicholas Dowley	One	Hugh Sherratt	Two
Abraham Tayler	Three	Richard Tomkinson	One
Richard Backe	Two	Roger Hargreaves	Three
Mtrs (Mistress)		Widdow Beach	One
Wedgwood	Four	Richard Michell	One
Francis Sherratt	One	Widdowe Burn	One
John Heath	One		
Richard Heath,			
gentleman	Four		

The properties in Endon were not large, the largest being a property occupied by Joseph Wilkinson who was churchwarden at Leek, but efforts so far have failed to locate the whereabouts of the property. Other efforts have been successful and it is possible to identify some of the properties. For instance:

Samuel Malkin	1 hearth at Lane Head
Charles Malkin	3 hearths at Yate House
Thomas Sutton	3 hearths at Hallwater
Richard Heath	1 hearth at Park Lane
Roger Tomkinson	4 hearths at Lane End
William Tomkinson	3 hearths at Park Lane
Richard Heath	1 hearth at Park Lane
Adam Mere	1 hearth at Endon Bank
John Ball	2 hearths at Endon Hill
Rolf Bentley	1 hearth at Yen Bank
Mistress Wedgwood	4 hearths at Endon Bank
Francis Sherratt	1 hearth at Claylake
Hugh Sherratt	1 hearth, a cobbler at Hollinhurst
Rose Hargreaves	3 hearths at Park Lane

Old windows and new at Reynolds Hey Farm. A.D. 1640.

Dated lintel over farm doorway at Reynolds Hey, Park Lane, dated 1640 A.D.
Note change in stone work at top left.

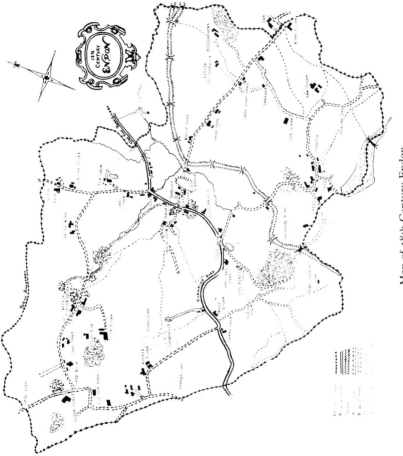

Map of 18th Century Endon.

The largest property in the district was at Wall Grange, where a Mr. Edward Downes paid taxes on eleven hearths. There are only two entries for Wall Grange, the other being Mr. Lyonell Harrison's payment on two chimneys.

At Horton, Tymathy Edge, gentleman, had eight hearths, the next in size being four in the name of William Keme. The largest in Gratton was two hearths, but at Longsdon the entry in the tax return reads, 'William Wedgwood, Esquire, seven hearths.' This was the William Wedgwood of Harracles Hall who was buried in Leek in 1677. In fact Longsdon possesed larger properties than Endon:

John Bateman, gentleman	Six hearths
Robert Hulme	Six hearths
Thomas Butley	
(Bulkeley of Stanlow)	Five hearths
John Reade of Bradshaw,	
Gentleman and his tennant	Six hearths

At Stanley, Thomas Fernihough, gentleman, and William Mollett, had three each and Richard Boughey had two. The remaining four were of one hearth only. At Bagnall, John Murrall, gentleman, Richard Bradshaw also a gentleman, had four apiece, whilst John Harding is credited with three. From these returns we learn that the Horton Constablewicke contained one or two large houses, though nothing to compare with the thirty-three hearths at Trentham Hall. Most of the houses were small, especially in Endon where something like twenty-two houses paying tax had only one hearth. To this one must add the seventeen or so which were excused producing a figure for rough guidance of thirty-nine out of fifty-seven, or about 70 per cent. of the people living simply in one-hearth houses, or were too poor to pay the tax at all.

However, the Horton Constablewicke as a whole compares favourably with Trent-Tame Valley where nearly 5 per cent. were living in houses of five or more hearths. This was not so in Endon. There was only one house with more than four hearths.[7]

In the return of 1666 the name of Thomas Bentley appears among those who were excused the tax. In 1668 Thomas Bentley was the churchwarden for the Endon Quarter at Leek. He died in 1696 and the inventory of his will is as follows:

33

Two cowes	... ...	6	00	0
One Twenter	... ...	1	13	4
Two Sterkes	... ...	2	00	0
Two Horses	... ...	4	00	0
One bed two coffers in little parlor	... ...	1	1	4
One bed in the little parlor	... ...		10	0
Two pairs of bed steds	... ...		12	0
One pras pot and a little kettle	... ...		4	0
Putor	... ...		6	8
Wooden Ware	... ...		4	4
One tabol, two chares, two stoules grate and tonges and sumother things	...		5	0
Husbandre ware	... ...	1	00	0
His wearing apparill and things	... ...	1	00	0
	The sum total:	£18	16	8

So in addition to the gentlemen with larger houses, there were the husbandmen with their meagre possessions and limited wealth.

References

[1] Leek Parish Church Records. Parish Chest.

[2] See John Wedgwood Will 1590. Lichfield Wills.

[3] *H.C.S.*, Vol. VI, N.S. Muster Roll of 1539, Part 1/1903. A. Gesturue, Gestrone, or Gessaraunte is a jacket without sleeves, on which were fastened small oblong plates of steel over-lapping one another.

[4] See Richard Sutton Will 1547. Lichfield Wills.

[5] *H.C.S.*, Vol. XV, 1849. Muster Roll of 1640.

[6] Hearth Tax Return 1666. Public Record Office, *H.C.S.*, Vol. 1925, p. 157.

[7] Thirsk, Joan: 'Horn and Thorn in Staffordshire', Earl Lecture, *N.S.J.F.S.*, Vol. 9, 1969, p. 1.

Chapter IV

ECCLESIASTICAL DEVELOPMENTS

St. Luke's Church

E ndon in more distant days was placed firmly in the diocese of Lichfield which was one of the earliest to be founded in England. Its first bishop was Chad. In more recent times, since 1541, the diocese of Chester has stretched to the Cheshire boundary, and this has remained the boundary between the dioceses until today. Endon is therefore in the northern extremes of the diocese of Lichfield. From the earliest of times the township of Endon was in the parish of Leek, and even after the establishment of a Chapel of Ease in 1730 the incumbent was a perpetual curate of Leek parish. For a while Leek parish was divided into four; Leek and Lowe, Leekfrith, Bradnop and Endon, under the Vicar and Warden of Leek. The four divisions of the parish were important since these were the areas of chapels of ease and provided a warden for a particular quarter at Leek Church.[1]

The patrons of the chapel were the Earls of Macclesfield, from its inception in 1730 until 1902, when the Earl at that time relinquished the duties in favour of the Vicar of Leek. This was because the parish of Endon was created in 1902 and a vicarage established. Endon, however, had already become an Ecclesiastical District in 1865, a role which was concerned mainly with civil administration within the Leek parish.

Since the term vicar has been used to describe incumbents since 1730, it is as well to point out that a perpetual curate would be responsible for the services at the chapel of ease, and to all the parishioners he would be 'Vicar', legally he was responsible to the Vicar of Leek, and shared patrons with the church there. Only since 1902, however, has there been a vicar of an independent parish of Endon.

The seventeneth century forms of nonconformity are represented by the presence of Thomas Buckley who lived at Dunwood and registered his house as a meeting place in 1693.[2] In 1751 the incum-

35

bent reported that there were some Presbyterians in Endon. He stated that some of the sixty-five families were of that persuasion but he does not give numbers and he continues that they had no meeting house. In 1830, the Reverend John Salt was reporting that there was no Lancaster School, no Dissenters' Schools and no dissenting chapels.[3] Several houses, however, were registered as dissenters' meeting places in Endon. John Hitchinor had one on 26th June 1805, Joseph Laken of Endon, a grocer, had another registered on 12th December 1814. Martha Machin registered her own house on February 28th 1815. Joseph Cresswell of Hazlehurst had a room registered at Endon on 20th April 1815. He was a writing clerk. John Heath of Endon, a farmer, registered a house at Endon Bank for use by protestant dissenters on 5th July 1824.[4] Methodism as a structured organisation came to Endon later than in surrounding industrial areas. Norton had a chapel before 1804, and Brown Edge had a Methodist Chapel in 1808. It would seem that Endon people were comparatively well-off and secure in their tenure not to want to engage in any social or religious change. It was not until 1835 that a Wesleyan Chapel was established in Endon village, but a Primitive Methodist Chapel was at Brown Edge, probably expressing the more radical views of the miners in that part of the parish. It was built in 1832. By 1851 the ecclesiastical census confirms that there were two Methodist Chapels in Endon, a Wesleyan and a Primitive. The papist return of 1706 shows only one, Elizabeth, wife of Andrew Heath.[5] By 1767 the churchwardens recorded, 'Paid the apparitor for four papers about the papists for Leek, Meerbrook, Rushton and Endon, four shillings.'[6] In this same year and in 1781 two unnamed men described as ribbon weavers are shown in a return of papists for Endon.[7] But Roman Catholicism did not attract any comment in the Articles of Enquiry or in the 1851 Ecclesiastical Census for Endon.

The Medieval Chapel

In 1295 the Audleys were granted the rights of a Chantry in a chapel in Endon. The priest appointed was to take an oath of fidelity to the Vicar of Leek, and was required to fulfil his office subject to certain conditions. According to a 'ledger' book of Dieulacres Abbey, the permission was granted on condition that only members of the Audley family, and their heirs should be baptised at the chapel. This condition was enforced in order to safeguard the revenues of the Vicar of Leek. However, several burials were recorded later for the family of Egerton of Wall Grange, members of which were buried at Endon before 1730 and are as follows:[8]

1570 William Egerton of Wall Grange
1613 Jane Egerton of Wall Grange
1615 Thomas Egerton of Wall Grange
1628 Timothy Egerton of Wall Grange
1663 Timothy's widow of Wall Grange

Where these burials took place, and the site of the original chapel, is not known, but footpaths of the district would suggest that the site was somewhere near the site of the present church. According to Loxdale the interments were made in 'ye chancel at Endon', suggesting, so it would seem, that the medieval church had been in existence down to 1663. A document of some fifty-eight years later suggests that there was 'a chapel or piece of building lately erected.' It is not clear whether the chapel was in existence together with 'the piece of building', or if it had been built as one structure. The Warden for Endon Quarter, acting for William Wedgwood Esquire as early as 1667, recorded in the churchwarden's accounts at Leek that 'ten shillings and eight pence was paid towards the getting of stone, walling the churchyard and laying steps.' If this relates to Endon Chapel it offers some light on the possibility of a part of the medieval chapel remaining until the late seventeenth century. A plaque inside the church gives 1719 as the year in which land for the church was given. It reads thus, 'In memory of Thos. Jodrell—late of Endon, Gent, who in ye year 1719 gave ye land on which this Chapell is erected and £5 per Ann. to the Minister thereof for ever, also the Profits of £200 to be distributed yearly to the Poor of Leek, Endon and Horton. He died ye 25th of September 1728 and was interred at Horton, this Chapell being then unconsecrated.'[9] The action of handing over the property is related in several documents one of which dated 1723 clearly states that the Vicar of Leek was to have all the rights, benefits, dues and privileges.

'To the Rt. Revd Father in God Edward Ld BP of Coventry and Litchfield

My Lord

Whereas there is a newly erected Chappell in the Township of Endon in the Parish of Leeke, and the people living in the said

37

Township are desirous to have a Curate licenced to read Divine
service in the sd Chappell, I therefore the Vicar of the sd parish
in Compliance with that desire, do hereby humbly recommend to
your Lordship the Revd Mr Willm Gardener to be licenced to
serve in the sd Chappell; Reserving to my self nevertheless all
such rights, benefits, dues and privileges, as have formerly been
enjoy'd by my predecessors, and do now of right belong to the
Vicar of Leeke; That the Benefit and advantage hereby reape'd by
the Inhabitants of the sd Township may not redound to the detriment of the present vicar or his Successors. In testimony whereof
I have hereunto put my Hand and Seal this 25th day of September
1723.   Aden Ley, Vicar of Leeke'"

I likewise nominate the sd Mr Gardener to be Curate at Maerbrooke,
where there is another Chappell in the same parish at witness my
Hand.   Aden Ley.'

A few weeks later another document was sent recommending John
Daventry for the curacy.

'The the Right Reverend Father in God, Edward Lord Bishop of
Litchfield and Coventry.

Whereas Thomas Jodrell of Leek in the County of Stafford, Gentleman, did by his Deed bearing Date the fourteenth day of September
Anno Dm 1721 for the consideration therein mentioned give grant
and convey All that Close or Parcell of Land situate within the
Hamlett of Endon commonly called Hilton's Croft, together with
the Chappell or Piece of Building lately erected on the same to
Charles Wedgewood of Haracles in the County of Stafford Esq.
William Bourn the younger of Little Chell, Gent. William Murhall
of Stafford, Gent. John Sutton of Endon aforesaid Gent. Luke
Bennett late of Mappleton in the County of Derby, Gent. Daniel
Nickson of Endon aforesaid Tanner. Simeon Sherratt of Endon
aforesaid Yeoman. Samuel Tomkinson of Endon aforesaid Yeoman.
William Whieldon of Endon aforesaid Dyer and William Ford of
Endon aforesaid Yeoman. To hold to them and their heirs upon
Trust to permit and suffer such a Minister as shall from time to time
be lawfully nominated presented and licensed to the aforesaid
Chappell to have, hold, use and enjoy the aforesaid Parcell of Land
and premises for the purposes of performing Divine Service there

and for his better support and maintenance. Now we the said Trustees whose names are hereunto subscribed by and with the consent of the said Thomas Jodrell testified by his signing these present do hereby nominate and recommend to your Lordship John Daventry of Stone in the said County of Stafford Clerk to the Minister or Curate of the said Chappell and humbly beseech your Lordship that he may be licensed thereto in witness whereof we have hereunto subscribed our names this fifth day of October Anno Dm 1723.[11]

> Thos Jodrell
> Charles Wedgewood
> Wm Bourne jun
> Wm Murhall
> John Sutton
> Luke Bennett
> Daniel Nickson
> Simeon Sherratt
> Samuel Tomkinson
> Wm Whieldon
> Wm Fford.'

Another of 1727 runs along similar lines, but offers other names as candidates for the curacy. Both are signed by Thomas Jodrell.

'To the Right Reverend Father in God Edward Lord Bishop of Litchfield and Coventry.

Whereas Thomas Jodrell of Leek in the County of Stafford, Gentleman, did by his Deed bearing Date the fourteenth day of September Anno Dom 1721 For the Considerations therein mentioned give grant and convey all that Close or Parcell of Land Situate within the Hamlett of Endon commonly called Hilton's Croft, together with the Chappell or Peice of Building lately erected on the Same to Charles Wedgewood of Haracles in the County of Stafford Esqr. William Bourne the younger of Little Chell, Gent. William Murhall of Stafford, Gent. John Sutton of Endon aforesaid Gent. Luke Bennett late of Mappleton in the County of Derby, Gent. Daniel Nickson of Endon aforesaid Tanner. Simieon Sherratt of Endon aforesaid Yeoman. Samuel Tomkinson of Endon aforesaid Yeoman. William Wheildon of Endon aforesaid Dyer, and William Fford of Endon aforesaid Yeoman. To hold them and their heirs upon Trust to permit and suffer such a minister as shall from time to time be

39

lawfully nominated presented and licensed to the aforesaid Chappell to have, hold, use and enjoy the aforesaid Parcell of Land and Premises for the Purpose of performing Divine Service there and for his better support and maintenance. Now we the Said Trustees whose Names are hereunto subscribed by and with the consent of the said Thomas Jodrell testified by his signing those present do hereby nominate and recommend to your Lordship William Brooks of Biddulph in the said County of Stafford to be Minister or Curate of the Said Chappell and humbly beseech your Lordship that he may be licenced thereto. In witness where we have hereunto subscribed our names.

> Thos Jodrell
> Ch Wedgewood
> Wm Bourne jun
> **Wm Murhall**
> John Sutton
> Luke Bennett
> Daniel Nickson
> Simeon Sherratt
> Samuel Tomkinson
> Wm Whieldon
> Wm Fford.'[12]

The legal document handing over the land to the church trustees is dated fourteenth of September 1721 a fact which is confirmed in the presentation requests dated September 1723, October 1723 and 1727.

In 1730 a petition was presented to the bishop asking for all the sacraments to be administered at Endon 'because of the many dangers of rains and waters when going to Leek for burial.'[13] It was not uncommon about this time for chapel burial grounds to be established in order to avoid the long journeys by funeral parties, often on foot, to the mother church. Resting or staging posts (halts) were often found and legend has it that one existed at Endon at the site of 'The Plough Inn' where there was suitably carved stonework and a date suggested some ecclesiastical connection. Alas, the stone has disappeared and the true function of the building cannot be determined.

The final agreement setting out the arrangements enabling the sacraments to be carried out at Endon was drawn up and signed. It is in the form of a lengthy scroll now kept in the parish chest at Leek.

St. Luke's Church, Endon in 1840. Reproduced by permission of the Trustees of William Salt Library, Stafford. Painting by L. J. Wood.

St. Luke's Church looking West. Painted by J. Buckler in 1844.
(William Salt Library)

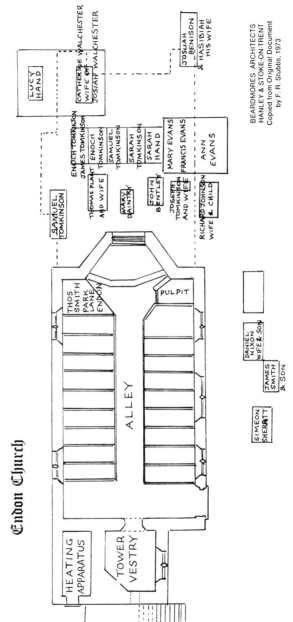
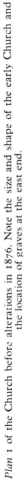

Endon Church

BEARDMORES ARCHITECTS
HANLEY & STOKE-ON-TRENT
Copied from Original Document
by F. R. Stubbs, 1973

Plan 1 of the Church before alterations in 1876. Note the size and shape of the early Church and the location of graves at the east end.

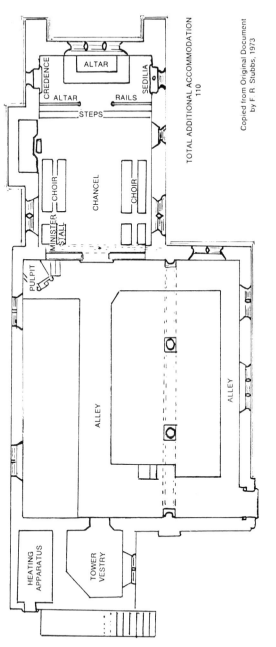

Proposed Chancel and Aisle

TOTAL ADDITIONAL ACCOMMODATION
110

Copied from Original Document
by F R Stubbs, 1973

Plan 2 Architects plan for Endon Church
1876.

To The Rt Revd Father in God Edward Ld Bp of
Coventry and Litchfield.

My Lord   Whereas these is a newly erected Chappell in
the Township of Endon in the parish of Leeke, and the
people living in the said Township are desirous to
have a Curate Licenced to read Divine services in the
sd Chappell I therefore the Vicar of the sd parish in
Compliance wth that desire, do hereby humbly recommend
to your Lordship the Revd Mr Willm Gardener
to be licenced to serve in the sd Chappell; Reserving to
my self nevertheless all such rights, benefits, dues, and
priviledges, as have formerly been enjoyd by my pre-
-decessors, and do now of right belong to the Vicar of
Leeke; That the Benefit and advantage hereby reapd
by the Inhabitants of the sd Township may not
redound to the detriment of the present vicar or
his Sucressors. In Testimony whereof I have
hereunto put my Hand and Seal this 25th day of Sept:
1723
                    Aden Ley Vic: of Leeke

I likewise nommate the sd Mr Gardener to be
Curate at Maerbrooke, where there is another Chappell
in the same parish as Witnes my Hand Aden Leys

A letter of 1723 nominating the Reverend Mr. William Gardener to be the
incumbent of Endon. In fact John Daintry became the first curate in 1730.
(Original at Joint Record Office, Lichfield).

This authorised services to be held at Endon and baptisms and burials could be performed. Marriages however, were not carried out at Endon, at least only a few bonds or agreements were recorded before 1753. In 1754 the requirements of Hardwicke's Marriage Act demanded that registers should be signed by partners and witnesses in the parish church, which would require a visit to Leek. This continued to be case at Endon until 1837 when civil registration under the Registrar General's office was established.

The first baptism was recorded in March 1730 and the first burial on 24th March 1731.[14]

Before we pass on to the well-documented era of the history of Endon Church, it may be fruitful to examine the churchwarden's accounts at Leek.

In 1724, the Wardens at Leek are listed as follows:
Abraham Taylor of Leek
John Sutton of Endon
John Wardle of Bradnop
Thos Wood of Frith
and the Vicar was Thomas Loxdale.

In the accounts for 1714 one reads of the long established Tythe Hay of Endon and Stanley (The first reference to Endon Tythe Hay was 1288—paid to the vicar of Leek as were the tithes of flax, eggs and geese.)

In the declarations made in the Easter Rolls of 1714 concerning Leek and its chapels, it would seem that a building did exist and dues were paid as outlined in the declaration.

'The Surplice Fees are payed as Follows:

For every *Churching* and *Registering* The Vicar of Leek has fourteen pence and the Clerk one penny. For every Burial, fifteen pence and Clerk fourpence, and every private bier that comes to the Church or threepence in lieu thereof. And for publishing Banns one shilling, and for marrying them, half a crown, and if with a licence, five shillings for the Clerk.

The same fees are payed for all things done at the Chappells of Meerbrook or Endon, with the threepence of the Bier for all persons buryed at either place or at Endon. The Curate or Warden if Paupers is answerable for it to ye Vicar of Leek who has also half a crown for every funeral sermon preached by any person in either chappel.

41

The Easter Roll and part of the Surplice Fees at Rushton have been lost, but now every wedding there pays at Leek and for every Burryall there ye Vicar has ninepence.

Besides all this the Vicar of Leek is to have all ye advantages of mourning cloth in ye Chappell of Endon or otherwise that the Curate of that place has. The Clerk of Leek besides ye due before mentioned has seed, oates or money given him at Easter. The Sexton of Leek has threepence payed by ye warden. Fourpence for two hours. Ye tolling of ye bell at Leek, Meerbrook and Endon, sixpence for a grave in ye yard, one shilling if in ye church and two and sixpence in ye chancell and five shillings for the Bell.'

1714 'The Tyth Hay of Endon and Stanley settled at the first upon ye vicars of leek is dropt into a modus payable as follows:

Endon			*Park Lane*		
The Ashes	...	4d	Mr Tompkinson	...	2d
Gatehouse	...	4d	The Lawn	...	4d
Knowls	...	4d	Dan Nixon	...	1d
Hollinhouse	...	2d	Roger Bridgwood	...	2d
Woodcockhurst	...	4d	Thomas Ball	...	3d
Holehouse	...	3d	Sym: Shirrot	...	3d
Lane Head	...	2d	George Hargrevs	...	2d
Fernyhough	...	4d	Ralph Colclough	...	4d
Moss House	...	1s 0d	Hollinhurst	...	2d
Lane End	...	4d			
Ann Ball, Endon Bank		4d			1s 11d
Wm Rowlys	...	2d			
William Fords	...	2d	*Stanley*		
Mr Sutton			Moss House (Wid Yate)		2d
The mill meadow	...	4d	Fr Mollats	...	2d
Mr Whywall	...	1½d	Ja: Yates	...	4d
Mrs. Endon	...	2½d	for Pilsburys	...	4d
			for Fernihoughs	...	1d
		4s 9 d	John Livery	...	1d
			Clough House	...	2d
			Upper Cloughouse		2d
			Stanley Head	...	4d
					1s. 10d

Note in ye Easter Roll that every farm while ye House is standing pays ye due tho: not Inhabited but that when the house is down and ye farm united with another the modus ceases—alsoe when a Plow land Farm is divided the Totall Summ is paid among the occupiers.'

It has already been shown that the habit of going to Leek for baptism and burial lingered on even after 1730, in spite of the difficult roads, and pews were held for Endon gentry at Leek parish church as a list of 1736 suggests:

Pews were allocated to the following: [15]

John Sutton	Hallwater
Thomas Sherratt	Park Lane
Sarah Fenton	Hollin House
John Wedgwood	Endon Bank
Hugh Sherratt	Holinhurst
William Murhall	The Knowles
Samuel Tomkinson	Lane End
Thomas Colclough	Park Lane

But services continued in the small eighteenth-century chapel situated on high ground overlooking the valley of Endon Brook, and almost within site of the mother church of Edward the Confessor at Leek.

Endon church was dedicated first as a chapel with John Daintry as the first curate of Endon and John Sutton, Samuel Tomkinson and William Ford as chapel wardens.

In 1751 the Rev. Enoch Tomkinson the next incumbent reported to the Bishop of Lichfield when he completed the articles of enquiry. Concerning the church he had the following points to make.

(1) no curate but myself

(2) 180 communicants: 30 at Whitsuntide; 50 at Easter

In 1786 Edward Fernyhough indicated the following were sources of income available to the incumbent at Endon:

(1) Glebe at Oulton with a new inclosure in the parish of Leek. tenanted by Jos Bayley

(2) £5 per annum for land at Henridding

(3) 6/8d received in Limehouse for a sermon to be preached on 29th May, Oak Apple Day

(4) £2.10s.0d. chappel croft and yard

(5) £3. 0s.6d. received for pews and sittings

(6) 1/11½d for burying and registering. [16]

43

On July 23 1830 a more detailed report was made by the Reverend John Salt:

Endon—perpetual curacy, chapelry near Leek

Patron—Lord Macclesfield. No tithes

General description—a neat small building erected 120 years ago. 200 seats

All the gallery sittings for the Poor

Roof—oak. covered lead

Walls—freestone good

Floor—bricks, even

Windows—good, new casement wanted

Doors—good

Pulpit and Desk—neat. Velvet cushion

Books—good

Seats—very neat and uniform, boarded floor

Galleries—two   Chapels—none

Organ—none   Benefaction tables—three

Vestry—there is one

Surplices—one. Another woollen

Linen—provided

Plate—Silver cup and plate

Iron chest for register—there is one

Register—from 1731

Cleanliness—attended to

Damp—not much

Table—neat.   Ornaments—none

Repaired by whom?—the township

Steeple

Square stone tower—good

Bells—one

Clock—none

Churchyard—kept by township—part has been turned into garden

Gates—poor

Drains—none, earth too high

Cattle—none

Divine Service—Two full services—Sunday

Other days—none

Sacrament—five times a year

Communicants—20
Incumbent—Reverend John Salt
What duty he performs—the whole
Parsonage—none
Income—£100 per annum
Glebe, an estate at Rushton Spencer (in 1809 it was worth £52).
Queen Ann's Bounty—amount not stated
Sunday School—40-50 children
Parish Clerk—John Mountford, appointed by the Minister at £5 per annum.
Churchwarden—William Hand.[17]

As a result of this examination it was decided to renew casements on Southside and one on Northside, to provide another surplice and to lower the earth outside the chapel, especially at the West end.

In 1841 a further report tends to support the overall view of the state of Endon church when it was recorded by the Reverend Daniel Turner that,

(1) The incumbent receives no tithes

(2) No land or farms in lieu of tithes

(3) The two farms Henridding and at Rushton Spencer were purchased with the Royal Bounty

(4) The living of Endon has not been augmented by any grants

(5) Marriages are not solemnised at Endon

(6) The Clerk's salary is £5 and the fees that he receives including those for grave-digging, may amount to about £3 more

(7) The chancel is repaired by the inhabitants and is in tolerably good condition

(8) The Communion Plate is very complete gilt with silver and of superior order

(9) Poor have charity amounting to £100 per annum—bread and money.

Continuing in operation throughout the period from 1771 until, at least, 1871 was a terrier of Endon church which was 'an account of the several seats and sittings belonging to the several persons there named, and their several entire properties to the best of my knowledge as being the surving trustee since the chappell was erected as witness my hand William Ford.' The Witnesses were John Murhall

45

and Thomas Dale and the incumbent is shown as Daniel Turner (1832-1864). The 1871 version was copied on November 20th of that year by the then churchwarden, George Foster.[18]

Copy of the Seatings of Endon Church

'On the 29th Oct. 1841 the following account was transcribed from the original writing, which is now in the possession of Mr Weatherby of Woodhead, by me Daniel Turner-Incumbent of Endon.'

An account of several seats and sittings on the North side of Endon Chappell belonging to the several persons here under mentioned, viz

NORTH SIDE

No 1 Mr Enoch Tomkinson
  2 Mr Richard Johnson
  3 Mr Samuel Tomkinson
  4 John Murhall one half the other half belongs to the Minister
  5 Mr Bennett of Lawn Farm— by purchase
  6 Lord Chief Baron Parker for Lane Head Farm
  7 Mr Willm Ford two sittings the remaining sittings to the Minister
  8 Enoch Tomkinson for Lane End Estate
  9 The whole of this pew belongs to the Minister for the time being
 10 Mr John Kidd's of Park Lane
 11 This pew also belongs to the Minister for the time being

Pews and sittings on the South Side of Endon Chappel viz

1 Mr. Thos Sutton
2 Mr Daniel Nixon
3 The heirs of John Wedgwood Esq for Endon Bank and Moss
4 The Minister's pew for the time being
5 Do   Do
6 Mr Thos Godwin on half Mr Thos Crompton the other half
7 The Minister's pew
8 Richd Needham for Holehouse
9 Mr Thos Sherratt of Park Lane

NB the Gallery to be free for the use of the inhabitants within the Liberty only dated this 20 day of Sept 1771
The several seats and sittings above mentioned belong to the several persons there named, are their several entire properties to the best of my knowledge as being the surviving Trustee since the Chappell was erected as witness my hand.
              Willm Ford

The above was copied on 20 November 1871 - Geo Foster, Churchwarden

Witness
John Murhall
Thos Dale[19]

Thus the eighteenth-century chapel continued to exist, not very well off and catering essentially for a predominantly agricultural community, and up to about 1840 without any challenge from Dissenting sects. The Plan (following page 40)[20] of the church of this period reveals its simplicity. The inside, as shown in a painting of the period, consisted of a simple nave with no aisle North or South, a fine collection of box pews, and a two-tier pulpit. The growing size of the population and the increased wealth of the parishioners led to an increase in the size of the church membership and the faculty for a structural enlargement was presented in 1876 by Reverend James Badnall along with Messrs. Tennant and Heaton, churchwardens, who declared that they proposed to remove the old chancel and build a new one. The proposals were displayed on the church outer door.

Something has already been said of the numbers of communicants and the secondary role played by the chapel to the mother church at Leek, both in connection with tythes and with regard to registration. (see pages 42-43). Perhaps the most significant figures are to be found in the Ecclesiastical Census of 1851 which provides the following,

C of E called 'Endon Chapel' 1730	80 free sittings 120 other ,,	Curate: Daniel Turner
	a.m.	Afternoon
General congregation	40	100
Sunday Scholars	40	40
	80	140

Remark: There is occasionally a night service with Stanley, where a mission church was eventually established by the Reverend James Badnall 1868. It was licenced for services on March 6th.

We have already seen that since 1865 Endon was an Ecclesiastical District and in 1902 was established as a vicarage with the Vicar of Leek replacing the Earl of Macclesfield as patron. In 1915 a vicarage was built and since that time the parish has enjoyed the full and equal rights relating to its position.

Perhaps the Visitation Return of 1906 records the most graphic picture. It states the facts of Endon Church.

Built 1730 (this, of course, is the date it became a Chapel of Ease of Leek parish). Restored 1877, 1879 nave, new roof and a chanel, South aisle, and South porch added Early decorated style cost £1,850. It consisted (in 1906) of chancel, nave, aisle, porch and embattled Western tower with one bell. The report continues to reveal some of the more detailed aspects of the church fabric's growth, at a time when offertory receipts amounted to morning: fourteen shillings and eightpence; evening: one pound five shillings and ninepence halfpenny.

In 1893 a stained glass window was put in in memory of George Smith. It was designed by Sir E. Burne-Jones Bart. The final extension was completed in 1898 when a North aisle was added, a gift of Mr Thomas Smith of Park Lane, thus giving the church the appearance it has today.

The organ was installed in 1906, when, so the report continues, the building was worth £200 per annum and was held as a gift of the Vicar of Leek.

Incumbents at Endon

Presentations for the appointment of curates were made in 1723, 1727, 1737, 1762, 1798, 1815, 1832, and 1864.[21]

The presentations of 1723 and 1727 have been referred to earlier, since they were concerned with proposals before the chapel was consecrated. The agreement to make John Daintry curate was made in 1730 by the Vicar of Leek. In 1737 John Daintry became Vicar of Leek himself and is featured in the church history there, perhaps most notably, because he was living in the vicarage when Bonnie Prince Charlie stayed there in 1745. He was followed at Endon by Enoch Tomkinson of Park Lane who remained there until he died in 1761. He was buried on October 5th.

Samuel Turnock is the subject of the next presentation in 1762. He too had a long stay at Endon remaining until November 1797. For a short period an officiating minister by the name of Thomas Bowness was placed in Endon under a sequestration order, as the parish registrar puts it.

The interregnum ended by the presentation of Thomas Middleton in 1798 who was followed by John Salt. He was recommended by
Clement Leigh, Rector of Newcastle
Thomas Butt, perpetual curate of Trentham
Thomas Coterill, perpetual curate of Lane End
as 'having been personally known to us for the space of three years last past, hath during that time lived piously, soberly and honestly: nor hath he, at any time (as far as we know or believe) held, written, or taught anything contrary to the Doctrine and Discipline of the Church of England.'

1832 saw John Salt replaced by Reverend Daniel Turner, a former master of Leek High School who acted as curate for thirty-two years until 1864, in fact, he and his successor covered the period 1832 to 1897 between them.

Speaking of Endon in 1872 and referring to his days at Leek High School, Mr. Joseph Challinor says of the Reverend Daniel Turner, his former schoolmaster: 'Many here would remember his geniality and eccentricity and that in his ordinary dress he certainly did not sacrifice to the graces. Mr. Turner sometimes, though not often, used the cane in his didactic capacity, and well remembered an anecdote he had repeated, that his father at one period used to thrash him every Monday morning, saying he was sure to have done something to deserve it during the week; also that when the operation went on he used to say, 'I love thee lad, I love thee, I lick thee because I love thee.'[22]

The memorial inscription in the South Wall of the chancel is 'In memory of James Badnall, BA, for thirty-three years vicar of this parish. Died, October 19th 1897.' He was incumbent during the years of development in Endon and his period covered the era of rebuilding the church. He was keenly interested in the Endon Club, the welldressing activities and local and national politics. The Reverend Percy Stowers followed him in 1898 and remained at Endon until 1902.

Since the establishment of an independent parish in that year, the vicars have been:

    1902   John Simon Morris
    1929   Arthur Eli Pavey
    1944   John Kingsley Ashton
    1957   R. Mackworth Dawes
    1966   Anthony J. Alban.

Nearer the present day, people remember the Reverend J. S. Morris whose twenty-seven years of office ended in 1929. Apart from his missionary work he was responsible for the high standard of music achieved during this period. He was a former choirboy of Canterbury Cathedral, and set a good example in vocal virtuosity gathering round himself a choir of considerable distinction. At the bi-centenary of the church in 1930, the memory of J. S. Morris was perpetuated by the presentation to the church of the beautiful choir stalls and two accompanying seats.

49

The church still contains four huge brass paraffin lamps and their shades, left in their original positions attached to brackets on the sides of the pillars.[23] Today the church is lit by electricity.

Endon St. Luke's Mission Church, Hill Top, Brown Edge

The present Mission Church known locally as 'Harvey's Mission' at the top of Broad Lane, Hill Top, was built in 1900. Two local builders Messrs. Simcock and Brooks carried out the construction work. Prior to 1900 the site on which the present Mission Church stands was occupied by three small cottages which were purchased by Mr. Herbert Heaton, a land agent living in Endon. He bore the cost of building the new Mission Church together with an adjoining caretaker's cottage, and presented them to Endon Parish Church. Also included in the gift was a three-acre field situated opposite. Mr. I. Harvey and his family were the first caretakers and they lived at the cottage until Mr. Harvey died, when one of his daughters and her husband, Mr. and Mrs. George Biddulph, took over and continued the work. The new Mission Church is built of stone with a tile roof, and has seating for approximately thirty people. Two of the members of this Church are at present members of the Endon Church Parochial Council and a firm connection is maintained between the two. The vicar of Endon celebrates Holy Communion at this Mission Church each month.

St. Anne's, Brown Edge

The consecration of St. Anne's, Brown Edge was on May 29th 1844. A local newspaper went on to describe the scene concerning 'this little edifice which has recently been built for the purpose of affordage of means of divine worship to the inhabitants of a boundary moorland district in the parish of Norton-in-the-Moors. As the appointed hour approached the highways and byways leading towards Brown Edge were thronged with parties intent upon witnessing the interesting ceremony.' The Lord Bishop of the Diocese of Lichfield stayed with Mr. H. H. Williamson and Mrs. Williamson at Greenway Bank Hall and performed the consecration ceremony. Included in the party were 'Charles Bowyer Adderley, Esq., M.P., and his lady.' Some six hundred people were present and after the sermon the service was concluded by the singing of the 119th Psalm. The site and £500 had been given by Sir Charles Bowyer Adderley. The rest of the cost of building was met by public subscription. The Patron was the Bishop of Lichfield and the first incumbent was the Reverend St. John Mitchell. On September 3rd 1844 an order in Council created 'a district to the church of St. Anne's built by voluntary contributions.'[24] Inside the church a slate tablet announces that this chapel was erected to accommodate three hundred sittings. It was built of local millstone grit stone with a tiled roof and two entrances on the South and West sides. Later Mr. H. H. Williamson arranged for a caretaker's cottage, stable and coach house to be built. The cottage bears the inscription: H.H.W. 1846. The building of a vicarage commenced in 1852, and was completed in 1853, and as if to reflect the mode of the age there was a coach house and stable on the vicarage drive. In 1855 the tower and spire were built, a gift of Mr. and Mrs. Williamson, costing £2,500. A year later the Williamsons bore the cost of installing a peal of six bells, another £316.6s.5d. Mr. Williamson also paid for the construction of a new approach road to the Church for his coach and horses. Hence 'Old Lane' and 'New Lane', Brown Edge.

In 1856 Brown Edge became an Ecclesiastical Parish quite separate from its mother church at Norton. The new parish stretched from Endon Parish Boundary in the east to the River Trent in the west. In 1860 an organ was installed in the church. Ten years later one of the more striking characters arrived as vicar. He was the Reverend R. G. Young, an Irish protestant who wore a black robe when he was preaching and made his visits round the parish either on horseback or with his pony and trap. He died in 1901, thirty-one years after his induction as vicar.

The turn of the century saw new problems, largely as a result of doctrinal differences and the church sank to a new low. The average weekly collections were fifteen shillings. This, added to the decaying church fabric, placed a tremendous burden on the vicar and the churchwardens, and a successful appeal raised £700. The repair work was carried out. In 1944 a further appeal was made and £600 was handed over for restoration. In 1948 a new organ was brought into use but not too successfully, and in 1951 it had to be overhauled at a cost of £1,000. Several additions have been made to the church furniture during the last twenty years and the church thrives, catering for a vastly changing community of people, slightly more than a century old, but boasting a state as an ecclesiastical parish which pre-dates the one at Endon.

The first entry in the baptism registers at Brown Edge reads: '12th January 1845. Levi, son of Thomas and Elizabeth Holdcroft of Sandy Lane, Brown Edge.' The father's occupation is shown as labourer. Since 1837 registration had been in the hands of the Registrar General and little significance can be attached to the number of entries in these registers, though occupations and the ability or inability of marriage partners to sign their names is interesting.

List of the Vicars of Brown Edge

1844   Rev. St. John Mitchell
1851   Rev. Samuel Pearson
1867   Rev. J. T. Willis
1870   Rev. R. G. Young
1902   Rev. Edwin J. Sturdee
1914   Rev. R. St. Clare Page
1920   Rev. Thomas Deane Lawton
1945   Rev. F. S. L. Ramsden
1950   Rev. W. T. D. Attoe
1957   Rev. R. G. Landsdale
1961   Rev. E. H. B. Richards
1967   Rev. E. Rastall

The Earliest Terrier of St. Anne's Church dated 1861

A statement of all and singular buildings, emoluments, dues belonging to the Incumbency of the new parish of St. Anne, Brown Edge in the County of Stafford and Diocese of Lichfield, delivered at the visitation of the Chancellor of the Diocese, held at Stoke-on-Trent on April 24th 1861.

(1) A residence for the Incumbent adjoining the churchyard with a garden, a small paddock and shrubbery belonging to the living and was erected as a parsonage for the Minister.

(2) The Incumbent receives annually £90 as an endowment from the Ecclesiastical Commissioners, also a further endowment from Queen Anne's bounty, interest at three per cent. on £94.3.2d. Reduced bank annuities, on £1,000 three per cent. Cordens

Fund and £1,000 at three and one quarter per cent. benefaction raised by Hugh Henshall Williamson Esq. to meet the Corden grant in 1853.

(3) The Incumbents Fees are as follows:

Marriage by Banns 3/6, by licence 7/-, publishing banns 1/-, churching 1/6, burials 1/6, brick grave 10/6, grave bricked to the surface £2, flat stone £1.1.0, grave stone erect 10/-, a small stone not exceeding two feet in length 5/- (for the poor), land for vaults £1.1.0. per square yard, opening vaults £1.1.0, monuments according to the custom in adjoining parishes.

For the bell ringers yearly £6 endowment on estate now belonging to Hugh Henshall Williamson of Greenway Bank Hall, and given by him through a deed enrolled in Chancery with £14 annually for poor widows, paid at Christmas in each year.

The owner of Greenway Bank Hall and the Incumbent for the time being are the Trustees. The estate is Woodhouse Farm under Marshes Hill lying North East of lands belonging to Stone House Farm.

Endowments have been made for the education of children trained in the tenets of the Church of England of three cottages (now two with a cow-house attached) and nine acres of land named Hobbs House and for a small house and ten acres called Hough Lane on the turnpike road to Endon.

These were done by H. H. Williamson, Esq. owner of Greenway Bank Hall, Sir George Chetwynd, and the Incumbent of Brown Edge for the time being trustees. Deeds have been enrolled in Chancery.

(4) The Communion Plate consists of Flagon, Chalice and Paten, all silver and iron chest.

The organ erected in the church was given by H. H. Williamson

Samuel Pearson, Incumbent

Joseph Sargeant
John Mountford   Wardens

In 1894 there was added an Electro Plated bread box and plate, the latter having an inscription, 'In loving memory of John and Caroline Jones, from their children.'

Mr. and Mrs. Jones were early headmaster and mistress of St. Anne's large school.

53

Memorial Tablets, etc. in St. Anne's Church

On the North side of the nave there is a large tablet inscribed as follows: 'In memory of Marie Williamson, wife of Robert Williamson and daughter of James Edwards of May Place who died January 12th 1862.' On the same side of the nave there is a marble cross cemented onto a black slate slab on which the inscription is cut, 'In loving memory of Hugh Henshall Williamson, Esq. who died 3rd of December 1867, at Greenway Bank Aged 84 years.' A stone plaque bearing the Williamson coat of arms is on the North Wall of the nave above the entrance of the organ chamber.

Between the two pillars which form the South West wall of the Chancel, there is fixed a copper plate measuring eighteen inches by twelve inches on which there is an inscription which reads as follows: 'The East window of the chancel was placed by general contributions A.D. 1874. In memory of May, wife of James Joseph Hefferman, M.D. of Her Majesty's Indian Army and eldest daughter of Robert Heath and Ann, his wife, who died October 13th 1872, aged twenty-eight years, also of William Heath of Greenway Bank, eldest son of the above Robert and Ann Heath, who died November 11th in the same year.' Both are buried in the family vault at Biddulph.

The window consists of three panels, the top centre one depicts the Resurrection, the painting of which was executed by the famous artist Sir E. Burne-Jones. On either side of this, and underneath in the centre, are portraits representing the Virgin Mary and the Apostles Peter, Paul and Mark, all of which are the work of an assistant who always distinguished his work from that of his master by including bunches of grapes with a prevailing tint of pale green in striking contrast to the deep colours of the master hand. Over the south door inside the church, there is a horizontal white marble scroll bearing the following inscription: 'In loving memory of the Reverend R. Goodwin Young, for 31 years Vicar of this parish 1870-1901, also of his wife Anna Maria Young. This monument was erected by parishioners and friends.'

On the South wall of the nave is the village War Memorial Tablet. The tablet is a slab of fine white marble provided by public subscription and was dedicated by Admiral Sir J. Slartin, K.C.B., of Linley Hall, Bishops Castle, Shropshire. The inscription reads: 'To the glorious memory of those of this parish who gave their lives in the Great War 1914-1918. I am the resurrection and the life.'

Killed in Action

Adams, Edward	Hall, Samuel	Sadier, William
Basnett, Edgar	Hall, Thomas	Sheldon, Joseph
Booth, John	Hancock, Samuel	Simcock, John
Bourne, Arthur	Hancock, Joseph	Stockton, Peter
Bowyer, William	Hargreaves, Harry	Turner, Allen
Ford, Isaac	Kennerley, William	Turner, Edwin
Frost, James	Moorcroft, George S.	Turner, Harry
Gunn, Frederick	Powell, Harold	Gaskin, Hugh

Died through War Service

Bailey, George	Holdcroft, Hiram
Goodwin, Joseph K.	Sheldon, Jesse

Ye that live in England's pastures green—remember us and think what might have been.

This tablet was unveiled and dedicated on the first of May 1927. During 1948 the organ was enlarged and renovated as the Village War Memorial for the 1939-45 World War. An inscription on the organ reads: 'This organ was enlarged and renovated by the people of this parish in grateful remembrance of Known and Unknown men and women who gave their lives in the course of Justice and Freedom, and in thanksgiving to the Almighty God for those who returned 1939-1945.'

In 1950 a litany table was given by Mr. and Mrs. J. Charles of Rock Cottage, and the inscription reads: 'In remembrance of Henry Bertram Eaton 1878-1944.' Also in 1950 a new reading desk made of light oak was given by Mr. and Mrs. Harry Proctor.

In 1958 a new altar table was given by Mr. G. H. Hall who at this time was one of the churchwardens. The inscription reads: 'In memory of Elsie May Hall who died March 27th 1955, and to commemorate her life long service to this church.' This altar was given by her husband and included with the gift were the silver cross, candle-sticks and curtains behind the altar. Also in 1958 Communion Kneeling Stools were given by the family of the late James H. Pointon, and the inscription reads: 'In memory of James H. Pointon, Lizzie Pointon, Maria Pointon and Samuel Pointon.'

55

ST. ANNE'S CHURCHWARDEN'S ACCOUNTS FOR THE YEAR ENDING EASTER 1881

Gross Receipts from Offertories	Deduct gifts to poor	for church expenses	Expenditure April 17th 1880 to April 19th 1881	£	s.	d.
			Balance due to Churchwardens ...	6	6	6
			Coal and Slack	2	16	2
			Oil for lamps and bells ...	0	7	11½
			Heating the church ...	2	10	0
			Attending to church ...	1	0	0
			Insurance	0	5	3
			Repairs and Materials ...	4	16	5
			Washing church linen ...	0	12	0
			Wine for sacrament ...	0	9	5
			Visitation Fees ...	0	12	6
			Blowing the church organ ...	0	5	0
£24 19 5½	£5 9 9	£19 9 8½	Cleaning the church ...	2	12	9½
				£22	14	0
Balance due to Churchwardens =		£3 4 3½				
		£22 14 0				

Examined and found correct:
T. Gilchrist, Easter 1881

R. Heath, Jnr.
George Turner } Churchwardens 1880-1881

56

'The Methodists in every place grow diligent and frugal; consequently they increase in goods. Hence they proportionably increase in pride, in anger, in the desire of the flesh, the desire of the eyes, and the pride of life. So although the form of religion remains, the spirit is swifly vanishing away.' John Wesley, aged 84 (1787).

At the end of the eighteenth century Methodism was firmly established in North Staffordshire. Preaching districts, or circuits, had been formed in both the Burslem and Leek areas, and the social and religious impacts of the new teachings were being felt among farmers and industrial workers. The origin of Wesleyan Methodism in Leek is associated with the Hammersley family who, before 1754, lived at a lonely farmhouse called Bryan's Hay, which is situated on the road between Newcastle and Leek, one mile to the east of Endon. As far as we know no records of the activities of this family at Bryan's Hay have been preserved and when the Hammersley family moved to Leek in 1754, they joined the Wesleyan Society there and preaching ceased in Bryan's Hay.[25] These, however, were early days in Methodism. In 1772, some years after the road passing Bryan's Hay had been turnpiked, John Wesley travelled along this the Newcastle to Hassop turnpike road passing through the village of Endon. An account of this journey which was made on horseback is recorded in his Journal.[26] On the 11th August 1772 John Wesley passed through Longnor on his way from Sheffield to Burslem and he records, 'About eight I preached at Grindleford Bridge. Before two we reached Longnor. After we had dined, a poor woman came in, and another, and another with whom we spent a little time in prayer and praise . . . at the end of the town the chaise broke down so I took horse and came hither (to Burslem) a little before preaching time.'

Wesley visited Leek for the last time on the 5th April 1788, when he wrote, 'I crossed over (from Newcastle) to Leek where for many years we seemed to be ploughing upon the sand, but at length the fruit appeared.' Again John Wesley travelled through Endon village along the turnpike road, but no mention is made of Endon in his Journal.

Probably the best known Methodist in this area, after Wesley, is Hugh Bourne who lived at Bemersley in the adjacent parish of Norton, and early in the nineteenth century was engaged in intense missionary activity in North Staffordshire.[27] He knew and frequently visited villages in the vicinity of Endon. He wrote on 'Tuesday February 22nd 1803 I went to Brown Edge meeting at night, we had a lively time, more people attended than usual and seemed serious.' On several occasions in his writi. ;s he mentioned Samuel Bennison of Annat's House, near Norton Green, and Miss A. Mear who lived at the Old Hall, Norton Green. 'Thursday 30th November 1809, I was at Miss Mear's Norton Green. Sh. was out . . . Hannah Heath, her servant, asked me to visit her brother at Milton.' The next day, 'I worked at Milton. At night I visited James Heath a young man, has been a boatsman and very wicked; has lain ill since last June. I was glad to meet with Hannah Heath there.' Her brother 'was blest. I believe he will be saved.' 'I visited Rowleys at Clay Lake, and brought Mrs. Rowley into liberty, and her daughter Ann also.'

Such were his connections in the area, and again on '7th August 1804 on Saturday while going through Endon, I seemed to have a call to visit Standley (Stanley), Bagnall Grange and Bagnall.' Later 'Old James (Crawfoot) preached at Bagnall . . . He tore up Old Calvin root and branch. Some that imbibed these opinions were present and were very much affected.' At Stanley James Crawfoot preached again 'we had a very moving time.'

In 1813 Hugh Bourne preached to 'a large company' of people at Dunwood and visited there again in 1816 to 'preach to the people' and 'renew class tickets.' The following year Joseph Armett of Dunwood threw open his house as a preaching place for Primitive Methodists.

The accounts of his local connections as given by Hugh Bourne continue 'Sunday 28th August 1808. I went with Thomas Cotton to Gratton. The meeting had not been published, however we got the people out and held meeting.' A year later he registered a preaching place at Gratton, the first to be registered by Hugh Bourne after his enforced separation from the Wesleyans, who by this time had taken on an air of respectability. Two years later he again raises the issue of the Gratton Camp Meeting when he stated on 'Tuesday 24th July 1810—Daniel Shubotham told me that there was a Camp Meeting appointed at Gratton next Sunday but one. At this I wondered that we had never heard of it. On this account I thought it right to refer my journey into Cheshire and Lancashire till after that meting.' On Sunday August 5th 1810 he recorded 'A camp meeting commenced at Blackwood Hill Green. It was a fine morning, but in a little time it thundered and rained and about noon it hailed and rained very heavily and we got the liberty of a large barn. This having a large pair of doors was convenient for out of doors and in, and it was a very powerful time all the day.'

But the stirrings of the Wesleyans had not been dormant. In 1816 Samuel, John, George (then 15 years old) and William Heath and their sister joined the Wesleyan Society at Gratton. Their father, who also became a Wesleyan Methodist, was later to erect a Wesleyan Chapel on his own ground in 1822. Thus starts the connection between the Heath family and the Methodist Society in Endon. John Heath came to live in the village at a farmhouse on Endon Bank, and in 1826 his brother George left Gratton moving to Rose Cottage, now called Barncroft, in Endon village. The two Heath brothers both became preachers and brought Methodism in an organised form to Endon.[28] For some years preaching took place at the farm on Endon Bank and at Rose Cottage. At first the reception was hostile but 'during this period (1826-1835) the hostility of the people softened and prejudices subsided' and in 1835 a piece of land was obtained on which to erect a chapel. The land was described as 'part of a certain close called Gate Field situated at a place called the Jawbones in Endon, one hundred yards or thereabouts.' It was purchased from Charles Heaton of Endon for the sum of five pounds five shillings, with an additional payment of ten shillings which was made to James Tessimond of Leek, a silk manufacturer. The agreement to purchase the land on behalf of the Society was signed by Thomas Phillips of Newcastle, a grocer, James Wardle, a silk manufacturer, George Bull, a grocer and Richard Cooper, a surgeon, all of Leek and James Hambleton, a farmer of Cheddleton, John Heath, a farmer, George Heath, a farmer, John Bailey, a miller, all of Endon. Also involved were William Heath, a farmer of Gratton, Richard Bailey, a farmer of Horton Hay, John and Joseph Corbishley both of Dunwood, farmers, George Harvey of Blackwood Hill, a farmer. The superintendent minister of the Leek Wesleyan Circuit at the time was Joshua Fearnside.[29]

The social significance of the occupations in this list suggests that the Wesleyans had now gained a degree of respectability and were men of some substance, in local terms at least. Another feature of the social position attained by this brand of Wesleyan Methodism was marked by the fact that all the signatories signed their own names suggesting at least a minimal standard of literacy at a time when some

59

fifty per cent. of the male population were illiterate. (For Stafford County the figures were 42 per cent. men, 61 per cent. women in 1839.)

The Leek Wesleyan Methodist Year Book states, 'it was largely by George Heath's efforts that a Wesleyan Methodist Chapel was erected in Endon in 1835, where a society of nine members was gathered within the sacred enclosures of Zion.' The chapel was described as being 'a plain but neat and commodious place of worship occupying a central and most eligible situation.' The cost of the building was £217. Following the opening of the chapel a Sunday School began in 1844 with eight teachers and forty-four scholars on roll.[30] The Moorland Poet, George Heath, was born in that same year at Gratton. He was a member of the early Methodist family mentioned above and owed much of the education obtained in his younger days to the Endon Wesleyan Sunday School. His poem 'Farewell to the Sunday School' is full of reminiscences of village Methodism, and what to the trustees had been 'a plain but neat and commodious place of worship' was to the Moorland poet 'a dear old place'.

'Farewell to the Sunday School on going out into the World' was written by George Heath and since the Sunday School he knew well was at Endon, it can be safely supposed that he had the days spent there in mind when he wrote the following lines:[31]

> Happy meeting sister schoolmate,
> Let us pause a moment here
> In this temple, memory hallowed
> And 'mongst scenes so strangely dear.
>
> For the time has come for parting
> Time to leave the dear old place
> Each to choose a separate calling
> Each to run a separate race.
>
> Therefore, let us pause a moment
> In this dear old hallowed pile
> Let us brace our souls for action
> Ere we enter on the toil.
>
> So that when deceit would lure us
> Sin 'ercome or passion rule
> Like a monitor before us
> May arise the Sabbath School.

The Ecclesiastical Census of 1851 records that the Wesleyan Chapel, Endon, erected in 1835, had seating accommodation for on hundred and ten people (no pew rent was to be paid on fifty seats), and standing room for twenty.

Thirty scholars attended the morning session of the Sunday School, thirty-three scholars and eighteen adults were present at the afternoon service, and forty-two people attended evening worship.[32] This on a day when the Incumbent of St. Anne's, Brown Edge was forced to record 'a very stormy wet day' against his entry, presumably in order to account for low attendances.

John Heath, a founder member of the 1835 Endon Chapel, died in 1862 and his obituary in the Leek Wesleyan Year Book says that he was 'a consistent and faithful Local Preacher for forty years.' Supported by men and women of devotion and purpose, the chapel prospered for forty years. However, in May 1875, the surviving trustees agreed to the 'sale of the chapel on condition that a new or more commodious place of worship was erected in a suitable situation.' The village was growing, Methodism was in its heyday, and a plot of land 'in a suitable situation' was found. It was at the spot where the old Endon meets the new, the junction of the roadways near the Fountain. The land was purchased from W. Orford, Esq., at a cost of one hundred and twenty pounds three shillings and ninepence, and the stone-laying ceremony of the new chapel took place on the 30th August 1875, the chapel being completed in 1876. It had by then cost one thousand nine hundred and twenty-one pounds, two shillings and ninepence.

On the 14th of October of the same year the 'dear old place' in the village centre was sold to 'John Walker of Endon, a farmer' for the sum of one hundred and fifty pounds, and was converted into cottages. The building still stands to this day in the centre of the old village. The surviving trustees of the 1835 Wesleyan Chapel were George Heath of Endon, John Corbishley of Dunwood and Joseph Corbishley of Dunwood, later of Endon. All lived to see the new chapel opened, but it has been recorded that the 1875 building 'owed much to Mr. R. Clemeson.' Other workers were Mr. Peter Walker, formerly of Norton and Mr. William Heath a local preacher of Endon, and to hear 'these three men pray in the after-meeting on a Sunday evening was a benediction.'

A Sunday School summary of 1887 provides the information that there were fifteen officers and teachers in the Sunday School, sixty-three scholars under the age of fifteen, and eight scholars over fifteen years of age. (There was no library at Endon Chapel, neither was there a Band of Hope.) The Conference Catechisms were used in the Sunday School which had an annual cost of twenty-six pounds, nineteen shillings, and Schedules for 1887 show that Endon Wesleyan Chapel had thirty-eight adult members of the Society,[33] a tightly-knit group, the only form of nonconformity in the village of Endon.

The chapel records show that during the first quarter of this century, the number of members of the Society and of scholars in the Sunday School do not vary much from the ones given in the latter part of the nineteenth century.[34] To a very large extent it carried on in a consistent but unobtrusive manner down to the present day.

From the descriptions so far it would seem that the people of Endon 'a pleasant scattered village' had little need of change in their way of life or mode of worship. Hugh Bourne's class meetings, his open-air religious services and camp meetings did not appeal to the more orthodox Endonian. In his writings, Hugh Bourne's references to Endon are of a casual nature, 'going through Endon', and on another occasion 'I went to Endon nearly'. By contrast there are many references of his ministrations in the adjacent village of Brown Edge where the majority of menfolk were coal miners. Here the vivid, fiery speeches and the constant urgings towards a change of life-style had an impact.

In 1803 Hugh Bourne who was then a Wesleyan visited Brown Edge each Tuesday and held religious meetings. Accounts of these are given by Hugh Bourne. He states 'Tuesday March 1st 1803. A very wet day. I had by desire to go to Brown Edge at night, which was rather a cross it being rainy . . . Going when it was wet and attending constantly when others would not or could not . . . When I came there I had the happyness of seeing a larger congregation than usual.'

'Tuesday March 8th 1803. I was rather to(o) late at Brown Edge. They had begun the meeting, my brother James and John Sarjant being there, and a greater congregation that I ever saw at that house. My brother James said that coming to the meeting he was overtaken by Little John who pretended to be set out again for Heaven, but this is very uncertain as he has had so many settings out: but James ordered him not to take any publick part in the meetings at present.' 'Tuesday 29th March 1803. I was at Brown Edge. I stopped a while after the meeting and found them very dark and ignorant although two of them had met in Mr. Wood's class.'

On 'Tuesday 23rd August 1803, I was at the tope of Brown Edge. We had but few, it being Norton Wake(s). I talked with J. Willat's wife. She seems to be going for heaven and betimes enjoys much happyness.'

The next day his brother James, who was preaching in Sarjant's house in Woodhouse Lane, talked with William Boardman 'who is seting out for Heaven.' William Boardman lived at 'Woodhouse' a 'thatched' seventeenth century property now known as 'Boardman's Bank.' In the early nineteenth century the Boardmans were farmers of twenty-six acres of land in Brown Edge, and a William Boardman had been warden at Norton Parish Church. The name Boardman persists in connection with Wesleyan Methodism in Brown Edge until the late nineteenth century. Hugh Bourne's account of James' meeting at Sarjant's house continues 'Brown Edge has been barren for many years, and has been tried and given up, but now it flourishes.' Two days later the colourful and sincere forms of expression were used to describe the pitfalls of Norton Wakes, when Hugh Bourne received good news of Little John who 'had so many settings out for Heaven' but on this occasion had not succumbed to the carousalling at Norton Wakes. 'They (the Brown Edge Class) informed me that Little John withstood the Wake.' However, there is no record of Little John being allowed 'to take any publick part in the meetings'.

On Easter Sunday in 1805, Hugh Bourne went to the Sacrament at Brown Edge. Later that same year Ralph Wood registered a meeting house at Brown Edge for the Wesleyans and James and Hugh Bourne. John Birchenhough, John and Richard Sarjant, James and William Scarlett and Thomas Mountford were witnesses to the registration. But the association between the Bournes and the Wesleyans was short-lived, for their separate styles became apparent and it was recorded that an estimated number of between two thousand and four thousand people attended the Mow Cop Meeting in May 1807.[35] The Burslem Wesleyans were strongly opposed to the camp meetings and later the Wesleyan Conference at Liverpool declared such meetings 'highly improper in England . . . and we disclaim all connexion with them.' However a small Camp Meeting was held in Brown Edge on Sunday, 16th August 1807. 'Many from Harrishead attended but no preachers besides Thomas Cotton and I', records Hugh Bourne. 'At two o'clock

63

we went in the *Chapel*. W. Skinner preached, we then returned to the common and continued till about six o'clock. Many came out to hear who scarce ever heard the gospel in their lives.'

There is little to indicate the feelings of the Brown Edge people towards Hugh Bourne, but they supported him on his numerous visits and his own personal attachment to the village was clearly shown. Perhaps it should be made clear that at this time Brown Edge was a remote cluster of workers' houses on the road between Norton and Endon. The houses in the main had been built only a few years earlier and associations with the more traditional centres of Norton and Endon were few. In many ways, it was an ideal place to foster the new wing of a new religion. In 1808 a Chapel was built in Sandy Lane, Brown Edge. Land was purchased from Richard Leake on which to erect a Chapel. Details of the transaction are as follows,

		Mr. Machin	Mr. John Riles		
1808		To Thos. Sparrow	6 Drs.		
May.	Instructions for conveyance from Richd Leake to you of a Plot Land on which to erect a chapel at Brown Edge and attendances afterwards consulting sevl times as the mode and manner of the Conveyance, etc.		13.	4.	
	Drawing same by which expence of two deeds was avoided for 38		1.	18.	0.
	Fair Copy for perusal			12.	8.
	Ingrossing		1.	5.	4.
	Attending execution			6.	8.
			4.	16.	0.
	Paid for Stamps and Parchment ...		2.	12.	10.
			£7.	8.	10.

Burslem Wesleyan circuit records show that the estimated cost of the building was one hundred and sixty pounds.

Hugh Bourne persisted with his camp meetings and subsequently on Monday, June 27th 1808 was excluded by the Burslem Circuit Quarterday Meeting from the Wesleyan Society. Nevertheless he continued his ministrations at the Wesleyan Chapel, Brown Edge, even though there was much discouragement and harassment by the Travelling Preachers of the Burslem Circuit. There are many accounts of the

A sketch made of Wesley Place, 1863. Note the early Methodist Church, now cottages and the well on the left. Drawn by H. W. Foster, November 19th, 1863.

Brown Edge Primitive Methodist class tickets 1876 to 1886. All relate to the Charlesworth family of Brown Edge.

continued success of the Brown Edge 'Wesleyans' who as adherents of Hugh Bourne would at this time probably be known as 'Bourneites'.

Hugh Bourne continues his report with such exclamations as 'I then went to Brown Edge . . . the Lord blesses me abundantly at this place', 'They go on well at Brown Edge. Old Bettesworth led the class and preached at two o'clock . . . I visited some at Brown Edge. I went with T.K. (Thomas Knight) to Brown Edge. He spoke from Matthew 20 verse 6. "Why stand ye all the day idle?" He was "strait".' Again he states that on Sunday, August 13th 1809 'I came to Brown Edge Chapel and was desired to take the pulpit. I went up and gave an exhortation, and then begun to give out a hymn. While doing this Thomas Hurd came (from the Burslem Wesleyan Circuit?) and it was a very dry time: the people wished me to have stopped in the pulpit instead of him.' He was not afraid to give his opinion of a preacher as he did the following evening when he was again at Brown Edge: 'Brougham preached, a dull time.' Some seven months later he heard James Crawfoot preach at Brown Edge and was satisfied that 'the work goes on well.'

Hugh Bourne's account of his activities in Brown Edge in his own words read: 'June 23rd 1810 I went to Brown Edge and some were assembled to hold a meeting on the Mountain (probably Marshes Hill). Billy Alcock preached first and I second. It was a powerful time. They told me I must go to Ramsor, so I went home and slept about two and a half hours and then rose up and went to Ramsor.' Undoubtedly Bourne was a man of great stamina. On another occasion he records 'I wakened ill in the night, ill in body, and grew worse. I rose up to go to Bagnal, Stanley and Brown Edge. At Bagnal I was laid under strong pain. I therefore sat down as I could neither stand nor kneel . . . I could scarce take any food today . . . my life hung in suspense before me . . . I was exceedingly ill all the way to Brown Edge. I could scarce talk and knew not whether I should come out of the pulpit alive or not . . . '

His account of the Brown Edge meeting that day brings to mind the contemporary scene and thoughts of the generation gap and juvenile delinquency. He records 'There were many young people and they were disposed to make disturbance. They had made great disturbance the Sunday night before. I immediately spoke to them before singing and then spoke from Solomon's irony "Rejoice O young men". When I had caught their attention I turned judgement upon them and struck them all serious . . . It was a blessed time to me and I spoke about an hour and sung a verse or two . . . some of the aged people were tried because I spoke all to the young people.' The next day he is obliged to make the comment in his diary 'being very ill'.

Some two and a half years after his enforced separation from the Wesleyans, Hugh Bourne records that Billy Turner was 'much tried' about the Brown Edge Society. Billy was afraid of the Travelling Preachers of the Burslem Wesleyan Circuit, and Hugh himself felt 'greatly discouraged at labouring so much in the old connection', and commented 'it is grieving to raise up the work and the Travelling Preachers to cut it down again.' However, he continued 'labouring in the old connection' and when he attended class meeting at Brown Edge on Sunday, April 13th 1811, he noted that 'there is a beautiful work here. Fanny Sherwin led class. It was a glorious time, several were brought in to Liberty.' Frances, or Fanny as she was known locally, married Samuel Barber, son of Francis Barber, who was 'the black servant of Dr. Samuel Johnson.' As a youth Samuel Barber was in the service of a Burslem surgeon and was influenced by the Burslem revival of 1805. 'In 1811 he married Frances Sherwin of the Brown Edge Society, he became a local preacher in 1807; he died in 1828 and was buried at Tunstall.'[36]

The summer and autumn of 1811 was a troublesome time for Hugh Bourne and the Brown Edge Chapel. There are no local records of this period, but Hugh Bourne's Writings provide some insight into the problems of this Wesleyan Chapel in a village of coal miners. He recalls how 'a Baptist preached at Brown Edge and threw the people off the inward work', and how 'James Crawfoot preached at Brown Edge and brought the work up again.'

On Monday, July 1st 1811 Hugh Bourne recorded 'There has been some embroilments at Brown Edge. I went thither and talked with the people . . . and all the rubbage was for the present done away.' But some two weeks later there was more trouble, 'I have now taken Brown Edge Chapel. Billy Turner flinches. He neglected his appointment last Sunday so I took the Chapel from him.' Hugh himself conducted evening service on Sunday, 21st July 1811, and on Wednesday of the following week he wrote, 'Yesterday and today I cleaned Brown Edge Chapel. At night James Crawfoot preached in it.' During the month of August he visited many local people making particular mention of Joseph Willat of Brown Edge and recorded 'I trust that

William Turner can do no more harm here.' At the end of October Hugh Bourne led the Brown Edge class meeting and 'had more faith in this place than ever.' He continued his visits to families in Brown Edge 'and had some useful times', but on Sunday, 27th October 1811 a sad note when he 'preached at Brown Edge and felt much for the people.' At this point it might be suggested that the Burslem Wesleyan Circuit officials had finally taken possession of the Wesleyan Chapel in Sandy Lane, Brown Edge, and had banished Hugh Bourne against the wishes of his supporters at Brown Edge. There is little doubt that the Wesleyans consolidated their position in Brown Edge, over the next eighty years.

The chapel is referred to as the Sandy Lane Wesleyan Chapel and it would seem that Hugh Bourne's connection with this chapel was severed. However, the early influences and associations of the hamlet with the pioneering work of the evangelist are significant. The point has already been made that he makes little reference to Endon in his writings. The many entries concerning Brown Edge speak for themselves and have been included, unaltered, in this passage to reveal the extent of his visits to Brown Edge and his concern for the religious well-being of the people. As the Wesleyan chapel's history enters the new chapter it is possible to draw some conclusions from the fact that Alderman Lawton presided at a meeting in Sandy Lane Chapel, Brown Edge in 1901 and said that he had with him a plan of the Burslem Wesleyan Circuit of 1822.[37] His father's name appeared on that plan and his father's first preaching appointment was at Sandy Lane. The 1839 Preachers' Plan of the same Circuit provides information that there were Sunday services at the Wesleyan Chapel in Sandy Lane, Brown Edge at 2-30 p.m. and 6-oo p.m., and that there was a preaching service on alternate Thursday evenings at 7-oo p.m. Watch Night Service was conducted by Mr. Baker assisted by Mr. Stevens, Snr., Mr. Timmis and Mr. Tunnicliffe. Friday, June 21st was Quarterly Fast Day, and Mr. Sidley was to preach at the Lovefeast on September 21st. A Lovefeast was originally a meal as a token of brotherly love amongst early Christians. Later it was usually a prayer meeting with a sacramental significance at which a loving cup filled with a beverage was passed around and sipped. An indication of the time involved in the weeknight devotional services is clearly shown against Thursday, February 21st 1839 when it states, 'the service will be continued about two hours.'

The names Sherwin and Sargeant appear in the Wesleyan Circuit Plan for 1839 and one is prompted to enquire whether or not these were the friends of Hugh Bourne who had remained loyal to 'the old connection'. Nevertheless the position of Sandy Lane Chapel is an interesting one. The tithe map schedule of 1843 for the parish of Norton describes Sandy Lane Chapel as 'Primitive Methodist', but the more official Ecclesiastical Census of 1851 confirms that it was a Wesleyan Chapel with seating accommodation for one hundred people. Rents were payable for fifty seats. Twenty people attended afternoon service and there was a congregation of ten at the evening service. Laban Leak, who lived at what is now known as Leek's Cottage in Sandy Lane, completed the census return and made no mention of any Sunday School Scholars or the inclement weather prevailing over St. Anne's.

In 1877 the chapel had no surviving legally appointed trustees, and on the 23rd of November of that year the following list of names of proposed trustees was affixed to the chapel door:

Thomas Mayer Oulsnam of Brown Edge, an earthenware manufacturer

Alfred Kirkham and

William Hiram Jones, both of Smallthorne, grocers

Frederick Stevenson Saddler

Peter Walker, grocer and

Edward John Walker, grocer, all of Norton

Thomas Blackshaw, chemist

James Malkin, earthenware manufacturer

John Sherwin Gardiner, draper and

Thomas Wardle, ironmonger, all of Burslem.

These subsequently became trustees of the chapel, and were socially and financially better off than the coal miners of Brown Edge. It was not until 1894 that eight local men, seven of whom were coal miners, were appointed trustees of the Wesleyan Chapel. The new trustees were Joseph Scarlett of Sandy Lane, James Sims, High Lane, Enoch Goodwin, Bank End, James Herbert Pointon, James Chadwick, Sandy Lane, William Goodwin, Lane Ends, James Goodwin, Sandy Lane and William Wiltshaw, a coal dealer of Sandy Lane, all of Brown Edge.[38]

The exact date of the opening of the Weslyan Sunday School is not known, but there are records which indicate that the Wesleyan Society in Brown Edge was providing some elementary educational facilities. The headmaster in his log book at St. Anne's School, Brown Edge records that on the 28th October 1875 'E. Mountford, the monitor, that left here a few months back has opened a school at the Methodist Chapel, to which I understand about twelve or fifteen scholars are gone.' The earliest available Sunday School records show that the Mountford family, who were farmers at Singleton or Singlet House, Brown Edge, were still involved in the work of the Wesleyan Sunday School in 1882. In the years 1882, 1884 and 1886, orders were placed to buy 'Infant School Books' and 'Easy Reading Books', and in 1890 the Sunday School staff agreed to the purchase of 'two dozen Easy Reading Books with the alphabet in.' There was no teacher shortage at this Sunday School in the late nineteenth century, when the secretary recorded that 'a teacher cannot take a class when there is another teacher at it.' It should be stated however, that there is no evidence to suggest a regular Wesleyan Society Day School in Brown Edge. A Bible class was formed in 1884 and John Mountford and Samuel Oulsnam were appointed its leaders. In May 1885 a Children's Clothing Fund was organised and handbills were distributed 'informing the neighbourhood of the clothing fund for Sunday School Scholars only.' The minimum contribution payable weekly was two pence.

Eli Hargreaves became an afternoon teacher in the Sunday School in 1882 and was appointed assistant superintendent in 1885, but his term of office was short-lived as the following tribute to him suggests: 'In deep memory of the late Eli Hargreaves of Wood-house Lane, died May 12th 1887.'

> 'E' is gone from here amongst us
> We shall miss his merry smile
> 'E' is gone to Heaven before us
> 'E' will wait for us awhile.
>
> Here the children too will miss him
> From the Sabbath School below
> His teaching when amongst them
> Was to serve God here below.
>
> Yes the teaching that 'E' taught them
> Was to do the will of God
> His teaching was to love the Saviour
> Whom for them did shed his blood.

The scholars too did dearly love him
Many a sorrowful tear was shed
On the day that we removed him
To his long and silent bed.

Nineteenth century chapel records contain accounts of Prayer Meetings at 7-00 a.m. on Sundays, numerous lectures, entertainments, tea meetings and missionary meetings. A list of foodstuffs purchased for a missionary tea in 1886 contained the following: one ham, three plumcakes, four plain, four currant and four seed loaves, four pounds of butter, four pounds of sugar, two quarts of milk, seven ounces of tea and two ounces of mustard. No indication is given of the total cost of the grocery bill on this occasion, but for a Sunday School treat in June 1890, one hundred buns were purchased from W. Holdcroft of Job's Pool, Brown Edge, at a cost of four shillings and two pence. Holdcroft's bakery was later transferred to Burslem.

On July 24th 1894 at a 'united meeting of the congregation worshipping at this chapel,' it was unanimously passed that Mr. Joseph Bratt be treasurer and Mr. James Pointon, secretary of the Building Fund, and proposed that 'twelve collecting books be got for members to collect with.' The meeting also gained strength from the fact that it was 'a long time since the desire to build a new chapel was expressed, and a longer time since the need to build arose.' Several years later in 1898, and no doubt after some collections had been made, three hundred and eighty-six and two thirds square yards of land opposite the chapel in Sandy Lane was given by the Heaton family of Poolefields, Brown Edge on which to erect a new chapel. The style of the architecture was to be 'debased Gothic', and the building was to accommodate one hundred and thirty people. The average number of regular hearers attending worship at this time was fifty, and the chapel had an adult membership of fifteeen. The stone-laying ceremony took place on Thursday, May 30th in 1901. It was a Fete Day at Sandy Lane, flags were flying and streamers were across the road. At 2-30 the people began to arrive on foot, by trap, by brake, and at 3-00 the road was full of friends who had come to see the ceremony. Foundation stones were laid by Mr. C. D. Heaton, Mr. R. Heath, J.P., Ald. S. Lawton, J.P., Ald. T. Arrowsmith, J.P., Mrs. W. Goodwin, Mr. J. Bratt in memory of Mr. S. Bratt, Mr. J. Mountford in memory of Mr. & Mrs. T. Oulsnam, in memory of Ernest Mellor by his parents and Mr.

J. S. Gardiner. The stone-laying was continued when a number of children laid stones on which their initials were to be carved later. Having performed the ceremony each child was presented with a small trowel to mark the occasion. Afterwards tea was taken by all in the tent erected behind the site of the new chapel. Building was completed in November of the same year, 1901, at a total cost of six hundred and fifty-nine pounds sixteen shillings and elevenpence, and when the chapel opened the old chapel was used to house the Sunday School.

The official opening ceremony of the new Wesleyan Chapel in Sandy Lane, Brown Edge, was performed by the Reverend Conrad S. Sargesson on Thursday, 14th November 1901 at 3-30 p.m. A '6d tea' was served at 5-00 p.m. followed by an evening meeting at 6-30 p.m. Speakers at this meeting included the Reverends Conrad S. Sargesson, T. L. Withington, James Feather, Mr. Wilcox and Mr. Edge.[39] This chapel was 'in the old connection', the Burslem Wesleyan Circuit. The head chapel in this circuit was Swan Bank the 'Burslem Wesleyan Chapel' of Arnold Bennett's 'Five Towns' novels where in 1901, the Reverends T. L. Withington and James Feather were ministers.

Councillor Sidney Malkin, a tile manufacturer, who then lived at 'The Limes', Porthill, but later at 'Westfields' in Endon, preached at the evening service in the new chapel on Sunday, 17th November 1901. Special music was provided by Norton Wesleyan Choir.

'Messrs. Scarlett and Pointon were duly appointed cleaners of the new chapel being paid the princely sum of £4 a year, finding own materials.' Other indications of the cost of church items at the beginning of the century are found in the chapel records. A wall was built in front of the chapel for £5, and a responsibility was put on 'Mr. Sandbach to get 12 chairs at 2/- each.' When in 1915 the chapel suffered as a result of a fire, the builder's estimate for 'making good all damage to floors, walls and ceiling, and providing a new cupboard' was only £9 15s. Other fire damages were three dozen bibles at tenpence each, baptismal register at five shillings and sixpence, book of offices, one shilling and sixpence, eighteen chapel hymn books and lettering at one pound, nine shillings, communion outfit two pounds, replacing crockery for tea meetings, one pound thirteen shillings and sixpence and two dozen teaspoons, six shillings. Fortunately for the chapel trustees, 'all this was covered by insurance'.

Though this may be regarded by some as the heyday of Methodism, the trustees had their problems which were of a different nature than those which were to beset the chapel trustees later. The records show that there were once four organists at the chapel: Mrs. Wiltshaw, Mrs. Hodkinson, Mr. Moses Pointon and Miss Weaver. The trustees 'agreed to have a rota . . . special services equally divided and taken in rotation.'

This Wesleyan Chapel situated at Sandy Lane in the civil parish of Endon and Stanley, in the registration district of Leek, was on the ninth day of November 1904 duly registered for solemnizing marriages therein.' A certificate was signed by Joseph Shaw, the then superintendent registrar for Leek.

Chapel office bearers in the first decade of this century included Chapel Steward Mr. J. Scarlett, Treasurer Mr. J. Bratt, Organist Mrs. W. Goodwin, Deputy Organist Mr. H. Pointon, Society Stewards Mr. J. Pointon and Mr. J. Talbot, Poor Stewards Elijah Mountford and Mr. F. Weaver. Sunday School Superintendents Mr. J. Scarlett and Mr. F. Goodwin. The Assistant Superintendent was Mr. J. Sims, and the Sunday School Secretary Mr. A. Pointon. On the 15th of October 1906 Mr. Percy Weaver was appointed Secretary and Mr. F. Forrester Treasurer of the Sunday School Children's Clothing Fund.

During the year of the national coal strike, 1921, £5 was donated to the Brown Edge Sub-Committee of the Norton Parish Relief Fund. Walter J. Jones was Secretary of this Sub-Committee. In 1932 electricity was introduced and electric light bulbs replaced the oil lamps in the chapel.

The 1808 chapel was now overcrowded with Sunday School scholars and 'the question of erecting a new Sunday School was raised.' With this in view two hundred and fifteen yards of land at the side of the 1901 chapel was purchased from Charles and Richard Heaton in 1938, and in February 1939 Mr. John Clarke, architect of Norton, submitted a plan of a building which would accommodate one hundred and fifty Sunday School scholars at an estimated cost of one thousand, one hundred and thirty pounds. However, Staffordshire County Council's road widening plans for Sandy Lane and the outbreak of war in September 1939 delayed the building of any permanent structure. In 1940 a wooden structure was purchased for seventy pounds and adapted as a temporary Sunday School building, the conversion costing three hundred pounds. From 1941 the 1808 chapel was an A.R.P. post until 18th June 1945 when it became the Beginners and Primary Department of the Sunday School.

The wooden temporary building was now too small for a Sunday School numbering one hundred and eighty scholars and there were pressures for a new church hall to be built. The Youth Club was affiliated both to the Methodist Association of Youth Clubs and to the Staffordshire County Youth Movement, and by the early 1950s sought larger premises. The inadequacy of the building is perhaps best illustrated by stories told of the Women's Bright Hour whose Thursday meetings on some occasions were in danger of being rained off. Consequently land behind the new chapel was purchased from Samuel Bullock Bratt in 1955 and this was added to when an adjacent piece of land which had formerly been the site of Brown Edge Workingmen's Club was acquired by the Trustees of Sandy Lane.

The need to build a new church hall gave added impetus to the 'Christian Giving Programme' of 1961 enabling the Sandy Lane congregation to build a new church hall, which was opened on 26th October, 1946 by Mr. C. H. Weaver, a former Sunday School Superintendent. The inaugural address on this occasion being given by the Reverend F. G. Bourne, a former Sunday School scholar.

Primitive Methodism

There may have been a note of sadness in Hugh Bourne's writings concerning events in Brown Edge when he preached there on Sunday, October 21st 1811 'and felt much for the people', but it was not a note of defeat.

Bourne's adherents or 'Bourneites', a separatist society without a name, adopted the name 'Primitive Methodist' in February 1812, and the first Primitive Methodist Plan appeared in the March listing a preaching place for Primitive Methodism in Brown Edge.

On Sunday, March 21st 1813 Hugh Bourne was again in Brown Edge 'and collected a few for a class.' Later in that month Hugh Bourne and William Alcock who preached that day at Brown Edge 'had a glorious time though we were few in number.' Steady progress was made, however, and in 1822 Richard Frost of Brown Edge opened his house for the holding of Primitive Methodist meetings, though by 1830 one John Petty a Tunstall preacher recorded of a number of Brown Edge families 'it might seem as if they have never heard the gospel; such was their ignorance. Some would not let me pray even for money; others inquired what was amiss.'[40]

On a plot of land at Pigeon Close in Collier's Road, which is today known as Hill Top, a Primitive Methodist Chapel built of local stone was erected in 1832. This chapel was in the Tunstall Circuit.

The Primitive Methodist Magazine of 1834 contained this report: 'Brown Edge Chapel, Staffordshire. Brown Edge, a country place, chiefly a common, and is about two miles from Bemersley, and our new chapel at this place was opened on Sunday, September 2nd 1832. The congregation is good and the Sunday School has one hundred and eighty-five scholars.'[41] A report of the Sunday Schools in the Tunstall Circuit in 1837 states that Brown Edge Primitive Methodists had one hundred and fifty scholars and a staff of six men and eight women in the Sunday School.[42]

A Primitive Methodist Preacher's Plan, also of the Tunstall Circuit in 1846, provides information that at Brown Edge on the 'Lord's Day' services were held at 2-30 p.m. and 7-00 p.m. and that there was a preaching service on a Monday evening every fourth week. J. Booth of Brown Edge was a preacher in this circuit. A Missionary Meeting took place on Sunday, 19th April 1846. J. Smith of Burslem was appointed to speak at the afternoon service being assisted at evening worship by P. Pugh of Chapel House and J. Alcock of Clay Hills.

At this time members of a Methodist Church were expected to attend a special weekly evangelical meeting called a 'Class Meeting' where members spontaneously related their own religious experiences.

Senior members of the chapel were appointed 'Class Leaders' assuming responsibility for the spiritual welfare and pastoral care of each member of their particular 'Class', whose names and addresses were listed in a register or 'Class Book'. Membership contributions or 'Class Money' usually a penny a week, were recorded in the 'Class Book', each member receiving quarterly a membership or 'Class Ticket'.

Hugh Bourne the founder of Primitive Methodism was a member of Brown Edge Primitive Methodist Chapel. He recorded 'Sunday, 26th March 1848. At class at Brown Edge, paid 3/- 2 quarters (Class Money). I preached to the children; it was rainy.' 'Sunday, 11th March 1849. I led class at Brown Edge. It was heavenly. The tickets were renewed. I paid 1/-.' No class books remain, but Hugh's writings inform us that on Monday evening, July 24th 1849, he preached at Brown Edge. 'My name is on the class book as usual. Praise be God.' Bourne's missionary activities had taken him on arduous journeys in this country and across the Atlantic to America, but in the eventide

74

of his life, Hugh Bourne frequently attended meetings at his own chapel in Brown Edge. He preached there on Monday, 3rd March 1845, his seventy-sixth birthday, attended the Good Friday tea meeting in April 1849 where 'We had three courses and I spoke three times. I was exhausted', was at class in Brown Edge on numerous occasions, at a revival meeting on October 1850, and in November of that year 'attended Brown Edge Anniversary. All Well.'

In 1852, though nearly eighty years old and failing in health, Bourne was at Brown Edge again, 'I laboured in the forenoon and at noon assisted in arranging the afternoon's service and was thrust into the lead to a large extent.' Hugh Bourne's last recorded entry concerning Brown Edge reads: 'Sunday, March 7th 1852. At Brown Edge during the week till today.' He died on October 11th 1852.

Other members of this chapel included John and Emma Charlesworth (nee Tomkinson). The 1851 Census material shows that John Charlesworth then an assistant coal miner was the son of William Charlesworth (formerly of Alton), nailmaker, in Brown Edge, and that Emma Tomkinson was the daughter of Francis Tomkinson a labourer of Brown Edge.

Other such examples of occupational interests of the early Primitive Methodists about the time of Bourne's death, are found in the Baptism Register.

The Ecclesiastical Return of 1851 was completed by the Chapel Steward, Isaac Ainsworth, of 'Burnfields' a farm near Marshes Hill, Brown Edge. In spite of inclement weather on the day of the religious census, forty-five people were at the afternoon service, and fifty people attended evening worship at the Primitive Methodist Chapel situated in a bleak remote part of the village.

The Primitive Methodists moved to larger premises in 1880 when it is said that this the first Primitive Methodist Chapel in Brown Edge became a Mission Church of St. Luke's, Endon. There are no local records giving the exact date of the commencement of the first St. Luke's Mission Church in Brown Edge, but documents show that this building 'formerly a chapel or meeting house' in 1893 was 'in the occupation of the Reverend James Badnall' who was then the Vicar of St. Luke's, Endon.[43]

On 20th September 1880 a plot of ground 'part of a close of land called the Far piece' some three hundred and three yards square, was purchased from James Turner the elder of Brown Edge for the sum of sixteen pounds 'to build thereon a chapel or place of worship for use of the people called Primitive Methodists.' Trustees of the proposed new chapel were James Turner the elder, farmer James Simcock, John Turner, William Hargreaves the elder, Charles Hargreaves, Samuel Heath, George Beardmore, John Stonier the younger, Rueben Sherratt, George Nicklin, Ralph Pointon, Charles Knight and Josiah Sherratt, all miners of Brown Edge, and Charles Beardmore of Norton Green, collier, Joseph Pickford, miller, John Sherratt, farmer, James Berrisford the elder, grocer, and Joseph Bratt, grocer, all of Brown Edge. All these signatories with the exception of George Nicklin and Ralph Pointon wrote their own name.[44]

This also was the chapel which served the miners of Brown Edge. Twelve of the nineteen trustees were coal miners who lived in Brown Edge, whereas at this time the Wesleyans of Brown Edge had only one trustee (out of a total of ten trustees) who lived in Brown Edge. The Wesleyan records suggest that this trustee was an earthenware manufacturer.

The site of the new Primitive Methodist chapel was some eight hundred and fifty feet above sea level, nearly the highest point in Brown Edge, and known locally as Jake's Bank. It is said that this chapel was built of stone quarried locally from common land known as Marshes Hill. A square stone building which would accommodate approximately 140 people, the chapel was in the Bradley Green (Biddulph) Circuit. In order to complete this building the trustees borrowed two hundred and sixty pounds from John Vaughan, no small undertaking considering the low wages of the miners at this time. However, the debt was 'paid in full' in 1895.

The first baptism in the new Primitive Methodist chapel was recorded on 31st October 1880, when the Reverend John Shepherd, Superintendent Minister of the Bradley Green Circuit, baptized Mary, daughter of Emma and George Beardmore, a collier of Brown Edge.

In 1909 the trustees purchased the remainder of 'the far piece' from Mrs. E. Turner and her daughter, Mrs. Esther Hollins of Brown Edge, for the sum of thirty pounds.

Annually on that Sunday in August nearest to Norton Wakes, St. Bartholomew's Day, this chapel held a camp meeting on Marshes Hill, probably the venue of Hugh Bourne's first camp meeting in Brown Edge in 1807. This event was discontinued in the 1950s.

Sunday School officials in 1915 included: Superintendents: James

Hodkinson and Daniel Hargreaves, Secretaries: Thomas Pointon and John Stonier, Treasurer: J. Hodkinson.

Bible Class and Sunday School teachers were Daniel Hargreaves, J. Hodkinson, Mark Frost. T. Pointon, Joseph Jones, Annie Frost, James Pointon, James Simcock, John Pointon, Eunice Dawson, Honor Dawson, Nellie Hall, Hannah Hodkinson, and Mr. J. Hargreaves. T. Pointon was the organist and A. Sherratt the conductor.[45]

The adequately staffed Sunday School needed premises other than the chapel building and in 1922 a Sunday School was built on to the North side of the chapel.

The Annual Report which was submitted to the Primitive Methodist Sunday School in 1924 shows that this was then a thriving chapel with eleven teachers and one hundred and thirty-eight scholars on roll. Fifty-three scholars were shown as being over the age of fifteen, and of these seventeen were members of the society. The report stated that the scholars were regularly taken to chapel services, International Graded Lessons were used in the Sunday School and there was a branch of the Daily Bible Reading and Prayer Union. The annual running cost of the Sunday School was thirty-eight pounds, seven shillings and sevenpence, according to Miss H. Hollins, Secretary of the Sunday School.

From this it might be assumed that Primitive Methodists were at this time more progressive than the Wesleyans in Brown Edge, whose records in the first quarter of this century make no mention of graded lessons.

Industrial strife and trade depression caused some people in this working class community to be unemployed, others were on short time. This induced the leaders of the Primitives in Brown Edge, well aware that 'Satan finds mischief for idle hands,' to construct a tennis court.

Arthur Pointon, junior, recalls that the menfolk of the Hodkinson family, Tom Pointon, Dan Hargreaves, Arthur and Jim Pointon, William Heath and Fred Simcock, assisted by other willing hands excavated the land, part of the 'far piece' purchased in 1909, and duly constructed the tennis court. Thus the young folk of the village were able to work off their surplus energy at a time of enforced leisure.

It is unfortunate that there is so little documentation about a chapel which must have contributed much to the spiritual and temporal needs of the folk in Brown Edge.

The Baptism Register clearly shows that this was the miners' chapel
Primitive Methodist Baptism Book at Brown Edge in the Parish of Leek and in the Tunstall Circuit
Baptisms solemnized in the years 1870-1879.

Born	Baptized	Child's Christian Name	Parents' Christian Names	Surname	Abode	Quality, Trade or Profession	By whom the ceremony was performed
	28 Nov. 1870	William	Charles Ann	Knight	Brown Edge	Colier	W. E. Saunders
	26 Dec. 1870	Maryann Goodwin	Joseph Maryann	Brownsett Goodwin	Brown Edge	Colier	Enock Mould
	17 Apl. 1871	Walter	John Emmer	Charlesworth Charlesworth	Sandy Lane	Colier	Joseph Heath
	7 Aug. 1871	Charlotte	Daniel Lucy	Simcock Simcock	Brown Edge	Colier	John Guest
	27 May 1872	John Thomas Goodwin	Joseph Maryann	Brownsett Goodwin	Brown Edge	Colier	W. E. Saunders
	30 Mar. 1873	Lucy	Daniel Lucy	Simcock	Sandy Lane	Colier	D. S. Prosser
	15 June 1873	Theodosia Mountford	Joseph Jane	Rogers Mountford	Brown Edge	Colier	D. S. Prosser
	17 Aug. 1873	George William	George Emmer	Beardmore	Brown Edge	Colier	J. Rowley
	30 Mar. 1874	Levi Goodwin	Joseph Maryann	Brownsett Goodwin	Brown Edge	Colier	W. J. Kirkland
	5 Apl. 1874	Ralph	John Emmer	Charlesworth	Sandy Lane	Colier	W. Foster

	23 Aug. 1874	John	George Harriett	Foster	Brown Edge	Colier	Geo. Eastwood
12 Nov. 1874	30 Nov. 1874	Maryann	Charles Ann	Knight	Brown Edge	Colier	W. J. Kirkland
16 July 1870	19 Apl. 1875	Shallcross	Enock Mary	Shallcross	Lane Ends	Colier	W. J. Kirkland
	10 Oct. 1875	Sampson	George Emma	Beardmore	Brown Edge	Colier	S. W. Thelwell
	9 Apl. 1877	John Willott	Thomas Sarah	Hood Willott	Brown Edge	Colier	J. Askin
2 Apl. 1877	23 Apl. 1877	Deborah	Charles Ann	Knight	Brown Edge	Colier	W. Evans, Tunstall
18 May 1875	23 Apl. 1877	Harriatt	John Elizabeth	Turner	Brown Edge	Colier	W. Evans, Tunstall
1 Apl. 1877	23 Apl. 1877	James	John Elizabeth	Turner	Brown Edge	Colier	W. Evans, Tunstall
	6 Jan. 1878	Maria	Benjamin Mary	Bentley	Sandy Lane	Colier	J. Baskeyfield
5 Dec. 1878	20 May 1879	George	John Edeth	Stonier	Brown Edge	Colier	J. Askin
28 July 1879	27 Aug. 1879	Samuel	John Elizabeth	Turner	Brown Edge	Colier	Rev. J. Askin
21 June 1879	27 July 1879	Sarah Ellin	John Elizabeth	Foster	Brown Edge	Colier	P. Sanderson
5 Oct. 1879	26 Oct. 1879	Elizabeth	Samuel Ann	Heath	Brown Edge	Colier	J. Frost

In 1851 John Charlesworth of Brown Edge was working in the mines at fourteen years of age. There are no records to indicate what influence, if any, Hugh Bourne had on this young man, or at what age John Charlesworth became a Primitive Methodist, but class tickets have been preserved which show that he and his wife Emma were members of the Primitive Methodist Chapel which was built on Brown Edge in 1832. Their son, Walter, and their youngest child Ralph were baptized at this chapel and in 1879 a grandchild, Sarah Ellin Foster, was also baptized there.

The early Methodists on Brown Edge held services in cottages and John Charlesworth was a man of the old ways. In addition to attending services at the new Primitive Methodist Chapel, he also held prayer meetings in his own cottage. In 1880 leaders of the chapel suggested that John should hold his prayer meetings in the chapel, but he refused and as a result was excluded from the Primitive Methodist Society in Brown Edge. Later he formed his own society 'a congregation of Protestant Dissenters called Free Missioners' who met in a wooden hut which had previously been a mission hall in Burslem. It was situated 'on the easterly side of the highway from Sandy Lane to Horton in the parish of Leek.' The area is now known as Hill Top, Brown Edge in Endon Parish. This independent society was organised like a Methodist Chapel and made its own preacher's plan. In June 1897 ninety-one square yards of land were purchased from John and Jane Lowe of Brown Edge for the sum of £7. The first trustees of the 'Free Mission' were John Charlesworth, now a farmer, his son Ralph Charlesworth, brother-in-law Frances Tomkinson, and his sons-in-law, John Foster and Frederick Lowe, all miners of Brown Edge.[16]

The Free Missioners were well supported by the people of Brown Edge especially at Sunday School Anniversaries, and the 'Mission' Church was too small to accommodate the large number of people who attended the special services in the early part of this century. From time to time a tent was erected in a field near to the Free Mission and a string band accompanied the singers. During one of the anniversary services the tent collapsed in a gale, and the afternoon service ended rather abruptly. Undaunted by this event the menfolk of the Free Mission re-erected the tent and it is said that the evening service proceeded as planned with just as large a congregation. Need-

BROWN EDGE FREE MISSION.

PREACHERS' PLAN—1915.

We Preach Christ and Him crucified.

Time of Service, Evening, 6.0	April				May					June			
	4	11	18	25	2	9	16	23	30	6	13	20	27
	2	3	8	0	11	0	10	13	12	15	0	14	6

PREACHERS

1 G Beardmore, Norton Green
2 H Berrisford, Norton
3 E Nixon. 23. Bleak-st., Burslem
4 G Mountford, 47, Leek Rd. Milton
5 ————
6 W Barnett, Smallthorne
7 J S Coates, 20, Gordon Street, Burslem
8 G Davies, 19, Wade Street, Burslem
9 J Wilcox, 116, Hot Lane, Burslem
10 E Davies, 17, Flint-st, Cobridge
11 J E Rushton, 30, Chetyn-st., Smallthorne
12 F Barber, Leek New Road, Burslem
13 C Bailey, Leek-rd, Baddeley Grn
14 J Kearns, 14, Furlong Lane, Burslem
15 W Leigh, 2, Gordon-st, Burslem
16 ——
17 M Stubbs, 29. Chell Heath-road Smallthorne

Manor Farm, Endon. From a painting of 1894. This is a view of the additional rear part of the house. The front bears the date 1638. (By permission of the Trustees of the William Salt Library, Stafford).

The First Primitive Methodist Chapel, 1832.
Later converted into three cottages.

less to say this was the last Sunday School Anniversary Service to be held in a tent on Brown Edge.

The Free Missioners depended, in the main, on both Wesleyan and Primitive Methodist preachers to conduct their services. In 1915 some of these preachers were becoming too modern for John Charlesworth, who was now nearing his eightieth year. He informed preachers on the Free Mission plan of 1915 that 'Any preacher who at any time feels he can no longer preach the old Doctrine will he kindly withdraw his name from the plan.' Later his grandson, also named John Charlesworth, a man of more moderate views, deleted this footnote from the preachers' plan.

John Charlesworth, senior, died in 1922 and is buried in St. Anne's churchyard, Brown Edge. His wife Emma is also buried there, her tombstone inscribed:

'A Christian here her flesh laid down,
The cross exchanging for a crown
In sure and certain hope to rise
To claim her mansion in the skies.'

A brick extension had previously been added to the wooden hut in order to accommodate an increasing number of members, and in 1922 structural alterations were made, the whole then becoming a simple brick and tile building. This also served as a Sunday School. In 1930 a vestry was added and the Free Mission Bible Class met here each Sunday.

The work was done by members of the Free Mission Church who were ably led by John, Wilfred and Ebor Charlesworth.

In 1951 an adjacent plot of land was purchased from James Dawson of Brown Edge which provided parking space for the cars of visiting preachers. But the advent of the motor car was to affect the chapel goers and prove to be a counter attraction to a Sunday at the Chapel or Mission.

On Sunday, March 17th 1963, the Free Mission closed, and the property and land sold to Thomas Dawson of Brown Edge. A modern bungalow now occupies the site.

The furnishings were distributed as follows: 'Chairs to Endon Church Mission, Brown Edge, Pews and Font to Baddeley Edge Methodist Church, Chairs, Pulpit, Organ Screen and Hymn Books to Norton Green Methodist Church. Chairs, Pews, Communion Rail,

Communion Tables and Chairs, Vestry Cupboard and Hymn Books to Hill Top Methodist Church, Brown Edge. Organ to Cross Gate Methodist Church, Hilderstone. Hymn Books to Sandy Lane Methodist Church, Brown Edge.

Other chapels have been adapted for use in different ways from the original intention. The early Primitive Methodist Chapel on Hill Top, opened on 2nd September 1832 was converted into cottages as long ago as 1894 and today bears the name 'Chapel Cottages', but giving no indication that Hugh Bourne himself was once a member there. The Wesleyan Chapel 'in the old connection', Sandy Lane, is now a draper's shop.

The Charity

No history of the Methodists in Brown Edge would be complete without the mention of the Charity (the Sunday School Anniversary Services). For many years it was the custom for the choirs from the Free Mission and the Methodist Chapels to tour the village on the Sunday before Charity Sunday, singing outside the cottages and collecting money for Sunday School funds. This involved walking several miles, breaking their journey at lunchtime in order to partake of sandwiches and tea provided for them by willing helpers.

The tour of the district would take nearly all day. Members of the choirs and other friends met at the chapel at 9-00 a.m. and toured half the village before lunch, and the other half of the village afterwards, often finishing at 5-00 p.m.

The Wesleyan Charity in Sandy Lane was the first to be held on the last Sunday in April, followed by the Primitives two weeks later, and the Free Mission in June.

On Charity Sunday morning the scholars, all dressed in their new clothes, their teachers and often the preacher for the day would meet at the chapel at 9-00 a.m. and form into a procession. Led by the village brass band they would march round the village stopping occasionally at some vantage point to sing a hymn followed by a short address from the preacher.

Their tour of the village completed scholars and teachers would disband, returning to chapel in the early afternoon and again in the evening to stand on the stage and sing special hymns. The choir also sang one or two anthems during the Charity services.

Many ex-Sunday School scholars returned to the village to attend these services and it was a favourite Sunday for family reunions. The chapels had large congregations at both the afternoon and evening services.

Probably as a sign of the changing mode of life in the village the choirs ceased touring the village in the 1950s. The first chapel to discontinue this custom was the Free Mission, followed shortly afterwards by the former Wesleyans and the former Primitive Methodists. Many of the older members of the chapels had passed on and not enough young people were interested in carrying on this traditional way of raising money for the Sunday School.

Chapels still survive in Brown Edge, but in spite of an increase in population, chapel attendances have decreased. The area has changed in character, middle class houses have been built and the extreme poverty of the nineteenth and early twentieth centuries has departed. So too, it would seem, must the chapels.

By contrast there is an adult membership of eighty-eight at Endon Methodist Chapel, well attended family services, a thriving 'Young Wives' group, an adequate number of officials and sufficient financial resources. It seems likely that as long as Methodism continues as a separate ecclesiastical body, there is a future for it in Endon.

References

[1] See Leek Parish Records for details relating to Wardens from each quarter and office of Warden of Leek.

[2] *H.C.S.*, Vol. III, 4th Series, p. 109.

[3] Articles of Enquiry (Visitation) Endon Returns. Joint Record Office, Lichfield (1636-1756), B/V/3.

[4] *H.C.S.*, Vol. III, 4th Series, p. 65.

[5] House of Lords Record Office, Papist Return, 1706.

[6] Extract from Churchwardens' Accounts, Leek Parish Church.

[7] House of Lord's Record Office, Papist Return, 1781.

[8] Information obtained from Leek Parish Registers referring to the Loxdale manuscripts (Thomas Loxdale p. 177). Also see *S.H.C.*, Vol. 9 (N.S.). Chartulary of Dieulacres.

[9] Plaque erected inside Endon Church to record granting of land by Thomas Jodrell.

[10] Presentation Records, Endon Joint (Diocesan) Records Office, Lichfield. (see illustrations for copy of script), 1723.

[11] Presentation Document, Joint (Diocesan) Records Office, Lichfield (Endon), 1723.

[12] Presentation Document, Joint Record Office, Lichfield (Endon), 1727, B/A/3.

[13] Thomas Loxdale, Vicar of Leek, and others, signatories to agreement setting up Chapelry of 1730. Scroll held at Leek Parish Church.

[14] See Parish Registers in St. Luke's Church, Endon.

[15] Leek Parish Church records—in parish chest.

[16] Articles of Enquiry, replies made to Bishop by Enoch Tomkinson, 1751. Joint Record Office, Lichfield, Endon Terrier 1786. B/V/3.

[17] Articles of Enquiry, replies made to Bishop by John Salt, 1830. Joint Record Office, Lichfield, A/V/1.

[18] Endon Terrier copied by George Foster, Churchwarden in 1871.

[19] It would seem that only the copy is now available for inspection.

[20] Plan made for submission by Messrs. Beardmores, Architects, Hanley and Stoke-on-Trent, 1876. Joint Record Office, Lichfield.

[21] Presentations for Endon. Joint Record Office, Lichfield, B/A/3.

[22] A remark made in an address by Joseph Challinor at a meeting in Endon in 1872.

[23] Sherlock, Robert: 'Church Lighting in Staffordshire Since the Reformation', *H.S.C.*, Vol. VI, 4th Series, 1970, p. 63.

[24] Lawton, Rev. T. D.: 'History of St. Anne's Church, Brown Edge', (1844-1944).

[25] Dyson, Rev. J. B.: 'A Brief History of the Rise and Progress of Wesleyan Methodism in the Leek Circuit', 1853.

[26] Wesley, Rev. John: 'Journal', Volumes 3 and 4.

[27] Bourne, Hugh: All quotes obtained from Xeroxed typescript copy of M.SS of Hugh Bourne's Self Review, Autobiography and Journal at Central Reference Library, Hanley. M.SS Rev. Dr. J. T. Wilkinson.

[28] Dyson, Rev. J. B.: 'A Brief History of the Rise and Progress of Wesleyan Methodism in the Leek Circuit', 1853.

[29] Endon Wesleyan Chapel Deeds, 1935.

[30] Leek Wesleyan Methodist Circuit Year Books.

[31] The Poems of George Heath, Memorial Edition, p. 246.

[32] Ecclesiastical Census, 1851.

[33] Leek Wesleyan Methodist Circuit Year Book, 1887.

[34] Leek Wesleyan Methodist Circuit Year Books.

[35] Wilkinson, Rev. Dr. J. T.: 'A Bi-Centenary Tribute to Hugh Bourne', Methodist Recorder, 30th March, 1972.

[36] Wilkinson, J. T.: William Clowes, 1780-1851.

[37] Burslem Wesleyan Circuit Magazine, Vol. 1, No. 6, June, 1910.

[38] Trust Deeds, Sandy Lane Wesleyan Chapel.

[39] Chapel and Sunday School Minute Books.

[40] Petty, John: 'History of the Primitive Methodist Connexion'.

[41] Primitive Methodist Magazine, 1834, Methodist Archives, London.

[42] Primitive Methodist Magazine, 1837, Central Reference Library, Hanley.

[43] Deeds of Chapel Cottages, Brown Edge.

[44] Trust Deeds, 1880, Primitive Methodist Chapel.

[45] Sunday School Minutes, 1 page only.

[46] Free Mission Deeds.

Thomas Parker, the first Earl of Macclesfield was born at Leek on 23 July, 1666. He was called to the bar in 1691 and on May 12, 1718 was made Lord High Chancellor. In 1721 he became the Earl of Macclesfield but was later fined £3,000 for corruption in the court of Chancery. The first earl died in 1727. His successors to the title were made and continued to be patrons of the chapel at Endon until 1902 when on the establishment of a parish the vicars of Leek became patrons. Apart from being landowners the family had little connection with the life of the village of Endon.

Chapter V

ENDON IN THE EIGHTEENTH CENTURY

I n some respects the eighteenth century saw a new awakening of
life in Endon, so far as matters related to the village community
were concerned. It was to become a centre in its own right. In
the Middle Ages there was a manor site, a park and a chantry. With
the departure of the Audleys and the change in the persons of the
lords of the manor, and with the post-Reformation supremacy of the
ecclesiastical parish of Leek, Endon, so it would seem, ceased to be
the centre it had been earlier. Beginning in 1538 when it was decreed
that baptisms,[1] burials and marriages must be registered, parishes
created earlier for ecclesiastical purposes became areas for neo-civil
administration and the vestry meetings, the offices of churchwarden and
constable took on greater significance as they assisted in the administration of poor law, the highways, charities, workhouses and schools.
Prior to 1730 Endon's history in these fields is contained and often
submerged in the documents of Leek parish church. Even after 1730
and the opening of the church, it did not assume full responsibilites
in these fields. Nevertheless, some records were kept in the village
and evidence is available for an impression of life in Endon in the
eighteenth century to be presented.

The Poor Law

Much of what we know as poor law sprang from an awareness in
Elizabethan times of a section of the community who were described
as poor and appear in records described individually as paupers. There
were two kinds of charity administered by the churchwardens—Outdoor and Indoor relief. The people receiving outdoor relief remained
in their own homes and generally speaking were infirm or incapacitated.
Those receiving indoor relief were catered for in almshouses or in the
workhouse. Endon had neither almshouses nor a workhouse within its
boundaries and all matters concerning relief were dealt with at Leek,
hence a churchwarden there for the Endon Quarter, to look after and
safeguard the interests of Endon at vestry meetings. One entry at

Leek reads: '1737, sent to the three chapels of Rushton, Meerbrook and Endon on the Sunday before churchwardens offer their accounts— any one concerned may have the opportunity of being present.'[2]

Endon	...	5s.	0d.
Frith	...	16s.	0d.
Bradnop	...	4s.	4d.

A similar one was sent in 1745. Several years earlier in 1724 bills had been paid for urchins at Leek—£1.6s.0d.

Some idea of the concern is revealed in an earlier entry, for 1662, where it states that the Bellot's legacy for the poor of Leek parish was administered and a sum of twenty pounds was distributed. Thos. Bulkley of Stanlowe distributed 'himself to the poor of Endon Quarter —£3.' Thomas Bulkley, gent, is shown in the Hearth Tax return of 1666 as being the possessor of property with five hearths at Stanlowe.[3] In 1664 Joseph Wilkinson, having six hearths in Endon (this was the largest property in Endon at that time) is shown as being responsible for 'what money hath bin disbursed by ye churchwardens of ye parish of Leek in ye yeare 1664 for ye Endon Quarter.'[4]

In 1676 Elizabeth Ash founded eight almshouses and garden ground for eight women of sixty years and upwards, and a yearly gift of forty pounds per annum, augmented by Lady Dethick, in 1678, and one hundred and ten pounds by two other benefactors, which were laid out in land, the rents of which were twenty-five pounds per annum. Also in the churchwarden's list were:

Miss Lowe William Watson 1688	£19	0s.
Thos. Joddrell	£2	10s.
Ann Jolliffe 1731	£33	6s.
Wm. Hulme 1690	£1	6s.
John Hulme 1694	£35	10s.

These charities became known as the town dole and were distributed at Christmas time, Endon presumably taking its 'Quarter' share.[5] The other benefactions relating to Leek, as shown by Griffith in 1860, do not refer to Endon.[6]

In 1778 an account for the disbursement to the Poor of Endon read:

To William	cash for 5 weeks	5s.	0d.
Easter	cash for one month	4s.	0d.
A payment made to Ipstones workhouse		5s.	2d.[7]

In addition a weekly payment of seven shillings and sixpence was made to Leek poor, presumably the amount due to the churchwardens for Endon Quarter. The connection with Ipstones workhouse at this period was very close and there were frequent payments of five shillings twopence, but no indication of any persons being lodged there from Endon. Because of the likely charge to be made on the rates if a bastard child was born to a poor girl, the man responsible, or any person found harbouring or giving shelter to the mother and child, could, if they were likely to become chargeable, be sent to the house of correction at the expense of the inhabitants of the parish.

In 1793 'Moses Bradshaw (was) sent to House of Correction at Stafford for getting Sarah Hollinshead with child and a bastard to be charged on the Poor Law.'[8]

In all, Endon at this time was connected with the workhouse at Ipstones, the workhouse and almshouses at Leek and the House of Correction at Stafford. However, there was some dissatisfaction nationally with the attitudes being shown to the poor and in order to present a sterner front, the Poor Law Amendment Act of 1834 was passed in Parliament. This placed Endon firmly in the Leek Poor Law Union. A new workhouse was built on the Ashbourne Road and during the nineteenth century there is firmer evidence of Endon people in the 'Union Workhouse'. Entries in the parish register read:
(buried) Ann Boulton, aged 2 yrs. died in Leek workhouse
(buried) John Dean, aged 4 yrs. died in Leek Union workhouse.

Not only 'the poor in very deed' suffered under the harshness of the eighteenth-century poor laws. The able-bodied poor were also subjected to some severity of retribution. Men of some substance who fell into debt were likely to be the subject of an order 'distraining off goods, etc., for nonpayment of rent arrears. In 1781 William Bennison produced the following list of possessions belonging to Joseph Garner:

Joseph Garner—Take notice I have destrained off the goods in the schedule underwritten for the sum of ten pounds for rent arrears due to the Overseer of the Township of Endon at Ladyday. In the house place. Dresser drawers, cupboard, three chairs, chest, whitetable stand, water tub, two solid irons, two iron pots, frying pan, bread iron, looking glass, bakestone, barrel, two stools, tin

oven, pitchers, tea kettle, grate, bellows, tongs and fire shovel, two candlesticks.
In the Parlour. One pair of bedsteads, three blankets and two sheets.
In the chamber. One pair of bedsteads, one blanket, two sheets, one sythe, one axe and one freal.[9]

There is little evidence to show what happened to Joseph Garner, or if he ever recovered from his brush with the bailiffs.

In 1787 some idea of relative values is given by the two entries debited in the Endon account:

To James Wood for Relief	3s.	od.
To Ale at meeting	3s.	od.
To Mary Badley for 5 weeks, being ill	9s.	od.[10]

The idea of having a celebration at the expense of the churchwarden's account was not new. In 1745 an entry at Leek was made:

'For treating the vicar, curates, schoolmasters and wardens and horse hire: £1.15s.6d.'[11]

Not all the people in need of charity were treated with compassion. The Settlement Laws caused many harsh acts and attitudes to be fostered. Since a pauper might become a liability on the rates of the parish, efforts were made against the settlement in an area of people likely to be an encumberance. Thus in 1819 Elizabeth Shaw, a single woman, had gone to live in Ipstones and being a papuer was chargeable to the parish there, not having gained legal settlement qualifications. An order was made which read 'we do therefore require you the said churchwardens and overseers of the Poor of the said parish of Ipstones to convey the said Elizabeth Shaw from and out of your said parish to the said parish of ENDON, and the said churchwardens of Endon to receive her.' In 1822 a Sarah Goodfellow was ordered to be brought back, under similar circumstances, from Wolstanton where she had gone to live.[12]

The problem of pests to farmers and others is highlighted in the churchwarden's accounts for 1723/24 when eighteen shillings was paid in Endon Quarter for seventy-eight hedgehogs, and at the same time eight pounds was paid for eight foxes. Ecclesiastical attitudes are reflected in the payment of Mr. Statham's bill for communion bread and wine for Leek, Meerbrook and Endon, which amounted to £14.1s.4d. A payment of three shillings was also made for altering the Common Prayer Books for Leek, Meerbrook and Endon. This was in 1745, a year well remembered in Leek for its association with the Jacobites and their visit enroute to Derby, and their return several days later. Not surprisingly an entry reads: July 1746 'Paid to ringers for victory over ye rebels—2s. od.' for celebrating the final victory over the Jacobites, at Culloden, in that year.

During this century many of the earlier Tudor timber-framed houses had extensions made to them and some of the classical outlines in design can be seen in farmhouses such as Manor Farm and Sutton House. It was the lesser yeoman-type gentry who were responsible for this development. One such person was John Sutton of Hallwater. Others were Thos. Sherratt, John Wedgwood, Hugh Sherratt, William Murhall, Samuel Tomkinson and Thomas Colclough. Perhaps the most stylish and wealthiest of these local leaders was John Wedgwood. It was he who left land in order that a school and master's house could be built.

John Sutton of Hallwater was a warden for Endon Quarter at Leek in 1724. He was a trustee of the chapel and was variously described as 'Gent'. Writing of his wife who died in 1738, John Daintry, the newly appointed vicar of Leek wrote:

'She was an obsequious wife—a tender mother—a rare economist— her temper was even—her passion calm—her understanding clear— her conversation was pleasant, instructive and pious, without any savour of pride, raillery, or affection. The whole course of her behaviour the constant series of her actions were the result of rational and religious principles, she died with the same character she lived —she was known to me several years—I never heard or knew she had an enemy and am sure she never deserved one. All this and more I know to be true.'[13]

William Murhall of Bagnall is well remembered for two things. One is the epitaph on his gravestone in Endon churchyard. He died on January 14th 1762 and the following is said of him for all to see: 'Part of what I possessed is left to others, and what I gave away remains with me.' The other story for which he is well-known concerns the unfortunate Scottish Jacobite who appeared before him as a county magistrate. The legend has it that he had the man skinned over a signpost at Leek and sent his hide to the tanyard at Endon to be made into leather for a drum head. It is an unlikely event even though the account seems credible in view of the local feeling against Jacobites who stole crops, cattle and horses.

References

[1] In 1538 Thomas Cromwell ordered that all baptisms, burials and marriages should be recorded in the parish church and registers opened for the purpose. This was the first time that any demographic records were ordered to be kept.

[2] Leek Parish Records. Churchwardens' Accounts, 1737.

[3] *H.C.S.*, Vol. 1925, p. 157. Hearth Tax Return, 1666.

[4] Leek Parish Records. Entry in Churchwardens' Accounts, 1664.

[5] See chapter on Ecclesiastical developments for details of the 'quarters' related to Leek parish.

[6] Griffin, G.: 'The Free School and Endowments of Staffordshire' 1860.

[7] Endon Parish Chest. Poor Law Records, 1778.

[8] Endon Parish Chest. Separate document commiting Moses Bradshaw to House of Correction at Stafford, 1793.

[9] Endon Parish Chest. Order served on Joseph Garner.

[10] Endon Parish Chest. Poor Law Accounts concerning payments to the poor of Endon.

[11] Leek Parish Records. Entry in Churchwardens' Accounts, 1745.

[12] Endon Parish Chest. Separate documents relating to settlement of Elizabeth Shaw and Sarah Goodfellow.

[13] A tribute to the wife of John Sutton written by the Rev. John Daintry who was incumbent at Endon between 1730 and 1737 when he became the vicar of Leek.

Chapter VI

THE TANYARD, THE MILL, THE HOUSES,
THE PEOPLE, THE PARISH REGISTERS

The Tanhouse, Endon
   *'Leather was needed not only for shoes and gloves, but for
   miners' protective clothing and for saddles and harness for
   all engaged in driving animals, carrying goods, and working
   the land'.* Joan Thirsk 'Horn and Thorn in Staffordshire.'[1]

I n modern times and among instances of local folk-lore, the tanhouse at Endon is perhaps best remembered as the place where
the locals attempted to tan the skin of a Jacobite rebel captured
by William Murhall in 1745. This, however, proved to be too much
of a job for the local tanners.

With a predominance of pastoral farming of cattle and sheep in
the area, it is not surprising that the tanhouse was built for a much
more serious use than the anecdote would suggest, and that with so
many hides available work was found for successive generations of
Endon folk. The poor law records of the early ninteenth century
suggest that there was not much succession of generations involved
when the Clowes children, who, born at Cheddleton, worked there for,
in the case of James, five shillings a week, and for Ralph, two shillings
and sixpence a week.[2]

The properties used for tanning consisted originally of two buildings, one fairly large and a much smaller one separated by a ten foot
entry.

The original stone can be seen in the wall and the additional stonework is easily recognisable in the modern structures. Today the
property consists of two houses, originally three. The original roof
was thatched, but this was replaced and made to cover the entry
thus joining the two buildings and forming a loading bay to and from
the loft. Here the leather was loaded into carts. The area at the rear
or north side was known as the yard and in it was a large soak pit

some twelve feet in width and ten feet deep. The pit was connected to the main public thoroughfare (Park Lane) by a sandstone path which was about four feet wide. Along this were brought the skins. Hanlers, the tanners' name for tannin, was used in the soak, and the first process was to place the skins in the liquid for a period of several hours.

Among the other terms frequently used by the tanners were:

KIP: a bundle of hides of young beasts made up of a specific number, but this varied from area to area.

LANDINGE GAWNE: a gawne or gallon measure used for ladling.

MATTERINGS: a term used by tanners for a liquid made of lime.

RUSSIA LEATHER: was a very durable oiled leather used in book binding.

SHAMESA FUSTICK: Fustick was a wood giving off a yellow dye used in tanning.

SHERES: were shears used for trimming.

STRICKE: a dry measure of half a bushel or a container of that amount.

BARK, BARKE, BAREKE: was used in the tanning process. It is the bark of a tree.

Much of this terminolgy has gone from the everyday conversation of Endon people, and since the tanyard closed in the middle of the nineteenth century, about 1840, it is unlikely that any old tanners will be about in the village to revive memories and recount stories of the Endon tanyard.

In 1847 Charles Heaton possessed fifteen acres of land on which he paid tithes.[3] He is described as land agent in 1851, a farmer of fifty acres. His son John was a land surveyor. However, though the church rate book of 1842 shows him as owner-occupier of the tanyard property, there is no evidence to suggest that he carried on business as a tanner. In fact it would seem that when he took possession of the property it had ceased to function as a tannery.

There are no people shown in the census of 1851 as tanners, and the property known as the tanyard, in Park Lane, was occupied in that year by a Thomas Plant, a wheelwright, aged sixty-four.

The premises known as the tanyard have from time to time been connected to the property now known as Sutton House, as witnessed in the will of John Sutton of 1744, and later with Hallwater House. We have seen that first the Suttons and then the Hand family conducted the business before the lands and properties passed to Charles Heaton about 1840.

The same Charles Heaton owned the property attached to Hallwater, and in 1854 he owned the 'house and garden' which was occupied by the incumbent of Endon parish, the Reverend Daniel Turner, Endon at that time having no vicarage.

The two references to tanners in Endon are in 1818 when W. D. Hand shown as of Park Lane and T. Tomkinson were recorded.[4] By 1834 only Mrs. Catherine Hand is shown in White's Directory. There are no other references a fact which suggests that, in Endon, tanning disappeared as an occupation in the first half the nineteenth century.

Endon Mill

At the beginning of this century another feature of Endon's continuous history became apparent. In medieval times references are made to the several mills in Endon, Horton and Longsdon, but it is difficult to place their position.[5] One of the earliest documents is dated 1805 when 'the land previously known as Crabtree Bank (part of Newfield) on one side of the stream and part of Ragonfield Wood on the other side of the stream, was acquired by John Lees of Stanley Forge from John Sant, and his son John, for the purpose of erecting a corn mill with permission to build a dam and divert the stream.' A mill and mill house were built and the course of the mill race which was supplied from the waters of Endon Brook nearly one thousand feet above sea level, can be traced on the site today. Unfortunately for John Lees, he became short of money and found it necessary to sell the whole property which in 1813 was in the hands of John Bailey. The Bailey family conducted the business of millers in Endon as is instanced by the many references in nineteenth century directories:

Post Office Directory of Staffordshire 1876: Bailey, Isaac, Miller, Endon mill.

Kelly's Directory 1880: Bailey, Isaac, Miller, Endon Mill.

Kelly's Directory 1892: Bailey, George Harry, Miller (water), Endon mill.

It was the Baileys who re-built the Mill House in 1825 at what is today known as Fields Mill. By coincidence or design the property today is owned by Mrs. Nora Hounslow, nee Morrey, who purchased the property from Mrs. Jessie Morrey, nee Bailey, in 1940. Thus up to that date the mill had remained the property of the one family since 1813.

In 1910 the mill ceased to operate, and in 1936 when the fabric had become unsafe, it was demolished. Thus ended the story of the Millers of Endon. Percy Williamson, however, wrote some details from which we learn:

(1) From the mill pond, over the mill wheel and out at the tail race, was a thirty foot drop.

(2) The mill wheel, was three feet wide and twenty-two feet in diameter, and could grind oatmeal, wheat, flour and coarser grists for animal feed, which would suggest at least three sets of stones.

(3) Because the mill was sited in a hollow, the grain could be loaded on to the top floor of the mill without the need of a hoist. The grain then passed through the machinery and was bagged off at a lower floor where it was collected by carts.

(4) The sacks of oats weighed ten score (two hundred pounds), but the wheat was bagged in eleven score four (two hundredweights).

(5) Most of the grain was grown on local farms; and in the autmun the mill was a very busy place.

The mill was indeed a busy place, but as corn growing declined, and animal feeds were supplied more conveniently, the mill fell into disuse, and the familiar sound of the rumbling wheels and the rushing water died away leaving older people to reflect with nostalgia and the young ones to wonder what it had all been about.

Gate House Farm

At this house there is a date, 1660, carved above the fireplace. In 1662 the Lord of the Manor of Horton was paid fifty-five shillings and threepence by one Christopher Malkin 'for admittance'.[6] It is not clear where the Malkins came from to take possession in 1662. In 1666 another Malkin appears in Endon at Lane Head, but perhaps some significance should be attached to the fact that the Vicar of Norton in 1561 is one Richard Malkin.[7]

Gate House Farm consisted in 1662 of forty-five acres, two cottages, fifteen acres called Emma's meadow, and twenty-four acres customary land.

The 1666 Hearth Tax shows Charles Malkin as paying on three hearths, but no indication of the official name of the property is given.

In 1688 an entry was made in the Leek parish registers: 'Geo Roades, Vicar of Leek and Ann Malkin of Gatehouse, married.'

It would seem that the property remained in the hands of the Malkin-Fenton-Jones and Grosvenor lines and was owned in 1847 by Mrs. Mary Grosvenor and consisted of one hundred and twenty-one acres and fifty acres.[8]

It is very likely that the several other people connected with Gatehouse, for example a baptism of 1692: 'Matthew, son of Richard and Elizabeth Benison of Gatehouse', and again in 1649: 'Jane, daughter of Richard and Anne Boulton' were tenants. There is an earlier baptism of Richard Boulton in 1688. Though Charles appears to have retained possession for a while no further names of Malkin appear in connection with the Gatehouse, and by 1847 the property had passed to the Grosvenors. In 1876 it was farmed by John Bentley who according to directories of the period was still there in 1880, but by 1892 the occupier was John Mountford. It is possible that there was another Yatehouse or Gatehouse within the parish of Leek, and entries in the Leek registers of some unfamiliar names relate to people not of Endon.

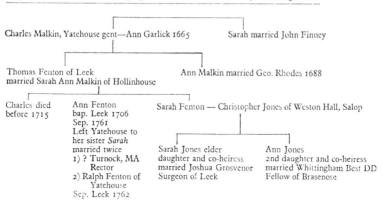

Christopher Malkin of Yatehouse prope of Leek 1662—Catherine Byron of Buglawton

Charles Malkin, Yatehouse gent—Ann Garlick 1665   Sarah married John Finney

Thomas Fenton of Leek   Ann Malkin married Geo. Rhodes 1688
married Sarah Ann Malkin of Hollinhouse

Charles died before 1715

Ann Fenton bap. Leek 1706 Sep. 1761 Left Yatehouse to her sister *Sarah* married twice 1) ? Turnock, MA Rector 2) Ralph Fenton of Yatehouse Sep. Leek 1762

Sarah Fenton — Christopher Jones of Weston Hall, Salop

Sarah Jones elder daughter and co-heiress married Joshua Grosvenor Surgeon of Leek

Ann Jones 2nd daughter and co-heiress married Whittingham Best DD Fellow of Brasenose

The Ashes

Another house which was among the earliest in Endon is The Ashes. It is believed that this farmhouse was once part of the Abbey of Dieulacres and on its dissolution the land came into the hands of the Bentleys where it remained until 1638 when it passed to the Bellots who later sold to John Debank. In 1796 the estate passed by marriage to the Sneyds of Belmont and Onecott before it passed to the Williamsons. The first of the Bellots of The Ashes to be buried at Leek was Edward, in 1649.[9]

It has two beautiful wide gables and mullioned windows, and is a fine example of a yeoman's house of the seventeenth and eighteenth centuries. In 1656, Thos. and Sarah Clowes are shown as tenants of 'Mr. Bellot's'. Thomas Clowes is shown in the Leek registers as a weaver, one of the earliest indications of a person's occupation to be found at Endon. The other one revealed was that of Hugh Sherratt, a cobler of Yen (Endon) Quarter. There have been claims that The Ashes was once a Quaker Meeting House, but there is little to support this.

Moving on into the nineteenth century, the Tythe schedule shows William Sneyd as owning and occupying one hundred and forty-three acres in Endon, The Ashes is clearly shown on maps of the eighteenth and nineteenth centuries and in Paterson's Roads[10] where an entry reads: 'Beyond Endon on the left is Ashes. S. Debank, Esq.' Cary's Roads[11] simply records 'Endon—S. Debank, Esq.' Both these comprehensive road guidebooks of the early nineteenth century single out the Ashes as the most important residence in Endon. In 1876 and 1880 directories show it as being farmed by Joseph and Hugh Mountford and in 1892 by Alfred Critchlow.

Wedgwoods of Harracles and the Moss

At the end of the Middle Ages in a case concerning the Moss, a document relating to Horton Manor Court shows how, 'In that part of Endon Quarter named Longston-Hamell near Stanlow is a small farm called Dearneford and before that Darple the estate of Mosse.'[12] Richard the son of Nicolas Mosse was executed at Stafford for the murder of Agnes Smith, and the estate of the Mosses, as a result, was forfeited to the crown. Ralph Edge, the lord of the manor, purchased it for forty shillings, a sum which was considered too small by the barons of the Exchequer and the property was sold to John Wedgwood for £10 in 1577. Although the next heir to the property, one Thomas Mosse brought an action it remained in the hands of the Wedgwoods. From Loxdale's manuscripts it can be deduced that the Wedgwoods held Harracles and the Moss, and that the family occupied both estates.[13] John Wedgwood of Harracles died in 1658, aged eighty-seven years, having survived his son at the Moss. However, they had earlier married into the property of Harracles when John Wedgwood of Blackwood married the daughter and heiress of John Shaw 'and had her Harracles'. Their son Richard was succeeded by John who is referred to in the document of 1577, and whose will was entered at Lichfield in 1590. He had married Mary Egerton. Ralph was baptised in 1577, Felicia in 1579, but his son and heir John Wedgwood, the one referred to above (born 1571), married a Miss Ford of Ford Hall, by whom he had John, Egerton, Mary (baptised 1608), William 1610, Esther 1612, Elizabeth 1614, and Andrew. It was about 1604 when John was born and it was he who was survived by his father, after having lived at the Moss with his wife Jane. In 1639 one John Jodrell married Elizabeth Wedgwood thus linking two names which were to figure prominently in Endon charities, the church and the school in the next century.

Harracles Hall passed from John Wedgwood in 1756 to Phoebe wife of Brooke Boothby and in 1790 was brought by Thomas Mills of Barlaston for £6,100, and after passing to his grand-daughter it was sold again in 1826 to Mr. Davenport, M.P., for £9,300.

Fernyhough and the Fernyhoughs

Erdeswicke and Harwood both make reference to a family named Fernyhough who owned an estate in or near Endon, also named Fernyhough 'though the estate was but small.'[14]

Thomas and William Fernyhalg were tenants of Lord Audley in 1307. Thomas rented 'three messuages and two bovates of land' in Endon, and William rented six acres of land also in Endon.

In 1350 a commission was set up to examine several complaints of riot and murder. In 1352 James, Lord Audley 'complained' that his son Sir Nicholas, and Roger, his son-in-law 'with a riotous following' had broken into and looted both Heighley and Redcastle parks. 'Among those who broke in with the young Audleys were such old tenants of the Audleys as Thomas Fernihaugh and Thomas of Greneway' though there is, in this instance, no mention of Endon.[15]

In the Endon Subsidy Rolls of 1327 the name 'Adam de Fernihaleugh' appears. In 1360 one Adam de Fernyhalgh served as a juror for 'Tatesmonslow' at Wolverhampton without any specific mention of Endon.[16]

In 1395 John de Fernyhalgh was bailiff in Leek and the 1539 Muster Rolls of Totmonslowe includes the names of Roger and John Fernyhalg.[17]

The name Fernyhough in connection with Endon reappears early in the seventeenth century when John and William Fernihough, gentlemen sold four messuages, four gardens, fifty acres of land, twenty acres of meadow, four orchards, fifty acres of pasture and 'all tithes in Endon, otherwise Yendon.'[18]

The parish registers of Leek record that on the 4th September 1640, Jocosa, wife of W. Meare of Fernihough was buried.

Sleigh, quoting from a deed, said that the Manor of Stanley was sold by William Stanley of Hootton, Richard Draycott and others to Thomas Fernyhough of Stanley on the 10th July 1660 for £900. The Hearth Tax of 1666 supports this, showing that Thomas Fernihough, gentleman, paid for three hearths in Stanley. Simon Fernihough occupied a more humble abode in Endon, paying for one hearth only.[19]

Fernyhough Farm, Brown Edge, is named in the Horton enclosures of 1813 and marked on the 1836 Ordnance Survey map. In both instances the location was that recorded on the enumeration sheet of the 1851 Population Census, when the farm was shown as being sixty acres in size. William Mountford lived at 'Fernyhough' at this time.

Some people recall that years ago at Fernyhough, Brown Edge, there were mullioned windows and an oak staircase. The property has since undergone extensive alterations and there is now merely the name on the gate 'Fernyhough Farm', insufficient evidence to prove that this was 'Fernyhough, near Endon, long enjoyed by a family of the same name though the estate was but small.'

Stanlowe Hall Farm is situated on a hill-top near to Longsdon Church, in a part of the old medieval manor of Endon.

In 1307 William de Stanlowe and John de Stanlowe were tenants of the Audleys, then Lords of the Manor of Endon, and a William Stanlowe was also named in the Subsidy Roll of Endon in 1327.

The Bulkley pedigree in the Historical Collections of Staffordshire, Volume 5, para. 2 indicates that the family 'de Stanlowe' was the Shyrard or Sherratt family of Chedulton and Stanlowe. Richard Sherratt of Stanlowe married Cecilia Alsop in 1441. The male line of the Sherratts of Stanlowe then failed (Richard's daughter Johanna married Richard Bulclough (Bulkley) of Perwych). Thus Stanlowe came to the Bulkleys early in the fifteenth century. In 1523 Humphrey Bulkley of Stanlowe married Johanna, daughter of William Egerton of Wall Grange. In the Hearth Tax of 1666, Thomas Bulkley of Stanlowe was charged for five hearths. He was buried at Leek on 24th July 1675. There is a memorial tablet to the Bulkleys in St. Edward's Church, Leek, which names Thomas Bulkley, late of Stanlowe, nr. Longsdon who died on the 19th May 1736.

From this time until the 1940s, Stanlowe was owned by this Bulkley family.

Pedigree of the Shyrards (Sherratts) of Chedulton and Stanlowe

William of Chedulton
|
Robert married Hawisia
|
William Shyrard married Petronella—1304
|
Nicholas Shyrard
|
┌───┐
| |
Henry married   Peter Shyrard of
Margareta—1382   Stanlowe
|
Richard Shyrard of Stanlowe married Cecilia Alsop 20 H6 (1441)
|
Johanna—Richard Buclough of Perwych and Stanlowe
|
Richard Bulkley Junior 1473 married Cecelia
|
Humphrey Bulkley married Johanna, daughter of Wm. Egerton of Wall Grange—1523.

Manor Farm

Built for Richard and Martha Tomkinson, it belonged to the Tomkinson family for nearly two hundred years. The stone over the doorway is marked RT/MT 1637, but some parts of the building are of an earlier period.

Wills for Tomkinson in Endon start in 1540, with one of John and one for Thomas in 1556. The 1666 Hearth Tax would suggest that the house contained three hearths and was the property of William

Tomkinson. There is a later Georgian addition which is divided from the older fabric by a long arched hall running across the width of the house.

Park Lane in the seventeenth century was more than a thoroughfare through the open spaces to the east of Endon, it was a district specifically referred to as such and quoted in the Leek registers without reference to Endon. Among the surnames are Harrison, Hulme, Tomkinson, Nixon, Brigewood, Ball, Sherrett, Hargreaves, Colclough and Sherratt.

Endon Bank—this is the name given to the area around the church, and there are many references to houses and cottages in this area—'on the bank.'

Sutton House

This name has only recently been given to the property. Like other properties it has been altered and added to by successive generations. There are parts of the building which suggest a wattle and daub structure of about 1490. It is heavily beamed and contains a fine Tudor hearth. It has more recent nineteenth century additions.

The Suttons as a family figure prominently in its history. The wills of the Suttons of Endon start in 1545 and show a continuity down to 1744 when one John Sutton possessed the tanyard and the lands around Hallwater.[20] Suttons figure prominently in Leek parish affairs, having been churchwardens for the Endon Quarter. A will of Jane Hand of 1803 makes the break complete and since that time the property has been in the hands of nineteenth and twentieth century style professional people. The occupiers of Sutton House have for several decades been associated with beagling. One such a person was Edmund Tennant, mayor of Hanley in 1870.

Hollin House Farm

The name of this house appears in 1567 when Christopher Malkin was involved concerning copyhold of lands and one tenement called Hollin House.[21] This and the connection with the Manor of Horton would suggest it is one of the oldest houses in the district.

In 1690 Charles, son of Thomas and Sarah Fenton, gent, of Hollin House, was baptised and in 1692 Sarah, daughter of the above couple was also baptised. Sarah Fenton before her marriage was a daughter of Charles Malkin of the Yatehouse. She died in 1762. Sarah married Christopher Jones as seen in the family tree of the family at Gatehouse.

Though there is no clear indication of Hollin House in the 1666 Hearth Tax return, we know that William Beech of Hollin House was buried on April 24th 1664. In the tax return is the entry, 'Widdow Beech, one hearth.' Could it be that the Beeches were the earlier occupiers of this house? In 1851 the house was in the hands of Jane Salt who is shown as a farmer of 120 acres. She was a widow with two daughters, Elizabeth and Margaret, and helped by three farm servants. In 1876 Charles Critchlow farmed at Hollin House and he remained there for about twenty years.[22]

Lawn Farm is situated in Park Lane, a building which has been redesigned over the years. It is believed to be four hundred years old reflecting some aspects of English social history such as the priest hide and the blocking of windows in order to avoid paying taxes. There are no references to the name Lawn Farm and since documents concerning the property have been lost it is difficult to identify occupants or to trace any names which may have had some association.

THE PEOPLE

Herbert Wilson Foster

Herbert Wilson Foster was born at Endon on 18th January 1848. His father George Foster was the Chapel Warden at Endon and an artist of some repute in the district. He attended the Hanley School of Art and was awarded a Bronze Medal in 1865, and in 1866 he won the Silver Medal of the Science and Art Department. This was followed in 1872 by the Silver Medal of the Worshipful Company of Painters, an award which placed him in high esteem as an artist.

During this period he used the summer house at Bank House as his studio, but shortly afterwards he had a house built in Orford Road, which was more suitable to his requirements. Many people in Endon sat for him and some of these works were hung in the Royal Academy.

In 1890 H. W. Foster moved to Sidmouth Avenue, Newcastle, and in 1891 he gained a National Scholarship at South Kensington, besides two silver medals which his work had earned him in Belgium. William Foster worked at one period for Messrs. Mintons of Stoke-on-Trent on the large panels of tiles for the new Victoria and Albert Museum, and remained with the company for some years as an artist. This employment was interrupted temporarily by a period in Paris where he went to study painting. After another period at Mintons he went to

Belgium to study and when he returned to England he took a post at Nottingham School of Art where he was in charge of the life class.

His pupils at Nottingham included such famous artists as Dame Laura Knight and her husband Harold Knight, also Mrs. M. Quillick, O.B.E., who designed the Queen's coinage. Many of his own paintings are to be seen in the village, and several have been used in this book to illustrate the local scene which he was so keen to interpret.

He was also fond of Nottingham, and his son, the Reverend L. Wilson Foster, M.A., Hon.C.F., recalls in a letter, 'When I was a boy my father took me on a sketching holiday each year going to some beautiful part of the country and coming home with a portfolio of water colours. I don't think there was not an interesting cottage or scene on the south side of Nottingham that my father had not sketched.'

Herbert Foster's wife was a pupil of his and an extremely fine artist. She sold many of her designs to the well-known firm of Raphael Tuck and Sons.

One of his last paintings in oil was of Queen Victoria, done especially for the centre board at the Endon well-dressing for the Jubilee of 1897. He frequently designed and helped with the dressing of the well. As if to underline the artistic fellow-feeling Foster was a great friend of George Heath the Moorland Poet, and during the time that George Heath lay ill he helped to provide him with books. The title page of the memorial edition of 'The Poems of George Heath' shows the concern of several villagers for the work of the moorland poet. Herbert Foster was responsible for the portrait and illustrations and the selection and arrangement of the works was in the hands of the Reverend James Badnall.

John Daniel

Even though Endon has claimed more agricultural connections than industrial ones, it is worth noting that at Endon there is a monument worthy of the attention of industrial historians. It is what is known locally as 'the grave in the field'. John Daniel was the man buried there and this extract from the Staffordshire Advertiser of 27th January 1821 serves to illuminate some of the darker mysteries of the gentlemanly and studious nonconformist who requested that he should be buried in unconsecrated ground:

'On Thursday the 18th inst., John Daniel Gent of Hanley aged 65 years, one of the proprietors of the long established concern the

New Hall China Manufactory . . . his mortal remains were conveyed in a hearse (attended by a number of his friends in carriages) to Endon in this County on Wednesday last, and interred in a piece of ground at the village belonging to him . . . he was committed to the 'House appointed for all living' without the observance of the offices of religion in any shape, conformably with the opinions of the Free Thinkers to which it is understood he had long been a disciple. The singularity of the occasion collected together a multitude of spectators on the road to Endon and at the place of interment.'

Some years later John Daniel's sister was buried in the same grave.

Joseph Bowyer

(an account written on New Year's Eve 1903 by G. H. Heaton)

Joseph Bowyer was born at Stanley on 24th January 1818, and died at Brown Edge on 28th December 1903. He was the youngest son of Mr. Samuel Bowyer. He first attended a dame's school at Stanley, taught by Mrs. Willott, and afterwards the Parochial School at Endon Bank, leaving the latter at the age of eight to go with his father's boat.

He was among the first to attend the Sunday School conducted by the Parish Clerk (Mr. James Baddeley) in one of the stone-built cottages in the village of Endon, whence the children were taken to service at the Parish Church, stowed away in the gallery, and solemnly kept in order by an official armed with a long stick. His earliest years of labour were devoted to the boating of limestone from Froghall, for Joseph Brindley of Longport, varied by occasional journies with the boat into the 'Black Country' of South Staffordshire.

When 16 years of age, his father died, and Joseph took charge of the boat in his own account, bringing his earnings to his mother with whom he continued to make a home, and carrying limestone from Froghall as before. Three years later, when only 19 years old, he made an expedition in charge of his boat to London, the object of his journey being to fetch some carved stone for the entrances to the great mansion at Trentham which the Duke of Sutherland was then building. Being detained for eleven days at Paddington canal basin, Joseph had opportunities for sight-seeing in the great city, and apparently turned them to account, for to the last he retained a recollection of the places of interest which came under his observation.

Returning to Trentham, he was a participator in the young Duke's coming-of-age festivities, and if the truth must be told, Joseph, among convivial friends in the Servants' Hall, recounting his London adventures, made slightly too free with the excellent home-brewed ale, liberally served but in a two-handled mug, and required to be assisted to his bed-chamber over the Stables.

Subsequently, during a period of seven years, Joseph found employment under Mr. Trubshaw, the contractor, in boating stone and other materials from various parts of the country for the building of Trentham Hall, so that he could boast of having had a not inconsiderable hand in the rearing of the present magnificent pile.

Stone flags from Yorkshire, and slates from Wales, formed some of the cargoes he carried, as he pursued the even tenor of his way along the canal system.

Later on, he conveyed stone blocks on which to rest the metals of one of the earliest railways in the country—that from Crewe to Stafford—only to find in a few years those blocks superseded by wooden sleepers.

Going back somewhat, Joseph was married to his first wife, Jane Wakefield, of Ladderedge, at Leek Parish Church, at the age of twenty-three. He took her to live at Post Bridge, Endon, where she died in less than three years afterwards and was buried at Endon, leaving behind two children. After completing his job at Trentham, and for the railway contractor, Joseph once more undertook the boating of lime and limestone, this time for Mr. Edwin Heaton, who then had kilns at Post Bridge, Endon, and in whose services he remained until Mr. Heaton relinquished the business.

Seven years after the decease of his first wife, Joseph married Sabra Sheldon of Brown Edge. The marriage took place at Stoke Church, and in due course they had thirteen children of whom, however, only four survived.

Some time later he boated coal and slack for Richard Deane, colliery proprietor of Norton, who owned as many as twelve boats.

His leisure time was spent in a becoming and orderly manner, for many years he was a member of Robert Heath's Bible Class at Brown Edge, a communicant and a great believer in the due and proper observance of the Sabbath. 'Not slothful in business, serving the Lord' may well be written as his epitaph, and may the example he left behind be a pattern for many of the younger generation in Brown

Edge and the neighbourhood against whom it is sometimes alleged that they love their dogs better than their wives and children, and a public house better than a place of worship.[23]

Edmund Tennant

An eccentric and curious character of the village was Edmund Tennant of Sutton House who created much interest during the second half of the nineteenth century. Precise in his ways and speech his expressions were invariably caustic, yet tinged with many a sparkle of sardonic humour.

'Old Teddy' used a stick in his later years and the tap, tap, of his walking aid was a frequent sound as was the chanting of small boys as they called 'owld Teddy' after him. With Noah Baddeley he was a devotee of beagling and frequently greeted his companion with the expression, 'Here comes the sporting cobbler.'

Charles Perkin—a village blacksmith—1890-1969

Charles Perkin was born at Kingsley, Staffordshire, the elder son of William and Sarah Perkin. The family moved to Bucknall where his father, a blacksmith, found employment, and Charles started to go to school there. Later his father took the smithy at Tomkin, and from the Bucknall school the boy was moved to complete his education at Bagnall School.

He became apprenticed to his father, and learnt the trade of blacksmith and farrier at Tomkin. At the age of twenty-one years, he took over the smithy at Endon, succeeding Mr. Edensor Gibson. He rented the premises from Mr. William Critchlow, the local builder, and paid an 'ingoing' of one hundred pounds, which was loaned to him by his father.

After his first year's work at Endon, and after living expenses had been paid, which included a new suit of clothes, he was left with a grand profit of half a crown.

Things rapidly improved, however, due mainly to his expertise in farriery, and his knowledge of shoeing difficult and lame horses. For this speciality he was sought after over a wide area and horse shoeing was his first love. He spent many days travelling to smiths' shops in the county and beyond to attend classes to further his knowledge. These classes were organised by the Staffordshire County Council, who engaged Mr. George Harris, a first-class farrier, to conduct the instruction, both practical and theoretical. He passed an examination in 1953 as Fellow of the Worshipful Company of Farriers. He attended shoeing competitions at agricultural shows throughout Britain, and was frequently among the winners, often gaining first prize. From 1930 until he died he was secretary of the Stoke-on-Trent Farriers. In 1937 he won the championship of Great Britain at the Royal Show, held in July at Wolverhampton, and was proud of the fact that a Staffordshire man had won 'The Royal' in Staffordshire. This crowned his efforts in the field of show competition farriery.

During the war years the shows were curtailed, but on their post-war resumption, he again entered competitions and though past middle age, won further prizes. When he was asked to act as judge he retired from competitive shoeing and gained the distinction of judging farriery at the Royal Show three times.

In 1951 he was made a Freeman of the Worshipful Company of Farriers and of the City of London, being invested at Guildhall, London, by the Master of the Farriers' Company and in the presence of the Lord Mayor of London.

He was a chorister at Bagnall School, and was given one shilling by the Reverend John Simon Morris of Endon, for singing soprano solo in the Harvest Anthem, and on his marriage to Miss Olive Clowes of Stanley in 1921, he came to reside in Endon and was promptly enrolled by the vicar there as a chorister in Endon Church. He served the choir for almost fifty years, possessing a fine bass voice, and taking solos at Endon and surrounding churches on special musical occasions.

He always took an active part in the affairs of the village, being Chairman of Endon and Stanley Parish Council, for a term. He was a member of the C.E.M.S. at St. Luke's Church, a member of the Endon Gardener's Association, and member of the Old Endon Rifle Club, and secretary with his wife of the Endon Choral Society.

He lived a full and happy life, and never appeared to worry. When he locked his smithy each evening he never took work home with him, and at 9-30 p.m. each evening he went to the Black Horse Inn to enjoy a drink and the company of his many friends.

His first wife died in 1951, and he remarried six years later, pre-deceasing his second wife. He had one son by his first marriage who now carries on the business of village blacksmith as Charles Perkin and Son Ltd.

He died on October 1st 1969 at the age of seventy-nine years after a short period of illness, and was buried in Endon Churchyard by the side of his parents, his wife, and his brother. He was truly the village blacksmith known and respected by everybody.

Percy Williamson

Many references have been made in this work which suggest that Percy Williamson was a true lover of the rural life as it was found in Endon. He was a keen artist, a designer of the flower 'boards' at the well-dressing, a writer of local history and a man of affairs at parish and district level. Reginald Twemlow now retired from his post as village constable has written the following lines, a tribute to Percy Williamson.

A man he is with no mean frame
Of England's yeoman stock.
An artist-farmer of local fame
And steady as a rock.

His knarled hands can take the plough,
Both pen and brush as well;
Creating beauty is his bent,
As many men can tell.

The Well in Endon, at his touch
Like magic is transformed.
The grey-faced stone, so hard and rough,
With greenery is adorned.

Fashioned is the old well's face
With floral motifs seen.
Portraits there depict life's race
And tributes to God and Queen

Perhaps some poet's birth is told
Upon the facade there,
Or maybe victory's tales unfold
In nature's colours rare.

No need is there for written scroll
The message to impart,
Enquiring eyes take in the whole,
And marvel at the art.

Each portion tells its flowery tale,
Remembrance to awake.
Uplifts the human heart so frail,
And inspires his word to take.

As years roll by and memories fade,
The written word will stand,
His debt to life he will have paid
By his creative hand.

The Endon Parish Registers

Thomas Cromwell instituted the registration of Baptisms, Burials
and Marriages in England in 1538. Because Endon was regarded as
part of the ancient parish of Leek, all registrations before 1730 were
made there. In 1730 Endon was established as a perpetual curacy,
registers were opened and the first burial recorded was in 1731.

All the entries are made in one book and are made chronogically,
thus baptisms, burials and marriages are mixed, however, there are so
few marriages, and all before 1753, that they can be discounted for
statistical purposes. The lack of entries relating to marriages before
1753 is important socially because it indicates that local people were
married at Leek. After Hardwicke's Act of 1754 it was necessary that
marriages should be made in the parish church. Endon being a chapel
of ease was not empowered to register marriages.

In the first ten years 1731 to 1740 some 64 baptisms and 33 burials
were recorded. From 1741 to 1750 the figures rose to 114 and 45
respectively. The steady increase continued to about 1760 when there
was a decline to 1780. From 1780 the numbers rise gradually through
to the year 1850. Throughout the period 1730 to 1850 there is an
excess of baptisms over the number of burials recorded at Endon and
in a climate of natural increase which was occuring generally after
1730, this is acceptable. However, the number of baptisms up to 1800
is nearly twice the number of burials. Burials were obviously taking
place elsewhere and it is not unreasonable to suppose that this was
at the old mother church at Leek. Presumably as families identified
themselves with their own church the numbers taken to Leek (or else-
were) for burial declined. The numbers of baptisms and burials for
the decennial periods are given below:

Period	Baptisms	Burials	Natural Increase
1731/1740	64	33	31
1741/1750	114	45	69
1751/1760	118	69	49
1761/1770	113	66	47
1771/1780	105	68	37
1781/1790	140	87	53
1791/1800	123	106	17
1801/1810	142	103	39
1811/1820	161	138	23
1821/1830	183	134	49
1831/1840	202	169	33
1841/1850	414	185	229

The natural increase is based on the assumption that the number of burials shown truly reflected the number of deaths in the community.

In 1837 civil registration commenced and this together with increased activity among nonconformists caused the Anglican registers to be uncharacteristic of the true demographic profile of the parish, as they had been perhaps with slight under-registration, prior to 1837.[24]

Little information of a personal kind is given and the entries are quite stark. In the baptisms we are told that Hannah Frost of Brownedge was baptised, that in 1794 Thomas Bowness, officiating Minister, was under a sequestration and that curate Thomas Middleton carried on the work of incumbent. Among the burials recorded are those of Rev. Enoch Tomkinson of Park Lane, buried, October 5th 1761, in 1762 Mr. Justice Murhall of Bagnall was buried, and in 1765 one Angus McBean of the Nook House, Dunwood was buried.

By 1845 the entries take on a tone more typical of the nineteenth century, with references to the workhouse and the tollgate. In 1846 on December 14th, Ann Bennison of Poolend Tollgate was buried, aged 84. But what tragic stories are told in the entries. Phoebe Brooks, Lady Green, Cheddleton, age 43 years, buried on 28th February, Sarah Brooks, Lady Green, Cheddleton buried on March 16th, age three weeks.

The registers do not go back far enough to enlighten us about the consequences of plague in Endon. Even the fevers which affected the area in 1729/1730 occur too early to affect the demographic image presented by the Endon registers. Thus we see a growth and an excess of baptisms over burials throughout. Some indication of the diseases affecting Baddeley Green can be gleaned from the following entries, though there is no indication given of the cause of death.

Entries read:

Mary daughter of John and Jane Hall of Baddiley Green was buried November 15th, 1812.

Another d. of above named John and Jane Hall, of Baddiley Green was buried. December 22nd 1812.

John son of John and Sarah Adams of Baddiley Green buried. 6th December 1812.

Edith daughter of the above named John and Sarah Adams of Baddiley Green, Labourer was buried. 6th December 1812.

Charles son of the above John and Sarah Adams of Baddiley Green, Labourer, was buried. 22nd December 1812.

An indication of the journeying to Leek, however, is shown by the following extracts from the Leek registers for the period before the Endon registers began.

1636   Thomas Crockett of Endon buried at Leek
1636   Joan daughter of Ralph and Eliza Cooke of Endon baptized at Leek
1637   John Warren vulgarly called Pedley of Endon buried at Leek
1638   Ellen Tomkinson of Park Lane buried at Leek
1638   Samual Tomkinson of Park Lane baptized at Leek
1638   John Bentley of the Ashes buried at Leek
1639   Joan Bentley of the Ashes buried at Leek
1639   Sarah Tomkinson of Park Lane baptized at Leek
1640   Mary Crockett of Endon baptized at Leek
1640   Anna Booth of Knowles baptized at Leek
1642   Cath Crockett of Endon buried at Leek
1642   Richard Tomkinson of Park Lane buried at Leek
1643   Will Sutton of Endon buried at Leek
1645   Ales Sutton of Yendon buried at Norton
1653   John Sutton of Yendon buried at Norton
1658   W. Sherrat of Clay Lake buried at Leek
1658   R. Heath of Park Lane baptized at Leek
1659   Hugh Sherratt of Hollinhurst buried at Leek

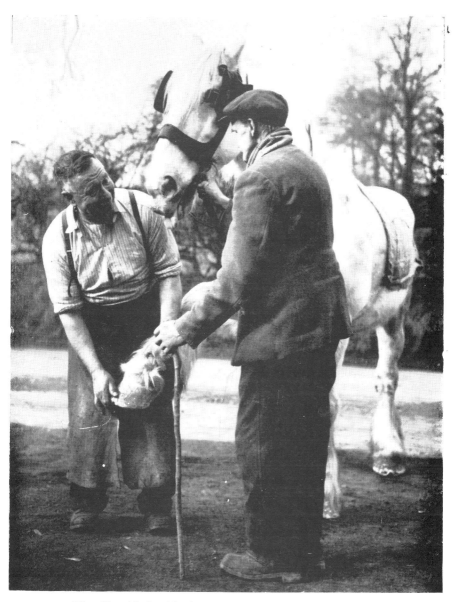

The village blacksmith of yesteryear—Mr. Charles Perkin at work.

MEMORIAL EDITION.

THE POEMS

OF

GEORGE HEATH,

THE MOORLAND POET.

Selected and Arranged by

THE REV. JAMES BADNALL, B.A.,

VICAR OF ENDON.

Memoir

BY FRANCIS REDFERN,

AUTHOR OF THE "HISTORY OF UTTOXETER."

Portrait and Illustrations

BY HERBERT WILSON FOSTER.

LONDON:

BEMROSE AND SONS, 21, PATERNOSTER ROW; AND IRONGATE, DERBY.

MDCCCLXX.

The title-page of the memorial edition of poems by George Heath, the moorland poet, selected and arranged by the Rev. James Badnall and illustrated by Herbert Wilson Foster, 1870.

1659 Thomas Sherratt of Hollinhurst and Mary Barlow of Norton married at Leek

1661 Thomas Sutton of Yen and Eliz Alport of Park Lane married at Leek

1662 Thomas Bentley of Yen baptized at Leek

1663 Mary Sutton of Yen baptized at Leek

1663 Jane Goodwin of Yen baptized at Leek

1663 Hugh Sherratt of Clay Lake baptized at Leek

1664 Ann Sutton of Yen baptized at Leek

1664 John Symson Churchwarden at Leek for the Endon quarter

1665 John Dennil of Stanley and Mary Tomkinson of Park Lane married at Leek

1665 George son of Thom and Eliza Meare of Endon Hill baptized at Leek

1666 Thom Pilsbury of Park Lane baptized at Leek

1666 Edna Rogers of Endon Bank baptized at Leek

1666 Tho. Pilsbury of Stanley Mill baptized at Leek

1668 Thomas Bentley of Yendon Churchwarden at Leek

1669 Will Cook and Mary Hargreaves of Yendon married at Leek

1671 Anne Bentley of Yen Bank baptized at Leek

1672 Mary Ford of Yendon baptized at Leek

1672 Mary Pilsbury of Woodcock Hurst baptized at Leek

1672 Ed Meare of Yen Bank buried at Leek

1675 Tho. Sherratt of Hollinhurst buried at Leek

1676 Rich Boughey of Stanley Head Churchwarden for-Endon at Leek

1679 Thomas Sutton of Endon baptized

1679 Joseph Hilton of Endon baptized

1679 James Coape of Endon Bank baptized

1683 Will Fallows of Limehouse serves as churchwarden for the Endon quarter

1686 Edward Mear of Morrice House guardian at Leek

1687 William Hulme of Clay Lake, one of the churchwardens at Leek

1689 Susannah daughter of Hugh and Ann Sherratt of Yen (cobbler) baptized

1692 John Clowes of Washy Brook in Endon quarter churchwarden

1694 Thomas Bentley of Endon Hill churchwarden

From the Church Wardens Accounts 1782 to 1818 (St. Edward's Church, Leek)

1782-83   Paid for Wine for Sacraments at Endon £1 16 0.

1786   Paid for Horse and Man to Stafford from Endon 8/6.
Wine and Bread for Endon 16/8.

1779   Paid Mr. Knight for Endon Chapel 13/9.

1801   Paid by John Knight of Longsdon Churchwarden for Endon £25.

1804   Chapel Warden for Longsdon Mr. Lockett.

1807   Mr. Royle Chapel Warden for Endon and Longsdon paid £37 10 0.

1809   Mr. Sutton paid £18 15 0. levy for Endon and Longsdon

1813   The Endon levy was raised to £100.

1814   Mr. Ball Churchwarden of Endon.

1815   Received off Mr. Ball for Endon £74.

1816   Received off Francis Ainsworth Endon levy £100.

1817   Received off Mr. Keates Endon Chapel Warden £100.

1818   Longsdon, Endon and Stanley levy £170.

At the Vestry Meeting of the inhabitants of the parish of Leek held in 1816 it was ordered that the sum of eight hundred pounds be collected by a rate throughout the parish towards further repairs to St. Edward's Church, Leek.

Number of people buried and shown to be from Endon from 1636 to 1689 = 14.

Number of children baptized and shown to be from Endon 1636 to 1689 = 23.

Number of marriages shown to be from Endon 1636 to 1689 = 4.

These figures do not represent the total activity involving people from Endon. It must be appreciated that before 1730 Endon people would be treated as other members of the Leek parish and only rarely would the name of the Quarter be given. These are the ones shown in the totals above.

References

[1] Thirsk, Joan: 'Horn and Thorn in Staffordshire', *N.S.J.F.S.*, Vol. 9, 1969, p. 1.

[2] Poor Law Guardians Minute Book, Leek, 1834/8, *C.R.O.*, Stafford, D/699/AG/1834-1838.

[3] Tithe Schedule, Endon Parish. Tithe Redemption Office, London.

[4] Staffordshire General and Commercial Directory, 1818. White's Directory, 1834.

[5] For Distribution of Water Mills in North Staffordshire see *N.S.J.F.S.*, vol. 9, For references to Endon and district mills in medieval times, see Chapter II.

[6] Horton Manor Court Records. *C.R.O.*, Stafford.

[7] Jack, J.: 'A History of the Church and Parish of Norton in the Moors'.

[8] Deeds of Gatehouse Farm, Endon (Private Collection).

[9] Leek Parish Registers, Parish Chest, Leek.

[10] Paterson, Daniel: 'Roads of England and Wales', 1811.

[11] Cary, J.: 'Roads', 1808.

[12] Horton Manor Court Records. *C.R.O.*, Stafford.

[13] Loxdale, T.: Manuscripts, *C.R.O.*, Stafford.

[14] Erdswick, Sampson: 'Survey of Staffordshire'.

[15] *H.C.S.*, Vol. XI, p. 273.

[16] *H.C.S.*, Vol. XIV.

[17] *H.C.S.*, Vol. VI, New Series, Part 1, 1903.

[18] *H.C.S.*, Vol. III, New Series.

[19] *H.C.S.*, Vol. 1925, pp. 160-161.

[20] Will of John Sutton, 1744. Lichfield Wills.

[21] Horton Manor Records. *C.R.O.*, Stafford.

[22] Post Office Directory of Staffordshire (Endon), 1876.

[23] This account of the life story of Joseph Bowyer was written by G. H. Heaton on New Year's Eve, 1903 at the time of Bowyer's death.

[24] The Registrar General's Office was established in 1837 and civil registration of Births, Deaths and Marriages became compulsory. Nonconformists, i.e., those who did not wish to have children baptised in the Church of England could register the birth with the Civil Authorities and have the child baptised elsewhere or not at all. For nonconformist chapels registering before 1837 see Register General's list of those registers lodged at Somerset House.

Chapter VII

THE POPULATION OF ENDON

Any attempt to estimate population for the years before official censuses were made is hazardous and fraught with difficulties especially in a small parish such as Endon. It may be possible to use listings, tax returns and periodic statements made by incumbents, if they exist, in order to estimate the number of people in the community at a given time.

The Hearth Tax return of 1666 shows a total of 57 households and assuming that each household contained four to five people, an assumption which is generally accepted as reasonable, we can use a figure of 4.2 or 4.5 as multiplier. Thus, using a multiplier of 4.2 we have a population figure of 240 for Endon in 1666.[1]

The incumbent, Enoch Tompkinson reporting to his bishop in 1751 said that within the chapelry of Endon there were some 65 families. The size of families in a given area or at a given time is difficult to assess, however we may use 4.5 as a multiplier which multiplied by 65 would indicate a population, in 1751, of 292, an increase since 1666, of some 52 people. Because the registers do not contain any entries before 1730 it is not possible to check the 1666 figure. However, by finding a multiplier for baptisms it is possible to arrive at an approximation for the years after 1730. Rickman's method provides a multiplier which is obtained by dividing the population figure for 1801 by the annual average number of baptisms during the decade 1790-1799. In the case of Endon the annual average is 12.[2]

Population figures for Endon, with Longsdon and Stanley in 1801 was 734. In 1811 it was 766. In the 1821 census the figures were broken down into townships and the figures read,[3]

Endon 445   Longsdon 350   Stanley 113

To what extent the three townships used the parish church at Endon is difficult to assess but it is safe to say that Endon represented about one half of the total population of the three. Thus in 1801 Endon population would be 367, a figure consistent with the steady growth since 1731.

Using Rickman's formula based on the figure of 367 we are presented with the following.

$$\frac{367}{12.0} = 30$$

Thus the population for each decade from 1741 is

1741	7.2 × 30 = 216	
1751	10.6 × 30 = 318	292 based on incumbent assessment of 65 families
1761	11.8 × 30 = 354	
1771	11.3 × 30 = 339	This drop is indicated on the graph, facing (page 128) when there is a fall in Baptisms from a new high in 1759.
1781	10.5 × 30 = 315	
1791	14.0 × 30 = 420	
1801	12.3 × 30 = 369	The levels of baptisms were higher in the decade 1781-1791 than in th. .. 1791 to 1800.

The figure for 1731 to 1740 of 216 is unreliable because this decade includes the first years of registration at Endon when it is likely that the old tradition of taking children for baptism to Leek lingered on and the newer practice of registering at Endon was not fully accepted. Thus there would be some under registration in the early days. The most significant jump in baptism is in the years between 1781 and 1791. (See graph facing page 128). Could it be that by now the social influences of turnpike road construction and canal building were causing the population to increase? Certainly the high incidence of baptisms suggests a young and virile community.

TABLE (a)

Population after 1801

	1801	1811	1821	1831	1841	1851
Endon			445	487	571	658
Stanley	734	766	113	118	122	
Longsdon			350	398	405	428

Here the increase is steady and more typical of the increase to be found in rural areas at that time. Price Williams states that 'The cause of

Statistical Tables of Endon with Some Comparisons from the Census of 1811

		HOUSES				Families Chiefly Employed in Agriculture	Families Chiefly Employed in Trade Manfr. or Handicraft	All Other Families not in the two Preceding Classes	Males	Females	Total
		Inhabited	By How Many Families Occupied	Building	Un-inhabited						
Cheddleton	Township	183	183	1	1	144	37	2	474	478	952
Endon with Longsdon and Stanley	Township	139	140	1	3	92	39	9	385	381	766
Grindon	Parish	69	74	1	3	60	7	7	206	197	403
Horton with Horton Hay	Parish	87	87	-	4	39	10	38	238	202	440
Leek & Lowe	Parish	832	835	6	3	125	599	111	1664	2039	3703
Leek Frith	Township	122	137	2	2	107	27	3	359	351	710

slow increase of the population (in rural districts with less than 2,000 inhabitants) between 1821 and 1851 is evidently in great measure due to immigration into the towns. The periods of greatest increase in the town population are co-incident with those of greatest decrease in the case of the rural population.'⁴ To what extent this is true of Endon is shown in the following table which compares the percentage rate of growth in rural districts under 2,000 with Burslem, the nearest large town and with the growth rate for England and Wales as a whole.

TABLE (b)

Percentage increases

	Rural districts with less than 2,000 pop.	Burslem	Endon	England and Wales
1811/1821	14.74	18.1	4.3	16.434
1821/1831	10.52	24.9	9.0	15.438
1831/1841	9.6	34.4	17.3	14.113
1841/1851	5.88	22.6	15.6	12.591
1851/1861	7.29	13.2	4.0	12.043
1861/1871	8.41	21.4	10.4	12.990
		Burslem only	Endon only	
1871/1881		4.2	13.9	
1881/1891		15.9	12.1	
1891/1901		23.1	7.1	

It would seem that Endon did not truly reflect the position of rural districts indicated by the Price Williams figures and the increases as shown for the population in England and Wales suggest that the increase at Endon was above the average for the country as a whole. The figures for natural increase in population suggest that for the first half of the nineteenth century Endon was a recipient community and that its population was steadily built up by people who came to live in the area, Table (c). On the other hand an examination of the figures for the urban parish of Burslem suggests that the growth at Endon was very slow by comparison and that it had more in common with the rural areas and with national increases rather than with the growth experienced in the pottery towns.

For census purposes, Endon is shown as in the Leek District which was divided into the sub-districts of Norton, Leek, Leek-Frith and Longnor. Adjacent districts were Newcastle and Stoke. An interesting demographic statistic drawn from the Registrar General's report of 1845 shows that the average 'living to death' age for the respective areas were: [5]

	Men	Women
Newcastle District	40.1 years	41.4 years
Stoke District	37.8 years	39.9 years
Leek District	49.4 years	49.6 years

Surely a commentary on the rate of industrial development in the respective areas.

TABLE (c)

	Natural increase	Actual increase	Gain/Loss in excess of natural increase or decrease
1801/1810	39	32	− 7
1811/1820	23	142	+119
1821/1830	49	42	− 7
1831/1840	33	84	+ 51
1841/1850	27	87	+ 60

Taking the natural increase in the population, which is obtained by subtracting the baptisms from burials, and comparing this with the actual increase as shown in the population census figures it is possible to determine whether people moved into or out of the area. If the natural increase exceeds the actual increase then the people must have moved out. If, on the other hand, the opposite is the case then people have moved in. The extent of this migration can be shown as a gain or loss. We have shown later in this chapter where people moved from into Endon, but outgoing ones (the losses) cannot be shown without a detailed survey of other parishes. Rarely did anyone travel more than 10 miles at the first migratory move. There were slight losses in 1801/1810 and 1821/1830. In the first fifty years of the nineteenth century Endon gained some 216 people from areas outside the parish.

Population of Stanley Township, Longsdon Township, Endon Chapelry, together comprising 5453 acres.

Year	Population	Increase in Population
1801	734	3
1811	766	32
1821	908	142
1831	1003	95
1841	1098	95
1851	1194	96
1861	1241	47
1871	1370	129
1881	1560	190
1891	1759	199
1901	1884	125

The census return of 1851 is available for detailed study and the information thus broken down is a good indicator of the socio-economic condition of the parish. The census for that year was taken on the night of Sunday, March 30th and every householder completed a questionnaire or schedule. The following day the schedules were collected by an enumerator who then copied the information into enumeration books which are held at the Public Record Office in London.[6] The sheets contain details of every house in Endon and from them the following information has been gleaned. It should be borne in mind that these returns are 'static' and relate to the conditions on the one night. It is possible by using the 1861 enumeration sheets for comparison to establish how conditions changed during the ten years. The 1871 sheets have been available since January 1972.

Population of Endon in 1851

		Adults	*Children*	*Total*	*%*
Male	...	214	127	341	51.83
Female	...	211	106	317	48.17
Total	...	425	233	658	100%

The boundary line of Endon parish runs through the village of Brown Edge and divides the township; consequently an area, slightly less than one-third, of Brown Edge, is in Endon parish. The differences, social and economic between the two villages is clearly illustrated in the findings of this examination. The complete area of Endon parish including the part of Brown Edge is taken as one unit however.

Initially, a simple break-down of the tables shows that there were more males than females in the area and that there was a high proportion of children. In the mid-nineteenth century this would indicate a youthful virile community made up of active workers, not dominated by large numbers of professional or retired people.

The returns indicate that there were 138 occupied houses and taking the population at 658 this would produce a household size of 4.77[7] persons. Work done in York for the same time shows size of household to be 4.70.[8] In North Lancashire/Westmorland 5.08.[9] For England and Wales, outside London it is 5.07. Both at York and in Lancashire/Westmorland there were households in excess of 13. (1.15% and 2.41 % respectively.) Endon had none of twelve or more. It can be clearly seen in the Table facing page 128 that Endon had a predominance of households, sizes 2, 3, 4, 5. In an agricultural community one would have expected larger households because servants lived on the premises and farm families were not subjected to pressures causing an early break-up but this is off-set by the size of the farms in Endon which tended to be, on the whole, small.

The demographic profile presented by the Age-Sex pyramid emphasises the large number of young people and particularly the excess of young women between the ages of 20 and 24 years who outnumber the men of the same age by two to one. The female servants as a group were the largest single class for women and were only third in size after farmers and agricultural labourers. The figures in Table (d) do not explain the reason for the small numbers of men in that age group, but with colliery workings developing at Norton and Burslem it would be safe to suggest that they had left for work in the industrial areas.

The census returns do not suggest that there was a great imbalance between unmarried males and unmarried females as a whole and the discrepancy of one between married males and married females may be accounted for by one husband living away on the night of the census.

The age structure of the population of Endon, 1851

Age Group	Males	% Pop.	Females	% Pop.	% of Pop.	Below Age of
0- 4	46	13.49	43	13.56	13.53	5
5- 9	49	14.36	34	10.73	12.62	10
10-14	40	11.73	36	11.36	11.55	15
15-19	32	9.38	33	10.41	9.88	20
20-24	21	6.16	40	12.65	9.27	25
25-29	29	8.50	25	7.88	8.21	30
30-34	20	5.86	23	7.25	6.54	35
35-39	20	5.86	13	4.10	5.02	40
40-44	17	4.98	9	2.84	3.95	45
45-49	15	4.40	8	2.52	3.50	50
50-54	13	3.81	11	3.47	3.65	55
55-59	14	4.11	16	5.05	4.56	60
60-64	10	2.93	11	3.47	3.19	65
65-69	8	2.35	8	2.52	2.43	70
70-74	2	0.59	6	1.89	1.22	75
75-79	4	1.17	1	0.32	0.76	80
80-84	1	0.29	—		0.15	85
TOTALS	341		317			

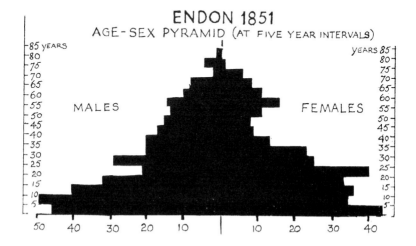

ENDON 1851
AGE-SEX PYRAMID (AT FIVE YEAR INTERVALS)

MALES   FEMALES

Place of Birth of Heads of Households in Endon in 1851

Over seventy per cent. of the heads of households in Endon in 1851 indicated that their place of birth was within five miles of Endon. This would indicate a close community with a good deal of inter-marriage. In this group were 98 persons but only 13 gave Endon as a birthplace. On the face of it this would seem to be an unusual happening and one might well attempt to account for it. The causes of the low number of Endon births indicated are not due to the movement of people but are more likely to be historical. The chapelry of Endon was still in Leek parish and a good deal of communication was maintained with that centre, thus, using the official name of that time many who were born in Endon, indicated this by entering the name of the parish of Leek as their birth place. Thus we have 30 shown for Leek but only 6 for Burslem. Brown Edge does not appear in the list hence the somewhat inflated figure of 27 for Norton where a similar, but less significant, situation arose.

Taking the population as a whole one sees the number of Leek indicated births as 209, Endon 109 and Norton 105. Here we have the same problem as when dealing with heads of households. Nevertheless the charts reveal the very high proportion of local-born inhabitants at the time of the census in spite of the fact that in the first half of the nineteenth century people were moving into Endon from the moorland areas around Leek, Horton, Cheddleton and Ipstones. The chart for heads of households is very similar to that for the population as a whole.

Places of Birth of the Population of Endon 1851

0—5 Miles

Place of Birth	No. of People	Place of Birth	No. of People
Leek	209	Biddulph	3
Endon	109	Longsdon Hd.	2
Norton	105	Werrington	2
Horton	33	Rudyard	2
Cheddleton	15	Blackbank	1
Burslem	14	Bagnall	1
Hanley	8	Wetley Moor	1
Leekfrith	6	Tunstall	2
Bucknall	5		
TOTAL 518			

Place of Birth	No. of People	Place of Birth	No. of People
Basford	1	Horstraw	1
Irlam, Lancs.	2	Dilhorne	1
Prestwich	1	Caldon	3
Haywood	1	Caverswall	3
Alton	7	Macclesfield	1
Checkley	4	Hillington	1
Foxt	2	Marston	1
Cheadle	4	Stoke	11
Wolstanton	4	Rushton	1
Cranage	1	Kingsley	4
Heaton	2	Acknor	1
Chester	2	Burton-on-Trent	1
Derby	1	Norton, Derby	1
Market Drayton	1	Red Street	1
Shenstone	1	Congleton	2
Prestbury	1	Grindley	4
Newcastle	8	Kingstone	1
Draycott	2	Buxton	4
Stone	5	Morton	1
Rushton	1	Whitchurch	2
Oncote	1	Headley	1
Allsmark, Cheshire	1	Marton	1
Lawton	1	Trentham	3
Ipstones	5	Cheshire	1
Eccleshall	2	Others	9
Roledge	1		

TOTAL 122

Places of Birth of the Population of Endon 1851

Place of Birth	No. of People	Place of Birth	No. of People
Kidderminster	1	Stonehouse, Glos.	1
Yarley, Derbyshire	1	Doncaster	1
Pendleton, Lancs.	1		

TOTAL 5

Over 100 Miles

Place of Birth	No. of People	Place of Birth	No. of People
London	1	Alded, Cumberland	1
Risborough, Bucks	1	Stonehouse, Devon	1
Middlesex	2	Saltash, Cornwall	1
Gunnerside	1	Falmouth	1
New Shelton, Durham	1		

Other than U.K. mainland

Londonderry	1	France	2

TOTAL 13

TABLE (e)

Comparison of Place of Birth of Heads of Households with that of the whole population of Endon 1851

Places of birth Distance from Endon	Heads of Households Number	%	Whole Population Number	%
Endon and within 5 miles	98	71.01	518	78.72
5—50 miles	34	24.63	122	18.55
51—100 miles	3	2.17	5	0.76
Over 100 miles	2	1.45	10	1.25
Overseas	1	0.72	3	0.45
Total	138		658	

It might have been expected that more people in the whole of the population were born from 51 to 100 miles from Endon than has actually been shown in the above table. In this case it is a smaller proportion than for heads of households (0.76 per cent. and 2.17 per cent.). One needs to look at the class structure to get a clearer picture since, in the mid-nineteenth century it was more likely to be the better-off who showed greater mobility.

Place of Birth of the Populace of Endon, 1851

Of those people born from 51 to 100 miles from Endon, one, the schoolmaster was born at Kidderminster and one, was the druggist born at Doncaster.

Of these people born over 100 miles from Endon, 3 were visitors. A pensioner born in Londonderry we know, from other sources, to have been a retired soldier and the two people born in France were the daughters of a person with a private annual income.

Social Structure

It is difficult to classify the social position of persons recorded in the census of 1851 because there are no social gradings of mid-nineteenth century society, similar to the five groups issued by the Registrar-general for today's population. It is possible to use the five successfully even though it is being applied to a society of 120 years ago. The one used in this analysis has been devised in recent times by Mr. Tillot of Sheffield University who worked on the social structure of Tickhill and has produced the following groupings and the occupations which could be safely included in each.[10]

Number of Persons in each Social and Occupational Group in Endon 1851

The population has been divided into eleven groups, according to their occupations. Some, where no occupation has been given have been grouped according to their status and/or age.

The sons and daughters of farmers have been placed in group 1b and have been classified as lower gentry. The adult males would presumably help with the supervision of the farm and remain at home. The details of this first group indicate that persons directly connected with agriculture account for 40.0 per cent. of the population. Endon was truly an agricultural community.

Shopkeepers and traders (group 2) were made up of five grocers and 4 butchers (with an extra two butchers' apprentices). One might think that for the population these numbers are high, however, in the absence of shopping centres and supermarkets a greater proportion of the villagers would shop locally.

The skilled non-industrial group (Group 3a) contained no less than 8 cordwainers and one apprentice. This was a flourishing local trade and owed some of its strength to the fact that there were a number of tan yards in the district and there would be a ready market for shoes in the pottery towns. Two blacksmiths, a general smith and four wheelwrights confirm the agricultural nature of the parish and the amount of service which was available in the village. The figures show that Endon was not at the hub of affairs and contained no large

128

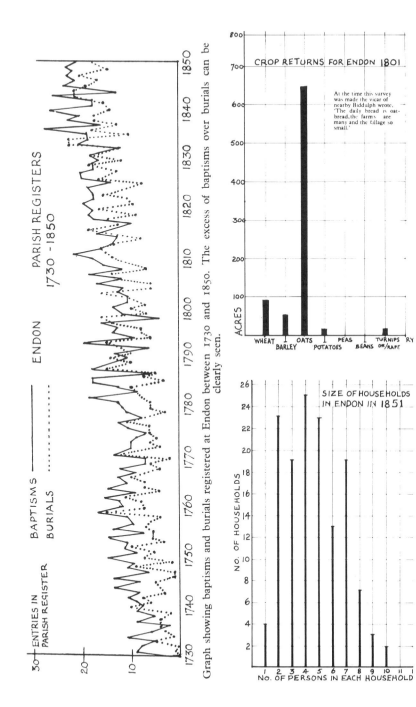

ENDON   PARISH REGISTERS 1730 - 1850

ENTRIES IN PARISH REGISTER

BAPTISMS ————
BURIALS ·············

Graph showing baptisms and burials registered at Endon between 1730 and 1850. The excess of baptisms over burials can be clearly seen.

CROP RETURNS FOR ENDON 1801

At the time this survey was made the vicar of nearby Biddulph wrote, 'The daily bread is oat-bread, the farms are many and the tillage so small.'

ACRES

WHEAT   BARLEY   OATS   POTATOES   PEAS BEANS   TURNIPS OR/RAPE   RY

SIZE OF HOUSEHOLDS IN ENDON IN 1851

NO. OF HOUSEHOLDS

NO. OF PERSONS IN EACH HOUSEHOLD

Place of Birth of Population of Endon in 1851

Place of Birth	Number of People	% of Population
Endon and within 5 miles	518	78.72
From 6-50 miles	122	18.55
From 51-100 miles	5	0.76
Over 100 miles	10	1.52
Ireland	1	0.15
France	2	0.30
TOTAL	658	

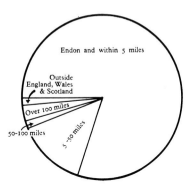

Place of Birth of Heads of Households in Endon 1851

	Number	% of whole
Endon and within 5 miles	98	71.01
From 6-50 miles	34	24.63
From 51-100 miles	3	2.17
Over 100 miles	3	2.17
TOTALS	138	

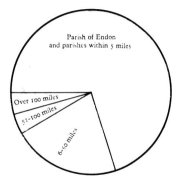

Marital Condition of the Population of Endon,
aged 16 and over, in 1851

	Male	Female	Totals
Unmarried	70	69	139
Married	112	111	223
Spouse deceased	17	20	37
	199	200	399

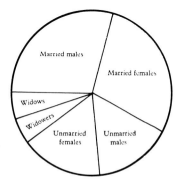

The First May Queen, 1868. The Rev. James Badnall is on the right.

At the end of a day of haymaking. This picture was taken in the fields opposite 'The Plough Inn', between the main road and the railway line. The area is now built upon. (*Left to right*) Braddock, George Adams, Jack Platt (boy), Hugh Carp, Ernest Gratton, Albert Holdcroft, James Bentley (On the load) Will Adams.

industries, a fact which is as true today as it was in 1851.

Group 5—the professional classes contain only four people, a druggist, the curate, the schoolmaster and a land surveyor who was a member of the Heaton family.

The sole member of group 6b (clerical supervisory) was the village police constable. The servants (group 7) included an ostler employed at one of the village inns.

Group 9, the semi-skilled and service workers contained four boatmen obviously employed on the Caldon Canal.

The 26 coalminers of group 10 all lived in the Brown Edge end of the parish and were probably employed at Norton colliery or what is now Chatterley Whitfield colliery or at the Black Bull, now known as Biddulph colliery, for neither Endon nor Brown Edge contained a colliery. The nearest was in Norton parish.

Of those not gainfully occupied 117 were classified as housewives (only one person was described as a 'farmer's wife'). Forty of the 'No Occupation' group were adult females and probably were acting as unpaid servants or were young women receiving a home training prior to marriage. Twelve people were visiting the parish temporarily their permanent residences being elsewhere.

List of occupational or social groups used in the analysis with occupations actually found in the 1851 census for Endon.

Group 1a *Agricultural Self-employed or Managers.*
Farmer.

    1b *Farmers Sons and Daughters (stated as such on the rank, profession or occupation column of the census form).*

    1c *Agricultural Labourers.*
Agricultural labourers, Farm labourers, Farm servants.

2   *Shopkeepers, Traders, Petty Entrepreneurs, not employing more than 5 persons (including apprentices and journeymen).*
Victuallers, grocer, butcher, cattle dealer, shopkeeper, beer-seller,—dealer, chaff dealer.

3a   *Skilled Non-Industrial (including apprentices).*
Wheelwright, cordwainer, milliner, dressmaker, tailor, stone-mason, blacksmith, brick maker, joiner, nail maker, smith, builder.

3b   *Skilled-Industrial.*
Potter, flint grinder.

4   *Manufacturers, Industrialists, Wholesalers and Managers of Large Enterprises (more than 5 persons).*

5a   *Upper professional.*
Druggist, Curate.

5b	*Lower Professional.* Schoolmaster, Land Surveyor.
6a	*Clerical* (non-supervisory). Clerk, attorney's clerk, attorney's articled clerk.
6b	*Supervisory* County Police Constable.
7	*Servants* (excluding farm servants). Ostler, House servant, servant, housekeeper.
8a	*Private Income Recipients.* Lady, independent, annunitant.
8b	*Pensioners.* Pensioner.
9	*Semi-Skilled and Service Workers.* Horse breaker, land surveyor's assistant, laundress, boatman, apprentice, foundryman.
10	*Coal Miners.*
11	*Labourers and Unskilled* (excluding agricultural labourers). Labourer, quarry man, stone quarry labourer.
C.	*Children* (those under 14 and all scholars).
H.	*Housewives* (wives and any one female in a household apparently solely occupied in domestic duties).
NO.	*No Occupation and Retired.*
V.	*Visitor.*

Between 1851 and 1900 the population was affected by the building of the railway and the development of a plot of land near the Fountain and the erection of villas after 1868.

In the twentieth century the population had risen steadily but there was a slight decrease in 1921 and 1931. By 1951 the population was approaching the 2,000 mark and by 1961 was well on the way to 3,000. The impact of the nineteenth century commuter habit may have caused some social changes in the village but these were nothing compared with the later changes in the period 1951/1971.

Population 1911/1961

Longsdon				Endon with Stanley		
2,708	acres	650	1911	1,583	2,745	acres
,,	,,	715	1921	1,512	,,	,,
,,	,,	617	1931	1,490	,,	,,
2,128	,,	691	1951	1,907	2,829	,,
,,	,,	639	1961	2,697	,,	,,

TABLE (f)
Number of persons in each social and occupational group in Endon 1851

Group	Male Adult	Male Children	Female Adult	Female Children	House-wives	Total	% of those gainfully employed
1a	38	—	4	—	I	43	16.73
1b	10	3	2	2	—	17	6.62
1c	42	1	—	—	—	43	16.73
2	13	1	4	—	—	18	7.00
3a	24	—	2	—	—	26	10.12
3b	3	—	—	—	—	3	1.17
4	—	—	—	—	—	00	0.000
5a	2	—	—	—	—	2	0.78
5b	2	—	—	—	—	2	0.78
6a	3	—	—	—	—	3	1.17
6b	1	—	—	—	—	1	0.39
7	4	—	29	7	—	40	15.58
8a	1	—	2	—	—	3	1.17
8b	1	—	—	—	—	1	0.39
9	7	—	3	1	—	11	4.28
10	26	—	—	—	—	26	10.12
11	18	—	—	—	—	18	7.00
TOTALS	195	5	46	10	I	257	
NO	18	—	40	—	—	58	
H	—	—	—	—	117	117	
C							
School	1	48	—	27	—	76	
Home	—	70	—	67	—	137	
V	1	3	6	2	—	12	
Illegible	—	—	1	—	—	1	
TOTALS	215	126	93	106	118	658	
	341		317				

References

[1] Hearth Tax Return, Endon, 1666. Public Record Office, London, *H.C.S.*, Vol. 1925, p. 157.

[2] For details of use of Richman's multiples see Wrigley, E. A.: 'English History Demography', London, 1966 and Census Return. Introduction 1831.

131

[3] See table of Nineteenth century population statistics for Staffordshire. Table of Population (1801-1901), *V.C.H.*, Vol. 1, p. 327.

[4] Price Williams, R.: 'On the Increase in Population in England and Wales', *J.R.S.S.*, vol. 43, 1880.

[5] Registrar General, Figures taken from Annual Reports of 1842-1845, Leek, Endon, Staffordshire.

[6] *P.R.O.* London many areas have enumeration sheets on micro-film in public libraries. The sheets for Endon are on film at the *C.R.O.*, Stafford.

[7] 138 houses holding 658 people gives a mean of 4.77 persons per household $\frac{658}{138} = 4.77$

[8] Armstrong, W. A.: The figures are taken from a paper in connection with researches in population problems in York. 'The Interpretation of Census Books for Victorian Towns'.

[9] Speake, R.: 'Historical Demography of the Ancient Parish of Warton', 1968, chapter VI.

[10] There are other variations of this. See 'Analysis of Census in Burslem, 1851', Stuart D. G., published by Department of Adult Education, University of Keele.

Chapter VIII

AGRICULTURE IN ENDON

W hen describing the West Midlands, the North and the North West of England, Joan Thirsk in her article 'Horn and Thorn in Staffordshire: the economy of a pastoral county', states that in this part of 'England horn and thorn-stock and enclosures —were ancient and long established features of the landscape.' Many observers believed and have stated that it was an inferior form of life, not as successful financially as corn growing and therefore supporting a poorer and more miserable people. The article continues 'It was a different life with different standards, which must be judged on their own merits.'[1]

So it is with Endon, a typical ancient pasture farming township in which the population lived in small and scattered places, and not in one village at the centre of the parish. This too has been used to show how easy it was to misread the signs. Such townships lacked an imposing centre because the people lived in farmhouses and cottages distributed throughout the area in what travellers from the English lowlands regarded as an uncongenial countryside. Thus this area and Staffordshire in general was often regarded as a poor relation.

Endon, it has been claimed, is a moorland community, and many of its customs and social activities have a good deal in common with the villages around Leek and with the area stretching south-eastwards along the Churnet river. The older farm buildings were of either stone or timber, and as is common in the moorlands area, the farms tended to be small family-size buildings. Going back to the seventeenth century we find that the largest property was six hearths in contrast with the thirty-three at Trentham and twenty-four at Keele.[2] Similarly, the wills and inventories of the same period suggest that the yeomen, who were in those days at the top of the social structure in this area, derived their wealth from the possessions of land and a few animals, mainly cattle, sheep, pigs and horses. There is nothing to suggest any extensive cultivation of crops except those which could be used mainly for animal fodder. Dr. Robert Plot shows how cattle and sheep sold at

133

Uttoxeter market were among the finest in the country. So too were the meat and dairy products.

In 1663 the inventory of the possessions of Thomas Bourne shows that it is a 'true and parfit inventory of all the goods and chattles', belonging to him.³ Not only did he possess cattle and tend them but he also had another trade. However, the value of his cattle totalled £10.00.00 compared with the 'loumes and geares belonging to his trade' which totalled £2.6.8d. More than half his estate of £47.12.10d. was taken up in 'debts owing him upon land and otherwise', which totalled £29.11.6d.

February 15th 1663.

A true and parfit inventory of all the goods and chattles of Thomas Bourne, late of Endon in the parish of Leek deceased.

	£	s.	d.
3 kine, 1 heifer and 1 stirke	10	00	00
Hoof and horns	01	01	00
loumes and gears belong to his trade ...	02	06	08
3 bedsteads and all	01	6	08
Sheets and linen	00	10	00
3 case and 1 box		10	00
Brass and pewter		16	00
Treine ware and some silver		6	00
Iron ware		5	00
Wearing apparell and moneys in his purse ...	1	00	00
Debts owing him upon land and otherwise	29	11	06

Sum is £47 12 10

Writing in 1686 Robert Plot says 'In the Moorelands they some-times lime this heathy sort of land three or four years before they plough it.' Of the machinery in use he writes 'after their corn is sown they cover it with harrows, not much differing from those of other counties; only in the moorelands I observed they were somewhat less than ordinary but very strong ones. But in the moorelands they never roll their barley, I suppose because they mow none, and therefore have no such instrument as a Roll among them . . . in the moorelands as they roll not, so they never mow their barley, but reap it with hooks, the land being generally so grassy there, that they would loose half their corn should they goe about to mow it.'⁴

Few of the farm inventories of this period show any large quantities of corn, barley or oats but the pastoral character of the area is clearly shown by the quality and variety of animals owned by the yeoman farmers, Richard Boulton of Horton died in 1731. The following is a 'true' inventory of his possessions.

	£	s.	d.
Purse and Apparell	5	0	0
13 cows and a bull	56	0	0
6 heifers	13	15	0
5 stirks	7	7	0
9 calves	4	10	0
20 sheep	6	0	0
17 lambs	2	10	0
3 work horses and colts	22	0	0
4 swine	4	0	0
Horses gears, cart, plough and 3 harrows ..	4	0	0
Tumbrels and all other husbandry ware ..	0	5	0
Hay	10	0	0
Cheese and Bacon	18	10	0
7 beds, brass and pewter	20	10	0
2 grates, fireshovel and tongs	0	12	0
3 Iron pots, 1 kettle and all iron ware ...		14	0
1 skreen chair, 16 chairs	1	0	0
3 tables and forms		10	0
4 table cloths also napkins		16	0
Clock cases and dresser of drawers ..	3	0	0
Cooper ware	1	0	0
	181	19	0

As if to record the news worthiness of anything which happened to a farm or its livestock the following entry appears in the parish records:

'On July 2 1742 a farm and barn in Endon was burned down by lightening and 2 calves were burnt and a cow of Mr. Nixon was killed in Park Lane and one of Thos. Yates of Old Field was killed by it.'

This was a pattern which was continued in the eighteenth century, though the increased activity in cottage industry tended to make husbandmen and yeoman farmers somewhat more independent. It was the limited return on farming at this time, which caused the local people to develop other skills. In Endon some turned to weaving, tanning, cordwaining and at Brown Edge to nailmaking.

In 1744 John Sutton of Endon described himself at a gentleman. To his son he left his tanhouse and tanyard with the 'small parcel of land lately enclosed out of the hamlet and added to the tanyard.' Tanning was an important by-product of a pastoral area such as Endon, because of the presence of so many stock farmers. Sheep and deer skins were plentiful and cattle hides were available in large quantities.

Enclosures in this area took place at the end of the Middle Ages, perhaps even before, if one is to go by the estimates made of the ages of hedges in the district. Several have been found to be six and seven hundred years old. These were old enclosures. Some later ones took place in the early nineteenth century as is shown in the Horton Inclosure Award of 1805. The following is a typical enclosure made at that time and it relates to Paradise.

Horton Inclosure Award 1805. New inclosures

'Tomkinson one rood and 5 perches near the Lane Head, bounded by the ancient road and south west wardly by old inclosure, to fence on North East.

To George Martin in right of the said Joseph Tomkinson freehold and tithe free estate called Hole House.' Plan IV (No. 336). Map 1815.

The field is known as Paradise to this day. It is a small garden-like field between the roadway and a brook, certainly too small for any useful purpose today.

The nineteenth century brought even more changes and a particular interest in milk production, though the farms remained small and were based on the old seventeenth century estates of the yeoman farmers. In the 1847 list nine hundred and ninety-two acres are shown as being divided agriculturally into:

600 acres of arable land

392 as meadow or pasture

———

992 acres.[5]

This total, however, is about half of the actual acreage of the parish and the proportions cannot be relied upon.

Of those listed in the schedule of that year the principal landowners were Samuel Philips, William Sneyd, the Earl of Macclesfield and George Thompson. Of the smaller landowners, William Basnett had one hundred and eleven acres on Moss Hill, Charles Hilditch had seventy-four acres at Fernyhough and twelve acres at Crofts Edge Wood. Alfred Hadfield had fifty-eight acres at Lane Farm. Thomas Sutton was owner-occupier of seventy-two acres in Endon, a wood (three acres) Hollinger (twenty-two acres) Hallwater (fifteen acres) and an acre called Jack of the Green. The trend however, was for mergers to take place and references are made to these indicating that the small holding held by a family of small farmers was being replaced by the modern concept of a farmer, a man producing crops, animals and dairy produce for sale. He was, in effect, producing a surplus to his own family's and his family's servants' needs. The 1851 census shows that there were forty-two farmers in Endon and their farms ranged in size from four acres to one hundred and fifty acres, though the size of two farms in the census is not given.

One thousand eight hundred and fifty-eight acres is shown as being farmed by forty farmers at an average of 46.65 acres per farm. Twelve heads of households were farm labourers and two men were shown as agricultural labourers which together with the forty-two people shown as farmers suggests that fifty-six householders were directly engaged in agriculture in 1851. This is a percentage of 40.58 per cent. of the one hundred and thirty-eight heads of households. It is possible that this figure may have been higher since some of the men shown as 'labourers' may have in fact been agricultural labourers. Of the sixty-five families in the village in 1751 it is very likely that proportionately more were dependent upon agriculture than in 1851. In 1811 it was 66 per cent.

Endon farms in 1851:

0- 10 acres	6 farms	11- 25 acres	7 farms
26- 50 acres	14 farms	51- 75 acres	6 farms
76-100 acres	4 farms	101-125 acres	1 farm
126-150 acres	1 farm	150 acres plus	1 farm[6]

From this table it will be seen that half the farms were between twenty-five and seventy-five acres in size. An advertisement in the

Leek Times on January 31st 1885 read:

'To be sold, forty tons of hay part harvested in 1882 and twelve tons of clover all got without rain. P. J. Kent, Endon.'

Haymaking in the summer, was a traditional and constant activity for centuries in Endon, possibly one matched for regularity by the processions of milking cows on the roadways and lanes between farm and field.

A survey made during the 1930s states that the area around Endon is mainly grassland and there is little arable farming except near Biddulph, at Rudyard, and around Cheddleton. The soil is 'rather poor and sometimes stoney.' The report goes on to say that farming throughout was based on milk production and some farms had a particularly high yield.[7] When a farm at Dunwood in the Horton valley was compared with a farm of a similar size (about seventy acres) east of Leek (Morredge, 1000 ft. above sea level) the Dunwood farm produced seventy gallons a day compared with thirty gallons on the higher land. Being near the railway and later easily accessible to the Potteries by road a large proportion of the Endon milk was conveyed out of the district which possibly accounts for there being little evidence of cheese-making on a large scale such as that found in the Cheadle district at the turn of the century.

The conditions on a local farm in the days before the 1939-45 war had been compiled in a land utilisation survey by J. Myers of Wolstanton. Writing in 1947 he described one as follows:[8]

Locality:	Longsdon, south west of Leek, at 500 to 600 AD Tenant farmer.
Area:	68 acres. Farmer has use of nearby common land.
Crops:	Hay.
Grass:	24 acres mowing grass.
Livestock :	Cattle. 37 shorthorn dairy cows Bull kept Sheep: none Horses: none. Two kept until October 1938. Pigs: none Poultry: 100.
Marketing:	Milk about 70 gallons a day sent to Manchester. Eggs to Leek Market. Calves sold immediately. Milking cows bought when required.

Purchased feeding stuffs: flaked maize, bran, a small amount of hay, no patent feeding stuffs used, own ration mixed, bedding straw bought.

Fertilizers used: Lime, basic slag.

Woodland: None, a few scattered trees.

Labour: Tenant and 1 man.

Additional Information: mixed soils, some clayey, some sandy. Some years ago crops included some potatoes, kale, cabbages, wheat, oats and mangolds. Formerly a few sheep and pigs. The fields in the past ten years have been steadily improved especially in the last three (1938-40).

A farm in 1972 following similar specifications could be described thus.

Location: Endon. 700-800 feet.
Owner farmer.

Area: 143 acres plus the use of 40 acres at Dilhorne.

Arable: None (excluding war-time ploughing, 1939-45).

Grass: About 60 acres grown for hay previous to 1968. Since then turned to silage making.

Soils: Heavy land. Does well in dry seasons.

Livestock Cattle: 170 mainly pedigree Friesians (100 cows and followers).
Turkeys: 3,000 Sheep: none.

Marketing: Milk about 300 gallons a day to Co-op Dairies, Hanley. Turkeys to Birmingham and Manchester markets (Christmas turkeys to Llandudno and Colwyn Bay).
Steer calves to Crewe market.

Purchased feeding stuffs: Straw bought

Fertilizers used: Lime, basic slag, general.

Woodland: There is a good deal.

Labour: Farmer, two sons and one man.

Between 1910 and 1918 about thirty cattle were milked by hand and the milk taken in churns by horse and float to Endon Station in time for the 7 a.m. train. Between 1918 and 1921 dairy farming continued with cheese making taking place in the kitchen. Whey was fed to the pigs for fattening. Even as late as 1932 there was no piped water, no bathroom and rainwater was collected in a large concrete tank, for washing and bathing. The bath was often carried in to be placed in front of the kitchen fire. The old stone flat sink which stood in the kitchen is now a garden trough. The main source of drinking water was a well operated by a hand pump. In 1936 a milking machine (Lister diesel) was installed and in 1937 electricity for lighting only was generated on the premises. At the time there were

70 cattle, 60 sheep (Breeding ewes), 1,000 free range layers, 4 workhorses, 3 young horses.

During the second world war (1939-45) about 30 acres were ploughed for corn, potatoes and roots for cattle. It was in 1942 that the first tractor was acquired for use on the farm.

The age of mechanisation had arrived. Today there are few horses and many tractors, but the Endon farmers continue the traditions of farming on the hillsides, a continuous succession for at least five hundred years.

FARMERS

1818 General and Commercial Directory

Dean, John
Saint, John

Tomkinson, T. (and Tanner)
Wain, John

1834 White's Directory

Basnett, William (Yeoman)
Bent, Thomas
Billinge, James
Critchlow, Ralph
Critchlow, William
Harrison, William
Mellor, Obadiah

Crompton, John
Oulsnam, James
Salt, James
Smith, Thomas
(Yeoman and brickmaker)
White, Samuel
Yates, James (Yeoman)

1850 Kelly's Directory

Adams, Johanathan, Clay Lake
Booth, Henry, Windy Harbour
Bowyer, William, Hen Ridding
Corbishley, John, Endon Edge
Critchlow, John, Endon
Critchlow, William, Knowles
Critchlow, William, Moss Hill
Gaunt, Josiah, Gate House
Glover, James, Hollinhurst
Grindley, John, Woodcock Hurst
Hall, William, Park Lane Head
Hammersley, Richard, Morris House
Harrison, Richard, Lane Head
Heath, George, Endon Bank

Heath, John, Lane End
Mountford, Isaac, Park Lane
Mountford, William, Fernyhough, Brown Edge
Ousnam, James, Park Lane
Salt, Mrs.
Park, Thomas, Park Lane
Smith, James, Park Lane
Smith, Thomas, Park Lane
Steel, John, Clay Lake
Stonier, John, Lady Moor
Thompson, Geo., Park Lane
Trubshaw, Charles, Stockton Brook
Weston, Charles

References

[1] Thirsk, Joan: 'Horn and Thorn in Staffordshire', the economy of a pastoral county. *N.S.J.F.S.*, Vol. 9, 1969, p. 1.

[2] Hearth Tax Return 1666, Endon. Public Record Office, London, *H.C.S.*, Vol. 1921, pp. 147-151.

[3] Lichfield Wills, Thomas Bourne 1663, Joint Record Office, Lichfield.

[4] Plot, Robert: 'The Natural History of Staffordshire' 1686, p. 344 (para. 24), 348 (33), 353 (42), 354 (43).

[5] Tithe Schedules, Endon Parish 1847. Tithe Redemption Office, London.

[6] Statistics compiled from the Enumeration Sheets 1851 Census. Public Record Office, London—and on micro films.

[7] Myers, J.: 'The Land of Britain', (ed.) L. Dudley Stamp, Part 61, Staffordshire (Region 3), p. 618.

[8] Myers, J.: 'The Land of Britain', (ed.) L. Dudley Stamp, Part 61, Staffordshire (Region 3), p. 618.

Chapter IX

ROADS, RAILWAY AND CANAL

Roads

There can be little doubt that Endon has been crossed by thoroughfares from the earliest times, and it is conceivable that the ridgeways along 'the tops' were used by the earliest men in the district. Since the Norman conquest and the establishment of the manor and the first chapel, pathways, bridlepaths and a through route from Newcastle to Leek traversed the district. One document of more recent times throws some light upon the tradition of collecting a highway rate in the Highway Parish of Woodcockhurst. It is a demand for one shilling and threepence calculated on three pounds at fivepence in the pound. It is dated 1897, but since Elizabethan times it had been the responsibility of the parishes to collect rates and procure men to maintain and work on road construction. For several centuries it was the responsibility of Leek parish to oversee the maintenance of roads. The system was not a success but sufficed until the industrial age when manufacturers demanded swifter and smoother transport for their manufactured goods. A description of the road from Endon to Leek before the turnpike era in this area, is to be found in the claims made by Endon people for the right to have a place of worship in Endon where they could attend without having to make the journey to the parish church at Leek. The chapel was built 'to remedy the inconvenience laboured under by reason of the great distance from Leek, and several waters running between the said places which cannot at sometimes be overpast without great danger.'[1]

In the early eighteenth century, up to 1712, Wall Bridge carrying the road from Leek to Newcastle was a small wooden horse bridge. The responsibility of maintaining the bridge rested with the inhabitants of Leek parish, and any money required was raised by a levy. The inhabitants raised sixty pounds in 1712, the cost of replacing the old bridge by a stone cart bridge. Longsdon township had two bridges, Horsebridge and Killenford Bridge over the river Churnet.

143

Newcastle was the principal town in North Staffordshire and communications with that town and Leek passed through Endon on the old road via Brown Edge through the village of Endon by way of Endon Edge, Stoney Lane, to the north side of the Plough Inn, called Littleworth, which in the early days of the eighteenth century comprised of cottages only, Brook Lane through the ford and then right by the site of the present-day well to cross the new road at right angles. From here it ran in the fields and crossed Endon Brook by a structure known as 'Mill Bridge', some three hundred yards down stream from the present-day bridge. This road can still be seen near the Endon Sewage Disposal Works.

Newcastle saw the turnpiking of the first road in Staffordshire. It ran from Tittensor to Talk-o-th-Hill, a distance of eight miles, and was turnpiked in 1714. In 1762, the Leek to Ashbourne road was improved and three years later approval was granted to the trustees of the Newcastle, Leek and Hassop turnpike to repair and widen the road from Newcastle to Hassop, in Derbyshire.[2]

The turnpike roads were opened by private trusts and the tolls levied by the trust, under supervision from Parliament, were to provide money for the maintenance and repair of the road. Trustees were to be men of substance, and were not allowed to be a trustee and at the same time hold an office of profit under the same trust. The trustees were compelled by law to appoint a secretary and a surveyor to administer the affairs of the turnpike trust in a professional manner. The qualifications on the Endon turnpike were such that prospective trustees should be in possession of:

(a) yearly receipt of rents of £50 or

(b) personal estate of £1,000 or be heir apparent of a person possessed of lands of a yearly income £100.

In the fifth year of George III (1765) an Act of Parliament was passed authorising a turnpike trust to be set up. The reasons for the new road as given in the Act were, 'the road has become very deep and ruinous and in many places goes over morasses, boggs and mountains, and is very narrow and incommodius and cannot be sufficiently widened, turned, altered, repaired and kept in repair by ordinary course of law.'[3]

The road, it was planned, should run from Newcastle via Leek to Hassop, near Bakewell, and was to have a junction from Middle Hills

Canal Bridge at Park Lane.

S. Turner's 20 seater Vulcan 'bus leaving The Fountain for Brown Edge.
This vehicle was purchased in November 1920 Turners also operated a
14-seater Sunbeam Charabanc and a 12-seater called 'Little Jimmy'

The Fountain. Looking along the road in the opposite direction—towards
Leek. The Station fields are on the right.

to the Macclesfield Turnpike road near Buxton. The list of trustees carried such local names as Thomas Beech, Thos. Heath, Joshua Heath, as well as the landowning gentry of Derbyshire, who had probably done much to bring about its extension into that County. They were Lord Grey, James Smith Stanley, Lord John Cavendish and the Marquis of Granby. The trustees were to meet at the house of William Davison, being the sign of The Cock in Leek, three weeks after the passing of the Act. The second meeting was to be at Monyash, Ashford, near Buxton, the third meeting at Burslem or Cobridge, and the fourth at Leek, 'and so on in rotation as often as it shall be necessary for putting the Act into execution.' Five trustees had to be present before a meeting could be held.

Provided also under the Act was a clause that no victualler or retailer of ale, beer or spirituous liquors, or any menial servant of any trustee, shall be capable of holding any place of profit under this Act. Parishes and places were liable to do statute work, in teams, the lists to be made by the surveyor, or, in his absence, the churchwarden. The Act also stated that 'No more than two days' work shall be done by any person or team who shall be inhabitants of Newcastle-under-Lyme, nor more than three days by any other person, or team, on any other part of the said roads.' This statutory labour was usually done in the spring round about the time of Easter.

The road was to be forty feet in width, milestones were to be erected and toll gates placed en route for the collection of tolls. No gates were to be erected within two miles of Newcastle and likewise there was to be freedom to travel between Bakewell and Monyash. Gates were at Cobridge, Endon and Endon side, Wallbridge, Leek Edge Moor, Flash and Flash side, Longnor, Monyash and Mabs Chain.

An example of the charges made were as follows:

Horse, mare, gelding, mule or beast drawing carriage   3d.

Horse, mare, gelding, mule or beast laden or unladen
and not drawing   ...   .   1d.

Drove of oxen, cows, neat cattle   ...   .   10d per score

Calves, hogs, sheep, lambs   ...   .   5d. per score

No person to pay more than once per day with the
same horses, mares, etc.

Half tolls were to be charged on Leek market day. Persons, cattle, carriages could travel between Newcastle and Leek for payment of one toll only. In the Derbyshire area the carrying of lime had concessions. In the Newcastle area it was coal which benefited by reduced payments.

From Cobridge there was to be a branch to Burslem and another one to Shelton to link up with the Shelton to Uttoxeter turnpike.

In order to prevent dishonesty at the tollgate, a system was devised whereby the 'gates' were auctioned to be let for a specified period to the highest bidder. The trust received the rents due and it was up to the occupier to ensure that the tolls at the gate were collected in order that he might be recompensed. Thus on August 21st 1788, the following notice appeared.[4]

TURNPIKE TOLLS TO BE LET
NOTICE IS HEREBY GIVEN:

That the tolls arising at the tollgates of the Turnpike Road from Newcastle-under-Lyme to Leek in the County of Stafford, called by the names of Cobridge, Oldfield Lane, Smallthorne Lane, Endon, Endon-side and Wallbridge Gates, with the houses adjoining each, will be let by auction to the best bidder, at the house of James Vernon, being the sign of The Dolphin in Cobridge in the said County on the twenty-fifth day of September next, between the hours of two and four in the afternoon, together or separately as shall be then agreed upon and in the manner directed by the Act, passed in the thirteenth year of the reign of his Majesty King George the Third for regulating turnpike roads.

The toll at Cobridge and Oldfield Lane Gates let last year at the sum of £228.0.0 Those at Smallthorne Lane at the sum of £77.0.0. Those at Endon and Endon-side Gates at the sum of £83.0.0. Those at Wallbridge at the sum of £65.0.0., at which respective sum they will be put up. Whoever happens to be the best bidder must at the same time give security with sufficient surities, to the satisfaction of the Trustees of the said Turnpike Road, for payment of the rent agreed for and at such times as they shall direct.

> Peter Swift
> Clerk to the Trustees of the
> said Turnpike Road

In spite of all the provisions for money, labour and material made by the Act of 1765, complaints were made in 1780 to the effect that 'the condition of the road, notwithstanding the utmost exertion of the trustees is so bad that post-chaises from Newcastle to Leek go another road two miles longer.' The Clerk to the Trustees, a nephew of Josiah

Wedgwood, by name Mr. Byerly, was called to a special meeting of the trustees to show 'the extent and condition of the turnpike road, the tolls and the revenues from it.' Some idea of the quantity of material used can be seen on examination of an agreement made between the trustees of the Newcastle to Leek turnpike and Joseph Holdcroft of Ball Green, who was the surveyor, stating that he had to repair the road for three years and put

> 198 tons of gravel in ENDON LIBERTY
>
> 15 ,, ,, ,, ,, WOODCOCK HURST
>
> 300 ,, ,, ,, ,, LONGSDON.[5]

The number of horses employed in haulage and the width of the wheels used on the wagons were often subjects for clarification by the regulations relating to tolls. The Newcastle to Hassop turnpike authorities allowed 'waggoners' to use more than the usual number of horses because 'it steadily rises to Leek which is about seven hundred feet above sea level, but on leaving Leek it climbs to one thousand seven hundred feet.'

The regulations were as follows (maximum):

10 horses for a *waggon* with wheels of six inches (width)

5 ,, ,, *cart* ,, ,, ,, ,,

5 ,, ,, *waggon* ,, ,, less than six inches (width)

5 ,, ,, *cart* ,, ,, ,, ,, ,,

The tollgate in Endon was situated at a point known today as The Fountain, at the junction with the side road from Stanley. References are made to tolls being collected from traffic using the side roads to Gratton and these are shown in the records as Endon side roads. A map of 1815 shows the toll house standing at the junction of Stanley Road (Station Road) on the opposite corner to the present-day Methodist Chapel. In 1807 William Debank Hand purchased land at Endon Tollgate for two pounds. He lived in Park Lane and was a trustee of the Newcastle turnpike road. By 1811 the road through Endon is shown in Daniel Paterson's Roads of England and Wales as being part of the cross-road between Chesterfield and Whitchurch. The route taken is clearly shown via Leek, Endon, Norton, Burslem (across the canal), Woostan (sic) and Newcastle-under-Lyme.[6]

The national and commercial directories for 1828 and 1830 show

147

that carriers were operating along the roads as follows:

John Wootton   from the Angel, Leek to Burslem.

J. Finlay   from The Red Lion, Leek to Newcastle.

J. Finlay   from The Marsh, Newcastle to Leek.

Wm. Warrell   from The Bird in Hand, Leek to Newcastle and Shropshire.[7]

Evidence of local connections with stage-coaching is to be found to the story of a stage-coach journey from Blackburn to London in 1824 passing through Manchester, Leek and Endon. It is a feasible account of the journey which took twenty-seven hours, though by this time the faster coaches were travelling between Manchester and London in eighteen/nineteen hours. The total cost was two pounds six shillings and fivepence for a traveller sitting on the higher outside of the coach and included payment to the guard, the coachman and the cost of meals and spirits. Local legend has it that there was an inn, known as the White Pheasant, where coaches could halt, change horses and rest passengers. The building is today known as The Mount, but there is little evidence to suggest any claims to large scale coaching traffic.

Some of the coaches passing through Leek en route to London were:

The Royal Mail	Nelson's Independent
The Telegraph	Independent
The Defiance	

It is perhaps worth noting that Messrs. Yelloways have run a motor coach service from Blackburn to London via Leek and Ashbourne for about fifty years.

It was shortly after 1815 that the first major alteration to the character of Endon Village was made. An examination of William Yates' maps of 1779 and 1799 shows the road clearly taking the route through the village, through the ford, and the right hand turn and away along the course of the existing road to Leek.[8] Similarly the maps of Smith 1801, Cary 1805 and 1806, R. Rowe 1813 and Pitt's topography of 1817 all show the road passing through the old village. However, Greenwood's map of 1820 distinctly shows the new, straight stretch of road from Littleworth, by the Plough Inn, to a point near the present day Black Horse. This is also illustrated on Phillips and Hutchins map of 1831 and 1832, and the first Ordnance Survey map of 1836. These changes caused the village to be comparatively quieter. The through traffic avoided the ford and the lanes such as Park Lane were intersected and farmlands which had grown together by convenience and tradition were separated. The impression that the new section was additional and something of an alteration is shown by (a) its straightness, (b) the more recent age of the houses fronting it, and (c) the way in which it affords a short cut to Park Lane without using village roads.

Perhaps the greatest structural alteration to affect the roads of the area, and to some extent the character of the Endon district, was the building of the new turnpike in 1842/4.[9] This new arm from the junction by The Fountain, near the present-day Methodist Chapel, provided a new straight road to Stockton Brook and from there into Stoke. It was an extension of the Uttoxeter and Blythe March trust's road, a direct link from the southern end of the Potteries to the Newcastle to Leek turnpike at Endon. As a result of these improvements the general direction of communication changed towards Stoke and Hanley and the present-day road over Brown Edge became, and has remained, in second place as a route between Leek and the Potteries.

With the arrival of the new roads and the increase in the volume of road traffic in the mid-nineteenth century, Endon tollgate became a busier place. Certainly the income was sufficient to support a family. The 1851 census shows, George Platt, aged twenty-nine years as the keeper. He had a wife, Ann (twenty-eight) and three daughters, Lucy, Angelyna and Emily.

Some of the mileposts between Newcastle and Leek are in situ, but are probably replacements of the original inscribed stone blocks. According to R. J. Sherlock they are made of cast iron and bear the name of 'S. N. Cobridge 1821', the initials he believes stand for Sarah Nicklin who practised as an iron-founder at Cobridge at this time. There were only two originals left in 1962, those at five and a half and six and a half miles from Newcastle, the others having been replaced by posts inscribed 'Hales, Cobridge 1879'.[10] Such is the importance of road signs to fast moving traffic that many of the smaller old signposts and mileposts have been removed and replaced by much larger ones.

The toll houses in this road were closed on November 1st 1873 when responsibility was taken over by the Highways Board, the forerunner of the County Council as the authority responsible for main roads. Today trunk roads such as the present A53 through Endon are the responsibility of the Department of the Environment.

The Canal at Endon

'They have enlisted me here in another navigation scheme to effect a junction between Cauldon Lime Quarries and our canal'

JOSIAH WEDGWOOD

The North Staffordshire area was not far behind the Duke of Bridgewater who first employed James Brindley to build the Bridgewater Canal from Manchester to Liverpool, in 1760. The famous canal builder then turned his attention to the Trent Mersey Canal and died in 1772 during the construction of the Harecastle Tunnel.

In the sixteenth year of the reign of George (1776) an Act of Parliament was passed enabling 'the company of proprietors of the navigation from the Trent to the Mersey, to make a navigable canal from the said navigation, on the south side of Harecastle to Froghall, and a railway from thence to or near Caldon in the said county.'[11]

The canal which became known as the Caldon Canal passed through Endon and was to be subjected to several changes during the latter part of the eighteenth century. Endon is at the summit level (484 ft. above sea level), and since canals need a constant supply of water the highest parts must be well provided for. No doubt Endon Brook was to do just this. The Caldon branch also served as a supplier of water to the Trent and Mersey, but as traffic increased, it, in turn, was deprived of some of its water. Consequently in 1783 Stanley Pool was constructed one hundred feet above the canal level to supply water to the system. This reservoir was later enlarged in 1840.[12]

The engineers could not let matters rest and a Bill was prepared and plans were laid for an intended canal from Caldon branch of the Grand Trunk canal near Endon and for a reservoir in the valley between Horton and Rudyard, together with a cut from the reservoir to the canal at or near Leek. The extension from Endon never materialised, though a reservoir was later built at Rudyard, but not in the position intended in these proposals. This survey was carried out by Hugh Henshall brother in law to James Brindley, James Barnett and William Cross. This was 1795. In 1796 another plan similar to the one above was put forward by J. Cary, who also intended greater use

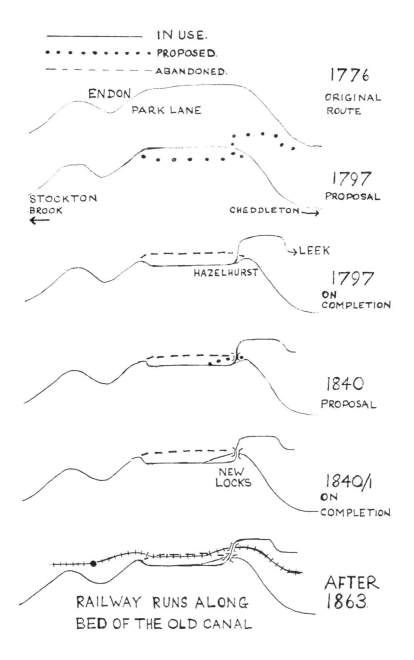

IN USE.
PROPOSED.
ABANDONED.

1776
ORIGINAL
ROUTE

ENDON
PARK LANE

STOCKTON
BROOK

CHEDDLETON

1797
PROPOSAL

→LEEK
HAZELHURST

1797
ON
COMPLETION

1840
PROPOSAL

NEW
LOCKS

1840/1
ON
COMPLETION.

RAILWAY RUNS ALONG
BED OF THE OLD CANAL

AFTER
1863.

of railways to Froghall and Caldon Low.[13]

Finally, the Act of Parliament authorising the construction of Rudyard Lake, as a reservoir, to supply water to the canal system, Caldon and Grand Trunk, at its highest point, was passed in 1797. The original plan was to feed the summit level at Endon, similar to the original proposal of 1795, but landowners and industrialists insisted that Leek should be connected to the canal system by a navigable cut. The new canal to Leek meant a higher summit level and the course of the canal and its three locks between Endon and Denford was to be altered. In 1797 the existing course was abandoned and the new channel ran along a high embankment and over the Endon Brook. The difference in level was twenty four feet and this was to be rectified by building a staircase lock at Hazelhurst which connected the new summit level extending from Endon to the old line and level of the canal at Denford. There was opposition to this proposal, chiefly from the man who had been appointed engineer to the new scheme, John Rennie. He suggested three separate locks instead of the 'staircase'. However, the 'staircase' was built, a new level established, and Leek was connected to the canal system. Rennie was a painstaking engineer, each bridge and aqueduct was individually designed and constructed, and the observant traveller along the canal or towpath, can see to this day the change in construction of bridges pre-1797 (Nos. 1-30) and post-1797 (Nos. 31-55).

It is also possible to see the abandoned bridge which carried Park Lane over the original canal. It is situated several yards on the Endon side of the existing canal and is easily discernable from the canal tow-path.

An unsuccessful attempt was made to link the Caldon Canal at Endon with the Peak Forest Canal at Marple in 1796. Estimated cost: £90,000, capital: £100,000, to be twenty-nine miles long and constructed by Benjamin Outram.

Perhaps the last but unfulfilled proposal was made in 1811 when an Act was drawn up to 'connect the Caldon Canal branch at Norton to Cheadle Heath (Cheshire) and the Bridgewater Canal at Sale Moor.'

By 1828 the system was a vital part of the industrial activity of this area. Limestone was brought down from Froghall, building stone from Caldon Low and copper ore from Ecton mines.

In that year Pickfords advertised barges from Leek to London, Liverpool and Manchester. Sutton and Company sought traffic to

Liverpool and Manchester as did Sampson and Gould. Coal was brought in the reverse direction as instanced by Messrs. Wharfinger, coal merchants with a wharf in Leek. Even as early as 1788 the Coalbrookdale Company of Shropshire supplied pumps and pipes to Ecton mines and these were transported from Coalbrookdale down the river Severn to Stourport, up the Staffordshire and Worcestershire Canal to join the Trent and Mersey at Great Haywood, then along the Caldon branch from Etruria to Froghall. From Froghall they were taken by horses to the mine. As a result of the industrial activity at Ecton, some three thousand one hundred and sixty-four tons of copper ore were sent from the mines to Swansea between 1819 and 1826. This was sent by canal boat to Runcorn and then by sea to Swansea.[14]

To supervise canal activity a Mr. John Steele filled the office of canal agent in 1851. He lived at Lake House (Beach Farm) and died in Stanley in February 1870. The Lock House on the towing path was occupied by William Hedale and his wife Elizabeth, then aged twenty-eight and twenty-five respectively. In the census of 1851 Hedale is described as a clerk from Burton, Staffordshire.

The reconstruction and planning of the canal was not finished however, and in 1842 the staircase built at Hazelhurst had to be abandoned and the present day three 'new' locks at Hazelhurst were built. These joined up with part of the original line abandoned in 1797 which was cleaned out and connected with the Froghall section by means of a brick aqueduct, leaving the remains of the old staircase to be seen to this day. The final constructional alteration came in the 1860s when the North Staffordshire Railway chose to use part of the bed of the pre-1797 canal as the foundation for the railway line. For a short distance east of Park Lane, the railway runs on top of the line of the old canal.

The railways in fact not only used the old canal beds as a permanent way, they saw the canals as a competitor for trade and gradually acquired sections of the canal only to let them fall into disuse and decay. The companies of North Staffordshire Railway and the Trent Mersey Canal Navigation, which included in the Caldon Branch, had been amalgamated since 1846/47 and the effect of railway attitudes generally towards canals was not felt in this area until after 1923. However, decay set in and only in recent times have efforts been made by preservationists and water sports enthusiasts to re-establish a through waterway to Froghall.

The Giant Hopper

As if to show how the two methods of transport might best be combined a hopper was sited at Endon Basin at a spot where the railway and canal are close together and easily accessible to each other.

The hopper was designed by Thomas H. Coleman, the son of Mr. J. H. Coleman, one time headmaster of Endon Parochial School. Built in 1917 it was used to transfer the contents of railway wagons into the holds of narrow boats on the canal. Crushed stone was brought down from Caldon Low by rail and transferred to the boats for transit to the Brumer Mond (now I.C.I.) chemical works at Middlewich. The wagons were clamped to the rails and turned over to allow the contents to fall into the boats with a regulated flow to avoid any possibility of damage.

The last boat to ply on the Caldon Canal commercially was operated by Mr. George Tomkinson of Stockton Brook. Motor lorries tipped coal slack into his boat at Endon Wharf and then the slack was taken to Cheddleton for use in the boilers there. Many local people still speak nostalgically of the skewbald pony which pulled his boat along the canal in Endon.

Perhaps the fact that the hopper was designed by a railway man helps to show the connection between the two modes of transport in the Endon and Churnet valleys. The two were interdependent and the hopper was the last piece of organisation which brought canal and railway together. Generally, however, it was the coming of the railways which caused the decline in canal traffic, perhaps less so in Endon, where the local boy, designer of the stone shute, had made good. He became a locomotive designer at Derby. The following is from an article in 'Chronicles of Steam' by E. S. Cox.

'Coleman, like H. G. Ivatt, came from the tiny North Stafford Railway, and like Ivatt, he had in his own field the same inborn flair for effective and even brilliant engineering. Without anything much by way of academic achievement, and abhorring public speaking and all communal activities such as Institution affairs, he nevertheless, by some hidden instinct, was able to hit the target of practical and effective design in nearly everything he undertook.

He reached his greatest heights in partnership with Stanier who knew what he wanted but was not always able to visualise it in precise terms. Coleman was able to interpret an initial idea and exploit it in a highly individual manner, and Stanier's biggest successes, the Duchess 4-6-2, the class 5 4-6-0, the class 8 2-8-0 and the class 4 2-6-4 Tank, all owed a great deal to Coleman. Indeed the first of these engines could almost be described as a Coleman product for it was he who proposed most of the modifications to the original 'Princess'. This is no detriment to general acknowledgement that the 'Duchess' was Stanier's masterpiece, for however much his henchmen may have contributed, it was Stanier who carried the full responsibility of decision to accept or reject each feature.'

Railways

Communications through the valley at Endon present a classic example of road, canal and railway running within a few yards of each other, and affording easy transport facilities between Leek and the Potteries. The railway, however, like the road and canal, is in the second phase of activity and does not rank among the first to be built in North Staffordshire, though the plans for the line from Macclesfield to Leek and through the Churnet Valley to Burton-on-Trent were presented in 1845.

In that same year the North Staffordshire Railway Company was formed with a capital of £2,350,000 in £20 shares. In 1841 the nearest railway station to Endon was Whitmore, seventeen miles away on the Grand Junction Railway. In less than ten years Leek had its own railway station when the line from Manchester to Uttoxeter was opened. Biddulph had already been connected to Stoke, so in 1860 an Act was passed authorising the building of a railway from the Biddulph Valley line at Milton junction to Leekbrook where it was to join the Churnet Valley line.[15] The line was built in the 1860s and opened, at first, as a single track, which operated until 1906, when it was made a double line. All the ballast and stone for its construction was brought from the Caldon Low quarries. The engineers engaged in the construction were Robert Stephenson, son of the famous George, and G. P. Bidder. It has been recorded that a Joseph Morris of Stanley, who was a porter at Endon Station in 1910, helped the surveyors engaged on planning the line and received twopence per day. He was then only a boy. Over the first twenty years of its existence, the line conveyed workers from Endon to the textile mills at Leek and to Bucknall Station for Hanley. This was used also by visitors to Hanley and those who wished travelled on to Stoke Station for connections to London. In reports of the well-dressing celebrations it is shown how some of the trains were delayed on account of the extra passengers to be carried to Endon. By 1885 the time-table was:

Rudyard	...		8.57			3.35	
Leek ...	...	7.30	9.05	11.35	12.30	3.43	7.27
Wall Grange	...		9.13	11.43	12.38	3.51	7.35
Endon ...	...	7.42	9.20	11.48	12.43	3.57	7.40
Milton ...	...	7.49	9.27	11.56	12.51	4.05	7.48
Bucknall	...	7.55	9.33	12.02	12.57	4.11	7.54
Stoke ...	...	8.03	9.44	12.10	1.05	4.19	8.02

Sundays
Three on Sunday leaving Endon for Stoke at 9.55, 3.30 and 8.18.

When one considers that the only traffic on the roads was horse-drawn, these times must have been of great significance in the lives of Endon people.

By 1899 the traffic had increased to nine trains in each direction and no doubt the increased traffic was a factor considered when the extra track was built in 1906. The influence of the traffic and the convenience it offered to passengers is best demonstrated by the amount of building of Edwardian villas which took place in Endon before the first world war. Bradshaw's Railway Guide shows thirty passenger trains per day in each direction in 1923. This was surely the zenith of railway operations along the Endon line.

Endon Station was a neat little station with two platforms, a level crossing, a signal box and a large building adjacent to it called Alder House, intended for use as a country hotel. The North Staffordshire Railway plans, however, never progressed beyond the initial stages and the property remained a private residence. 1923 may have been the peak year for Endon rail traffic, but ominous signs were looming. Motor buses were operating along the roadways and the North Staffordshire Railway was swallowed up by the London Midland and Scottish and Endon saw the new livery of the L.M.S.

Some idea of the intensity and the decline of railway traffic can be gained from the following extracts from a table produced from Bradshaw's Guide for the Victoria County History of Staffordshire: [17]

	1859	1875	1890	1904	1923	1958	1965
Congleton and Macclesfield	18	18	23	26	31	44	36
Uttoxeter (from Stoke)	11	12	20	32	26	41	49
Biddulph Valley	—	4	5	6	9	—	—
Potteries Loop Line	—	39	70	95	104	14	—
Audley Branch	—	—	7	6	24	—	—
Leek Branch	—	10	13	14	30	—	—

The numbers in each column indicate the number of trains on a normal weekday in each direction.

Excursions were operated at holiday times and at weekends and one could actually travel from Endon to Blackpool without having to change trains and for the price of five shillings return. A timetable of 1932/33 was as follows:

A thin line between the hour and minute figures indicates p.m. **173**

STOKE-ON-TRENT, LEEK, RUDYARD LAKE AND RUSHTON.

Another interesting feature of the early twentieth century is the amount of milk dispatched by railway. Mr. Brookes of Gratton Hall regularly sent churns from Rudyard Station to Longsight, Manchester for a nominal amount of one shilling and threepence a day.[18]

The decline set in after the second world war. Trains were used less by the travellers, and on Saturday, May 6th, 1956 at 5.56 p.m. the last passenger train along the line passed through Endon Station. The line was sometimes used for excursion traffic until 1963, and memories of former glories were conjured up as the old L.M.S. steam locomotive 'City of Manchester' regularly hauled a goods train through Endon to Stoke at 1.20 p.m. each day. Today the line is back to single track, used only for mineral trains hauled by diesel locomotives and heading goodness knows where. In a hundred years the history of the Endon line had gone full circle.

A journey along the line today

The railway constructed in 1867 runs closely alongside the canal and the roadway. When we leave Milton Junction travelling towards Leek the line becomes a single track operated by the tablet system. The former British Aluminium Company's factory, now a mixed industrial complex, is passed on the right and a bridge takes the line over the private Foxley arm of the Caldon Canal. Milton Station, now in a disused state is reached in a matter of a few hundred yards. The line then passes under the Leek New Road and on up the valley towards Norton Green, leaving Bullers' Electrical Porcelain factory on the left. The sidings here are now closed and the line passes over the Caldon Canal and the River Trent.

The railway travels partly on low embankments and partly in very shallow cuttings with Baddeley Green, ERF Engineering Co. Ltd. and Allied English Potteries' factory on the right. Norton Green is in the distance to the left. Travelling parallel to the Caldon Canal we come to the Staffordshire Potteries Water Board pumping station at Stockton Brook, with evidence of the days when it had its own unloading wharf. Recrossing the Caldon Canal, the line passes through a short tunnel before going through what remains of Stockton Brook Station. This is in a deep cutting. Passing behind Victorian villas on the left, the newly constructed playing fields of Endon Secondary School come into view. The fields formerly belonged to Moss Farm. On the right the Caldon Canal has now reached its summit level. Beyond the canal can be seen the remains of Stanley Mill, which was used to burn and grind flintstone for use in pottery making. At the mill there are remains of Stanley Forge, where iron was puddled by the old 'open hearth' process. As we approach Endon Station the remains of the sidings and goods yard are seen. Here the line was double track until August 1973 when one track was removed. Formerly a siding ran out of Endon goods yard and was used to take flintstones to Stanley Mill. The potters' slip was brought back in trucks hauled by a Stoke-built battery electric o-4-o locomotive. The siding crossed the Caldon Canal by a swing bridge which pivoted in the centre of the canal. This bridge was constructed by Hartleys Ltd., Engineers in Etruria, Stoke-on-Trent. Near to Endon Station was a raised embankment leading to the canal loading bay and trucks containing limestone were pushed by a locomotive to a point where the whole truck was tipped mechanically sideways and its contents spilled down a steel slope into a hopper, and then into the awaiting narrow boats.

Mr. Eric Morris, a foreman ganger on the Endon line, tells of the occasion when a locomotive, in taking a 'run up' to push the trucks up the embankment, started from the Station Master's house, and, gathering momentum, pushed the leading truck of coal over the stop block causing the truck to plunge into the canal. A steam crane was needed to lift the wagon from the water on to the rails.

Endon Station stands with the remains of waiting rooms, toilets and platform. The booking hall was demolished in 1970. The signal box was removed in January 1974 and the level-crossing over the Endon-Stanley road is now a modern open-type, controlled by lights. On up the Endon valley, the 'new' part of Endon is to the left together with the Plough Hotel. St. Luke's Church stands on the hill, above Hallwater House and Farm in the valley below. Park Lane passes over the line by means of a bridge before the Caldon Canal reappears on the right, but at a higher level. Endon old village is now over to the left with the Black Horse Hotel situated on the main road (A53). Also seen is Endon new sewage disposal works (L.R.D.C.) opened in 1970 on the site of the old works which was constructed in 1920-21. The course of the pre-1797 canal is on the left not far away from the old turnpike road (Corkscrew) and the route of the new road passing through the modern cutting, avoiding the hazardous 'Corkscrew' bends.

On the right now are the Hazelhurst new locks and Lock House, where the Leek branch of the Caldon Canal moves over the long embankment across the Denford valley. The railway passes through this embankment, the canal being carried over the line in a cast iron trough.

Perhaps the best way to conclude the story of the railway is through the eyes of a schoolboy.

'From 1915 to 1918 I went to school at Newcastle, going by the train leaving Endon about 8.40 a.m. The signalman at Endon Station box would stand with the door open and ring a handbell about five minutes before the train was due to arrive, a useful check, as it took roughly this time to walk down the path from the main road and get your ticket, if you were not a contract ticket holder. Sometimes I was late and only half-way down the Station Fields, as they were then called, with the train coming under Park Lane bridge, demanding a lengthy sprint followed by a breathless collapse onto a seat.

Farmers brought their own milk to the station in horse-drawn floats, crossing the lines and unloading the tall churns onto the platform. Occasionally a late-comer would find the crossing gates closed with the train approaching. Angry shouting would ensue before the signalman, busy with his routine duties, would be available to open the gates, reprimanding the culprit at the same time.

The Leek trains were usually made up of a six-wheeled coaching stock, comfortably upholstered but hard riding. At speed there was a considerable amount of sideways jolting, due no doubt to their short length, and on the standard 22 foot rails of the Company the rail-joint tattoo was much faster than on the 60 foot rails of the neighbouring L.N.W.R. giving passengers an illusory impression of high speed. Nevertheless, the timings were tight, with brisk acceleration and braking. I always got the impression as we shot down the 1 in 70 bank to Bucknall Station that the train would not be pulled up in time.

Motive power was shared mainly between 2-4-0 and 2-4-2 tanks. They were worked hard and evidently kept in first-class condition. I imagine that on restarting after a stop they were in full gear with the regulator well over, for the exhaust was often explosive and accompanied by a shower of char on carriage roofs, or in the road and on passengers leaving a Leek train at Endon.

Entry by train into the Stoke area was always interesting. A sharp look-out was kept for any of the larger engines, particularly No. 38, the 4-4-0 tender engine and the only one of her class. I compared her with the L.N.W. 'George V' and 'Precursor' types, and wished she had 6 foot 9 inch drivers instead of 6 foot, a larger boiler and shorter chimney; but I realised she had been designed specifically for the work she had to do and I was happy to see her.

The engine on the morning train took water at the end of the Stoke down platform before going on to Market Drayton, so we did not have to change. The Manchester train of five 8-wheeled coaches would be standing in the bay, headed by one of the handsome 4-4-2 tanks.

Returning from Newcastle I had to change at Stoke, with a half-hour wait for the Leek train due to leave about 5.35. This was part of the busy rush period with trains continually running in and leaving, the loop-line traffic predominating; all doing good business. From amongst the scurrying crowds of passengers, the loading and unloading of parcels and mail and the occasional rumble of a passing goods on one of the centre lanes, I liked to watch and hear the porters as they strode smartly alongside the waiting trains, calling out with voices loud and clear their relevant destinations.

Then my train would come in, heralded by cries of 'Now all Leek way—Leek train.' A mad scramble for an empty compartment by six of us lads, then down with the blinds, sometimes a foot up against the door handle to restrain an unwelcome would-be entrant, or a craning of packed heads out of the window if any pretty girls were in sight.

I got on friendly terms with some of the engine crews on the Leek trains. After tea, with homework done, I would often walk from my home in the old village to the station to meet the evening train returning to Stoke, have a short chat with the driver and fireman, sometimes handing them a jam pasty specially made by my mother, or an apple each because I had heard that they were good for the nerves.'

John Critchlow.[19]

References

[1] Quoted in petition from parishioners at Endon to Bishop of Lichfield and Vicar of Leek for the establishment of a chapel of Ease at Endon.

[2] Local Acts, C.R.O. Stafford. 5 Geo. III 1765 also see articles *H.C.S.*, Vol. 1934, pp. 1-157 and *T.N.S.F.C.*, lvl, p. 3.

[3] Preamble to Act setting up turnpike trust. 5 Geo. III 1765.

[4] See 'Geographical Aspects of the Development of Transport in North Staffordshire During the 18th Century', by Annie Longton Thomas, *H.C.S.*, Vol. 1934.

[5] The small amount required for Woodcock Hurst relates to the Endon side road.

[6] Paterson, Daniel: 'Roads of England and Wales', 1811.

[7] Details from Slater's National and Commercial Directories 1828/30/46/ 62.

[8] This route through the village is clearly shown on maps before 1820. The by-pass was constructed about this time and should not be confused with the new road to Stoke which was planned in 1839.

[9] Act 3 and 4 Vict. cap 116 (local and personal) S.R.O. Q/RUt (1840/41).

[10] Sherlock, R. J.: 'Industrial Archaeology in Administrative Staffordshire: An Interim Report', *N.S.J.F.S.*, Vol. 2, p. 96.

[11] Act. 16 George III cap XXX 1776.

[12] Inclosure Map and Schedule. Stanley 1815. Horton Parish Church Records.

[13] For details of several proposals for extension and development along the Caldon branch see Acts of Parliament (local and personal), C.R.O., Stafford.

[14] The life story of Joseph Bowyer (1818-1903) tells the life-story of a worker on the canals of the nineteenth century.

[15] The Stoke, Biddulph and Congleton Railway was authorised in 1853. The Endon line connected this with the 1845 line at Leekbrook.

[16] Time table from an advertisement in The Leek Post and Times 1885.

[17] V.C.H. Vol. II, page 329, Table II (Table of trains etc.)

[18] Bills and Receipts, C.R.O., Stafford.

[19] The article was written by John Critchlow for the 'Five Towns Magazine'.

Chapter X

ENDON A CENTURY AGO

For centuries Endon remained a quiet, scattered community with a small cluster of houses, none of them very large, around the ford, carrying on distinctly agricultural pursuits with a social structure pyramid somewhat squat; the rich not so rich and the poor fairly poor, as the workhouse records have shown, but not so impoverished as some of the labourers on arable soils. There the pyramid was more elongated with an almost peasant-like working population and a very wealthy landowning gentry, who dominated the scene both socially and politically. In Endon there grew up a sturdy spirit of independence which few would deny, and it could be claimed that in Endon 'Jack was as good as his master.' This was typical of the moorlands of Staffordshire, and although barely on the border, Endon still boasts its moorland connection, perhaps more so during this century as it turned away from the barren industrial scene and found a connection with English customs and folklore through welldressing and maypole dancing. Domestic industries had been carried on in farmhouses and cottages before the century began and were to decline before it ended. Nevertheless, the industrial occupations were still mainly connected with the land or with the care of animals, and it is not surprising that farm labourers were the predominant occupational group. In 1811 in Endon, Longsdon and Stanley, ninety-two families out of one hundred and forty, some 66 per cent., were chiefly employed in agriculture, whilst thirty-nine families (28 per cent.) were employed in trade, manufacturing or handicraft. This left no more than nine families occupied in other ways. The families included those heads of households who chose not to work and were described as gentlemen and annuitants.[1]

In accordance with a trend found in rural areas there was a fine balance between the sexes, the males numbering three hundred and eighty-five and the females three hundred and eighty-one. In Leek in 1811 there were one thousand six hundred and sixty-four males against two thousand and thirty-nine females a situation caused mainly by the labour demands of the textile industry. In some colliery districts of North Staffordshire, the reverse was the case on account of the demand and the correspondingly high wages for men in the coalmines. At this time Endon was on the turnpike and canal route to Leek and the story of Joseph Bowyer[2] and his travels on the canals of England though not typical of all Endon folk, does give some idea of the opportunities for travel available to people who happened to live near a waterway. To what extent the well-dressing celebrations could be afforded by a down to earth community is open to conjecture. We do know, however, that before Mr. Thomas Heaton arranged for the well superstructure to be erected halfway through this century, that the only spring water available was in the field above the present day well, not a readily accessible place, not one suitable for 'constitutional' and other forms of village chatter.

There was, of course, the ford crossing the main turnpike road providing a focal point to village activity, here was the smithy, the village inn occupied and conducted by one James Gosling, a victualler, the weavers' cottages and other properties, one of which was owned by Charles Stubbs and carried on as a shop. We know too that the church and the schoolhouse stood above the village and nearer to Littleworth, the site of the cottages which later became The Plough Inn. In a document of 1816 John Yates an innkeeper, is shown as customary or copyhold tenant of the manor of Horton.[3] He died and his son James Yates, a miller of Stanley took over. Though John Yates is described as an Innkeeper, there is no indication that 'The Plough' was in existence as such. It is not until 1839 that it is so named, the land on which the dwellinghouse or tenement, now The Plough Inn stood was described as 'Greenstyles, otherwise Littleworth.'[4]

By the mid-century 'The Plough Inn' had established itself as a hostelry and the property was owned by Thomas Hopkinson and occupied by the Innkeeper Thomas Atkinson, neither of whom were involved in the transactions of 1839. By the turn of the century the inn was the place for Friendly Society Dinners, political party and electioneering meetings, and as a meeting place for villagers and travellers alike. The other Inn was owned by William Philips and occupied by Mark Greatbatch, and it would seem that this was about half the size of The Plough, its rateable value in 1842 being seventeen pounds against the Plough's thirty-five pounds.[5]

The household of The Plough in 1851 consisted of Thomas Hopkinson, aged fifty-four and described at a victualler. He had a wife, Ann, aged fifty-five, and three children, Elizabeth thirteen, Henry, twelve, and William who was four. Also living there was Sarah Ogden aged fifty and described as an annuitant from Stand in Lancashire. Ann Ogden is shown as a house servant, aged twenty-one and it appears that she was related to Sarah Ogden, being born in Prestwich, Lancashire. The household was completed by the presence of one Thomas Birch aged twenty-two, a servant of the head of the household and described as Ostler. He is the only Ostler shown in Endon at this time.

The directories reveal that in 1876 Henry Platt was the innkeeper at The Plough, and Charles Adams was at the Black Horse. In 1880, Henry Platt was still at The Plough, but Richard Frederick carried on a business as a butcher as well as running the Black Horse. He was still there in 1892, and The Plough was in the hands of Mrs. Matilda Platt.[6]

There can be little doubt that the smaller Inn described above is the Black Horse, though the name is not recorded in the rate book or the census. We have already seen that the occupiers were Thomas Gosling, aged thirty-six and his wife Mary who was thirty-two. He too is shown as Victualler employing one Jane Gratton, aged twelve, as a house servant. His own children are shown as John aged five, Mary three, Elizabeth two, and Ann seven months. The other interesting feature about public houses is to be found in 'The Basnett Arms', run by Susanna Mottram who is shown as a grocer and beer seller, married and living with her daughter Betty Basnett and Job Basnett, aged fourteen and ten years respectively. Also living there were John Dicken a sixty-six year old servant and John Limour aged seventeen. This inn was situated close to the canal and presumably supplied refreshment to boatmen and farm labourers in the area around Waterfall cottages. The inn was later known as The Moss Inn and has since been demolished.

In 1820 William Basnett is shown in a Land Tax[7] canvas book as a landowner along with Charles Adams, Thomas Crompton, John Dean, Richard Myatt and Thomas Tomkinson. In 1854, James Basnett was the owner/occupier of a stone quarry at Endon Edge, and a brick kiln at Stoneywood.

The number of people employed in stone quarrying as labourers was two, but three people worked as stone masons, though of these two were father and son, named Charles and John Hollinshead, of Waterfall cottages. Also living in Waterfall cottages was Thomas Hollinshead, aged thirty-four, described as a Stone Quarry Labourer, Charles Goldstraw was another quarryman living at Claylake. It is worth noting that besides his son, aged twenty-eight, at home, Charles Hollinshead had daughters aged twenty-two, nineteen and sixteen, and sons aged thirteen and three. This family had not been subjected to an early 'break-up' as a result of economic pressures and one can assume that the job of stone mason was a financially rewarding one. Besides the brick kilns at Stoneywood, there were two others held by Thomas Smith, who paid one shilling on a rateable value of eight pounds. For the one kiln occupied by Harmah Thomas the amount was four pounds, and for the three brick kilns owned by John Alcock at Longsdon, the rateable value was twelve pounds. Nevertheless only one brickmaker appears in a mid-century occupations list, and after 1851 there is no record of Smith, Thomas or Alcock. Thomas Clewes had a lime kiln (rateable value ten pounds) at Stanley Moss in 1842.[8] There was another lime kiln at Postbridge owned by Edwin Heaton.

The cottages belonging to the Endon Friendly Society in 1854 were situated in the centre of the village and were occupied by:

1. Samuel Fynney, whose house had a rateable value of five pounds, and he was a horsebreaker by trade.

2. Thomas Gratton (rateable value two pounds) was a tailor with a family of five children, aged twelve years and under.

3. George Beresford (rateable value two pounds) lived next door. He was a farm labourer with a family of five children of ten years and under.

4. Ralph Alcock was a stone mason (rateable value five pounds) aged twenty-nine with a family of two.

5. Next door to Beresford lived Benjamin Harrington with his wife. He was a butcher and the butcher's apprentice, one Joseph Millward, aged fifteen, lived with him.[9]

Among those scattered around outside the village, Edward Nathan was at Waterfall Hall, George Boulton at Holehouse Farm, Edward Swift at Moss Hill and Thomas Woolliscroft at Harracles Hall. Perhaps the best indicator of the changing character of the owners of such properties and of the social changes taking place in Endon in the second half of the nineteenth century are reflected in the events of

1884. In that year Alderman Hulme, of Dunwood Hall, died, aged 75. He was a native of Burslem, a pawnbroker and a Liberal and held the office of Chief Bailiff of Burslem in 1877/78, the last years of its existence before the creation of the new office of Mayor of Burslem. Thus he was the last chief bailiff and the first mayor of Burslem. He is buried in the Hulme family vault in Endon churchyard.

At the top of the hill on the road to Newcastle was Brown Edge, though part of Endon parish, the community there was experiencing a newer and more severe impact. Coalmines had opened nearby and many young men were to find employment as colliers. The domestic industries of Brown Edge also took on a different activity, that of nailmaking. Only a few were nailmakers, but at least enough to drive home the point that the two communities were forming separate characters, a notion which was to be reinforced later in the century when the people of Brown Edge 'went down the road' to be the servants and to take in the washing of the more residential and socially superior people of Endon.

But this was, as yet, a railway age away, and the earthiness of the two communities at this time was sufficient to ensure their association continued.

In 1820 the people of Endon responded to the popular appeal made to working people by the friendly societies. Some fourteen per cent. of Staffordshire's population was now in one such organisation or another, and thus an annual village ritual was established as the loyal members of the Endon Club presented a show of solidarity and strength in late June annually for the rest of this century.[10]

The early days of this century are often described as the golden age of the stagecoach, and since Endon was on the turnpike road it is often suggested that it was involved in posting and stabling. There is very little, however, to suggest any of this activity, except on a minimal scale, and concerned only with traffic from Leek and Buxton to Newcastle and the Potteries.

The main routes from Manchester to London at first followed the route of the present day A6, but after accidents at fords and with swollens rivers in Derbyshire, it was decided to take the safer route to Derby, so it was in 1786 that the first mails were sent by coach from Manchester to London, and they took the route via Macclesfield, Leek, Ashbourne and Derby. Claims have been made that 'The Mount' (once the home of Charles Heaton) was once a staging post for stagecoaches travelling to the North.[11] This may bear some truth, but in lists of posting stages made in the early part of this century by Cary[12] and Paterson,[13] no mention is made of inns at Endon, though Leek and Newcastle figure quite prominently. Endon would be on the route for stagecoaches and wagons going South via Macclesfield, Leek and Newcastle, because the Macclesfield to Congleton road was not turnpiked until after 1820. Suffice to say that Endon's part in the stagecoach age would mainly be concerned with refreshment for those travellers passing through during the day. Perhaps one should also remember that before 1820 the roadway passed through the centre of the village and not along the bypass which was only constructed in that year. The Plough was not shown before 1839, and the inn in the village even as late as 1851 did not employ an ostler.

Parish constables were concerned with the preservation of peace in the villages. For Leek the parish constables in 1842 were:

Enock Baddley	labourer	Endon
John Glover	farmer	Longsdon
William Glover	miller	Stanley
Richard Harrison	farmer	Endon
Richard Knight	joiner & moulder	Stanley
Samuel White	farmer	Longsdon[14]

Some nine years later, the enumeration sheet shows that one William Hand was the County Police Officer, giving the office a more 'professional' touch, and reflecting the influence of Sir Robert Peel's efforts to provide more security, and perhaps a more reliable service.

Nevertheless, it was an age of severe and almost inhuman punishment. In 1831, Thomas Turnock, aged thirty-four years was sentenced to death for breaking into the house of Thomas Bosson of Endon on August 5th, and stealing one pair of breeches and eight shillings and sixpence in silver coin. This sentence was commuted to one of transportation for life, but whatever the outcome for the prisoner, the sufferers were his wife and children. In 1838 Hannah Turnock, now aged forty, described in the poor law records as 'washer, earns a little, husband being transported, has two children, Hannah aged ten earns nothing, and Thomas aged seven.'[15]

As a result of their plea for assistance, they received an allowance of twelve pounds of bread from the Guardians of the Poor at Leek. Endon appears very rarely in the list of offences dealt with by

Stafford Assize, possibly because of its association with the parish of Leek, and its inclusion in the lists under that name. However, the following are local offences from official sources related to sentences passed at the Staffordshire Assizes, 1832-45, upon persons convicted of crimes in Leek and the district around:

Thomas Turnock (34) for breaking into the dwellinghouse of Thomas Bosson, of Endon, on the night of the 5th August 1831, and stealing one pair of breeches and eight shillings and sixpence in silver coin, was sentenced to death.[16]

Joseph Mellor (33), for breaking into the dwellinghouse of Samuel Kinsey at the parish of Leek, on 28th January 1832, and stealing there-from two loaves of bread and part of a cheese, was sentenced to death.

James Gibson (23) for assaulting William Gibson at Barnswood in the parish of Leek, on the 21st March 1839, putting him in bodily fear and danger of his life, and attempting to rob him, was transported for life.

Samuel Clark, alias Cobb (26), for assaulting and stealing from the person of William Scarratt, on the 18th May 1840 at Leek, two £5 promissory notes, eight sovereigns and one half sovereign, two half-crowns, and a calico purse, was transported for the term of fifteen years.[17]

Joseph Boden, alias Bowden (26), for stealing a dark brown cart mare, on 27th November 1832, at the parish of Leek, the property of Hannah Smith, was transported for life.

Joseph Godson (27), for breaking into the parochial chapel at Rushton, on the night of 14th December 1832, and stealing a Bible, a Prayer Book, a surplice and communion table cloth, the property of the inhabitants of the Chapelry of Rushton, was sentenced to death.

Daniel Tipper (22), John Lovatt (21) and James Smith (23), were tried for assaulting William Gould on the Highway leading from Leek to Macclesfield, on the 26th December 1832, and stealing from his person a gun, a watch, three soverigns, thirteen shillings, from his person a gun, a watch, three sovereigns, thirteen shillings, Tipper and Lovatt were sentenced to death.

Samuel Mellor (19) and William Hulme (18), for breaking into the shop of Thomas Mycock, in the parish of Waterfall, in the night of the 19th July 1833, and stealing a soldering iron, a pair of shears, and other articles, were transported for life. Hulme had previously been convicted of felony.

Thomas Osborn (21), for breaking into the dwellinghouse of Richard Fallows in the night of 19th February 1837, at Leek, and assaulting, beating and putting him in bodily fear, and stealing from him two waistcoats, one bolster case, and one crown piece, was sentenced to death.

John Beardmore (30), for stealing, on the 13th June 1836 at Caldon, two rams, the property of Thomas Mellor, was transported for fifteen years.

William Taylor (20), for feloniously uttering on the 7th February 1838 at Leek, a counterfeit note for the payment of £5, well knowing the same to be false and counterfeited, with intent to defraud the Governor and Company of the Bank of England, was transported for the term of his natural life.

James Nicolls (31), for stealing on 12th July 1838 at Leek, one sovereign, two half-crowns, and other articles, the property of John Dabitt, was sentenced to one year's imprisonment with hard labour.

Besides the activities associated with well-dressing and Oakapple Day, the summer of 1885 saw great excitement in Endon. It was the occasion of the creation of the new Leek Parliamentary division, in which Endon became number nine district with the instruction that people were 'to poll at Endon and revise at Endon.'[18] However, before the reform was implemented the situation in Endon, Longsdon and Stanley was as follows:

Population 1881	Inhabited Houses 1881	Ownership Voters in 1885 (A)
1560	310	95
		paying rates on assessment of £12 a year.

For district ten, the township of Horton and Horton Hay with Blackwood and Crowborough, the figures were:

1201	236	83

The term ownership voter means a person entitled to vote in respect of the ownership of property whether of freehold, leasehold or copyhold tenure, and does not include a £50 rental voter. The extension of the franchise and the creation of the new Leek division caused a correspondent to write in the Leek Post and Times of 1885:

'Sir, The great measure of electoral reform which shines a fitting aureole around the 75th birthday of the most popular statesman of our time is fraught with interest to we denizens of the metropolis of the moorlands now about to give its own name to a wide electoral area.'[19]

Gladstone had extended the borough household franchise to the counties (Leek, of course, was not an ancient parliamentary borough) and the area generally saw an increase in the number of voters.

The changes are revealed for Endon in the following table:

	Freeholders	Occupiers	Total number last year	Revised increase
1884	110	94	204	
1885	102	204	306	102

In 1867 working men in towns had been largely admitted to the franchise. The Act of 1884 which was to apply to the new Leek constituency enfranchised the agricultural labourers and put about two million new voters on the lists in Britain. Even though the number affected in Endon was small, the increase in the number of voters in the Leek division was five thousand, five hundred and seven. This is called the Country Franchise Act. Every occupier or lodger in town or country paying ten pounds a year in rent was given a vote. However, since this was the first occasion on which the division had returned an MP, it is pointless to attempt to compare the influence made in terms of the total electorate or on the result of the election in party terms. Mr. Harry Davenport the Conservative candidate was seeking election, as was the Liberal, Mr. Charles Crompton, Q.C. The result of the first election in the Leek constituency was:

Charles Crompton (L)   ...   4,225
Harry Davenport (C)   ...   4,063

The issues were somewhat remote from the parochial affairs of the village, and the speeches made by visiting politicians are academic. One must also remember that, at this time, not all men were entitled to vote and no woman was admitted to the polling booth, though judging by reports in local newspapers some attended Mr. Crompton's meeting at 'The Plough Inn'. Could this be the beginnings of a suffragette lobby in Endon? It would seem not to be so.

171

The Leek Post and Times of July 4th 1885 reports an earlier meeting, 'a largely attended meeting of Conservatives was held at "The Plough Hotel", Endon, on Wednesday night, when addresses were delivered by Mr. H. J. Davenport, M.P., and Mr. John Robinson, J.P., D.L. Mr. Thomas Smith (Park Lane) was unanimously voted to the chair. The main point of Mr. Davenport's address read:

In a village like Endon if the people were entirely in favour of shutting up public houses, I do not think that it is right that they should have the power to say that the minority should not have reasonable opportunties for refreshment.

Presumably this was an argument against the Liberal, and particularly the nonconformist view. The other issue, and the major one at the 1885 election, was the Liberal proposal to disestablish the Church of England. Mr. Davenport's statement may be taken as a comment on the attitudes towards this question. However, the report continues 'he was sorry he could not stay any longer as he had to catch the nine-twenty-five at Stoke. The honorable gentlemen then left the room amidst a round of hearty cheers.'

In the November of 1885 when further support was needed for the candidature of Mr. Davenport, a meeting was held at the Black Horse at Endon when again it was reported that Mr. Thomas Smith presided and was supported on the platform by the Reverend James Badnall and others.[20]

Though issues such as Free Trade, the Budget and Irish Home Rule were occupying the attention of most politicians at this time, the Leek newspapers carried letters expressing approval of or opposition to the disestablishment of the Church of England, and it is along these lines that Charles Crompton chose to address a meeting at The Plough in August 1885. 'On Friday, August 4th, Mr. Charles Crompton addressed a meeting at the Plough Hotel, Endon. The chair was taken by Mr. Arthur Nicholson, a mill owner of Leek, who was supported by Mr. Woodall, M.P., and several influential gentlemen of the district, a few ladies being among the audience', so says the Leek newspaper which continues by reporting that Mr. Crompton said 'he should be prepared to vote for the disestablishment and disendowment of the English Church when the constituencies of England had pronounced in favour of a measure to that purpose.' Victory or not there was no disestablishment in 1885 when the Liberals took three hundred and thirty-two seats to the Conservatives two hundred and fifty. But the Parliament was short-lived and the Liberals were defeated in 1886 on the Home Rule issue.

The historical significance and the ever-present importance of Free Trade to the mill owners at Leek and the agriculturalists of Endon is well illustrated by a correction which the Conservative candidate thought fit to enforce upon the local newspaper. Harry T. Davenport (Conservative) asked for the correction stating that he was *not* in favour of putting a duty on corn. The newspaper had apparently reported that he was in favour. The Editor wrote 'the mistake we find on enquiry was a telegraphic one—the negative having been dropped between Leek and Stoke.'

Perhaps the effects of the growing concern in the electorate for matters political, and the increased involvement of the people are shown in the table of the population, aged over twenty, who were voters in Britain:

	1831	...	...	...	5%
After	1832 (First Reform Act)		...		7.1%
„	1867 (Second „ „)		...		16.4%
„	1884 (Third „ „)		...		28.5%
„	1918	...	...	...	74.0%
„	„ 1928 (Equal Franchise Act)				96.9%

In Endon in 1884 out of three hundred and ten occupied houses, only two hundred and four people had a vote, in effect two thirds of all householders were enfranchised. After 1884, three hundred and six householders could vote, indicating, roughly, a complete manhood suffrage in Endon for householders. But Endon had other things to bother about. The British and Foreign Bible Society—Leek Auxiliary proposed to extend their village work still further and to seek an opening for the society in Endon. The Wesleyan Chapel held its Harvest Festival and tea meeting which was presided over by Mr. G. F. Ford (The Mayor of Burslem).

It was commonplace for children to be absent from school at harvest time, and quite a number were engaged 'for agricultural purposes in March at this time.' In fact in August the children were affected by the corn harvest, the commencement of the potato harvest and the Annual Flower Show, for which those who were not already absent from school, got a half holiday.[21]

AMICITIA, AMOR ET VERITAS
FRIENDSHIP, LOVE & TRUTH

After 1793 basic regulations for friendly societies could be approved locally by magistrates, but during the Napoleonic Wars some societies were suppressed because of the fear of them harbouring revolutionaries. In 1801 there were seven thousand Friendly Societies with a total membership of six hundred thousand people, but the most prosperous years were 1873/4 when the membership was four million. The movement commonly related in people's minds to sick and burial funds, had a great impact on society, providing an insurance against hard times which the state, as yet, did not provide. The Endon Club was founded in 1820, mainly for artisans and workers in agriculture with the title Endon Friendly Society, and bore the motto: *Amicitia Amor et Veritas*. In 1828 the club purchased a piece of land from John Frost, related to which a document dated April 16th reads 'Received from Mr. Thomas Lockite, High Steward of the Endon Club, the sum of one pound as a consideration for a Bit of Copyhold Land with a house at Endon belonging to the Club, and of another new building and containing about twenty-five square yards or thereabout, and I hereby promise at any future time to make the Club a good title to it if they will be at the expense of it.   John Frost

X

his mark

Witness: I. Tomkinson and John Dean.[22]

The club owned property in the village, presumably wishing to invest its wealth in local securities. A church rate book shows Endon Friendly Society as owner of several properties in 1845.[23] Enoch Tomkinson and William Salt each occupied houses which had a church rateable value of £5. The 1854 ratebook shows the Club owning properties and paying 1½d. in the £ rate for the upkeep of the church on the cottages, as follows:

		Rateable value
Property occupied by Thos. Gratton (House Endon)	... ...	£2
Samuel Fynney	... ...	£5
Ralph Alcock	... ...	£5
Thomas Dale	... ...	£5
Richard Doorbar	... ...	£2
George Beresford	...	£2[24]

A document of 1859 relates how the 'Reverend Daniel Turner of Endon in the County of Stafford, Trustee of the Endon Friendly Society, and Sampson Bratt, a grocer, and High Steward of the said Society' made an agreement with 'John Jackson of Norton in the Moors, Police Officer, and James Mayer of Norton, aforesaid publican', allowing Jackson and May to become tenants of the public house, outbuildings and garden, by the name or sign of The Plough Inn at Endon. The rent was £45 per year. So it would seem the club had a sound investment. The society finally sold their interest in the inn in the 1870s during the chairmanship of the Reverend James Badnall, vicar of Endon.[25]

An important regulation of the club read 'members of this society are required to bring the surgeon's certificate before they will be allowed sick pay, every sick member to renew his certificate from the surgeon every week, and to pay up all arrears night before the feast, or be fined two shillings.'[26] The feast was held on the first Thursday after Midsummer Day each year. Attendance at the feast was compulsory, proper substitutes had to be found, but in the event of a member not answering to his name 'before going to church to walk in procession' he was fined sixpence. The public display of membership solidarity and the strength of the organisation by an annual show of numbers was a feature of working class life in the nineteenth century, and can be seen in the displays made by some trade unions up to the present time, though not in Endon. A report of 1873, one of the pinnacle years for friendly society activity, shows a membership of four hundred at Endon and describes the activities on June 26th. Some indication of the concern of the clergy for the behaviour of the membership, who from time to time were known to smoke pipes in the procession and even in the precincts of the churchyard is clearly indicated. The account goes on to record how the vicar advised, exhorted and warned the men before they left the church for their dinner at the 'Plough Inn'.

It is interesting to note how the society which began as a piece of working-class self-help in times of great poverty and industrial unrest was by 1873 acquiring a degree of respectability and was to consider inviting 'the leading gentry' to the annual feast.[27]

Members dressed in a regalia, mainly consisting of a brightly coloured blue sash bearing the motto of the Society, and each carried a wand or staff in the hand. Smart headgear was also worn. Not only did the occasion involve working men, children were given the day off and the school closed as instanced by the entry in the school log book which read: 'June 28th 1872. The attendance this week has been lower. Thursday was a holiday on account of the Endon Friendly Society.'[28] Of the annual Club day the Rev. James Badnall wrote in 1873:

'On Thursday, June 26th the 53rd Anniversary of the Endon Friendly Society was celebrated. In the morning, the Endon Band accompanied the Committee to the residence of the High-Steward, Mr. J. Bratt, of Sandy Lane, who to his own credit and to that of the Endon Society, has thus far well fulfilled his office. At half past one, the entire members, over 400 strong, assembled together and in a very orderly manner walked through the village to the Church. One can remember the time when pipes were the predominant regalia on the road of march—and even into the Church Yard. To the credit of the Society be it said, these are annually by degrees becoming discarded, we hope they will disappear altogether. By all means let the good collier or any other member of the club have his pipe of tobacco before the procession begins, but not in the procession. A pipe and a wand look bad together. Inside the Church no number of men could possibly have behaved better; there were few who did not kneel during the prayers. Thanks to Mr. Ford, the Churchwarden, there was not the same confusion as on former occasions in taking or leaving places. The short and simple service began with the singing of the glorious old hundredth, Prayers and Hymns. The Vicar then preached the sermon. He advised, and exhorted, and warned, and then the men who had been very attentive left the Church to their dinner. Every praise is due to Mr. and Mrs. Jackson of the Plough Inn, for the excellent dinner they provided and which 400 hungry men made short work of.'

The Rev. James Badnall acted as Chairman, supported by Mr. Ford, Mr. Robert Clemison and the High Chief Steward on his right, Mr. Hall on his left. The usual loyal and local toasts were proposed and responded to with vigour. Mr. N. Baddeley the Secretary, who gave a statement of accounts, which showed the club to be in flourishing condition not withstanding several heavy drawbacks during the year. About £300 had been spent on sick cases, still a saving of £80 had been effected and 17 new members had been added. The accumulated funds at the lowest estimate amounts to £3,000. A deal of the fund

ENDON FRIENDLY SOCIETY.

No. 325   William Shaw   Member.

| SURGEONS : T. HALES, ESQ. DR. GAILEY. | HIGH-STEWARD : MR. JOSEPH BRATT. | SECRETARY : SAML. WILLOTT. | CHEQUE CLERK : MR. NOAH BADDELEY. | TRUSTEE : MR. H. MOUNTFORD |

1884—1885.	July 12	Aug 9	Sept 6	Oct 4	Nov 1	Nov. 29	Dec. 27	Jan 24	Feb. 21	Mar. 21	Apr. 18	May 16	Jun. 13	Feast Jun. 25
Contributions -			3/			3/		3/		3/			2/6	
Surgeon - - -														3/
Funeral - - -												9/6		
Fine 6/1			1/2											
Total - - -			3/2			3/		3/		3/		10/6	5/	

☞ All Members are requested to attend or forward their Contributions between the hours of Six and Eight in the Evening, from Michaelmas to Lady-day ; and between the hours of Seven and Nine in the Evening from Lady-day to Michaelmas ; at which hour the Club-room door will be closed, and no person can afterwards be admitted to pay Contribution. Fine for non-compliance with the above, *Two Shillings.* No Contributions to be received without a Card. ALL APPLICATIONS FOR SICK PAY MUST BE MADE TO THE CHEQUE CLERK. Funeral expenses to be paid according to Rule.

An Endon Society Club Card 1884-1885.

The Cottages in Endon which were once the property of Endon Club.

Inside 'The Plough Inn', late nineteenth century.
Painting by H. W. Foster.

Inside the old 'Black Horse', late nineteenth century.
Painting by H. W. Foster.

being invested in cottage property. The society has had to contribute rather heavily to the expense of improvements necessitated by the rural sanitary authorities order.

In closing this account, may one or two suggestions be made to the Committee and Officers of the society.

1. Would it not be as well to issue invitations to the leading gentry to the Anniversary dinner. To enlist their sympathy with the society by becoming honorary members.

2. Might not better provisions be made for the after dinner speeches and could it be arranged that the members of the Club as well as the officers take a part in the after dinner proceedings, hear what is to be said on their annual gathering. Thereby showing interest in the welfare of their Society.

By 1878 Endon club had a reading room and at a meeting held in October of that year it was proposed 'that those members residing more than three miles from the schoolroom be required to pay one penny (extra) for each night in attendance. Later, on February 6th 1879 the Reverend J. Badnall submitted specimens of periodicals recommended by the Pure Literature Society and it was resolved 'that several of them should be taken in for the use of the Room.' It was also proposed and carried unanimously 'that a separate room be provided for Reading apart from that now used for games.'

In 1890 the officials were:

Surgeons—Dr. Lindsay   High Steward—Mr. Joseph Bratt
       Dr. Gailey   Secretary—Samuel Willot
Check Clerk—Mr. Noah Baddeley, and the Trustees were
Mr. H. Mountford and Mr. J. Mountford.
The contributions were one shilling per week.[29]

The feast as an annual occasion continued until after the turn of the century, though the importance and significance of the occasion diminished and finally disappeared. Similarly the occasion ceased to be a holiday for schoolchildren.

In 1914 the trustees are shown as Thomas Wilshaw and Herbert Myatt but about this time inroads were being made into the supremacy of the private self-help organisations by the introduction of state provisions for health, sick and unemployment pay. There is the story of James Pickford aged 91 who had been a member of the Society for over seventy years, who walked from his home in Brown Edge to have dinner with Mr. Platt, the landlord of The Plough, then walked from the inn round the village and back to his home. The account states that he did this, alone, sometime in 1910 on the day on which the Friendly Society usually held its feast. It was the first time for over seventy years that he had made the walk alone.

About the time of the high-noon of the Endon club other forms of activity were occupying the attention of the villagers. Endon established itself as a pioneer of Association Football in the moorlands, when on November 16th 1876 'a meeting was held in the schoolroom, at Endon, for the purpose of forming a club to play under the rules of the Sheffield Association. Mr. G. H. Heaton presided. It was stated that a suitable field had been offered and the meeting was adjourned for a week. Sufficient members were obtained, to justify the existence of such a club, and after some practice games the club played Normacot on December 23rd 1876.'

This was the first recorded match which took place in the moorlands under the rules of the Sheffield Association.

Endon succeeded in winning the match by one goal to nothing, after an exciting struggle. E. Baines had the credit of scoring the goal which was loudly applauded.

The Endon players were: G. H. Heaton (capt.), C. D. Heaton, F. Heaton, W. S. Heaton, R. Ford, F. Powell, E. Baines, H. Lee, Houltby, Bradbury and W. Heath.

On Boxing Day, Endon were successful in their second match, defeating North Stafford Railway Clerks by one goal to nothing.

On December 31st 1876, the Stoke 2nd team beat Endon one goal to nothing.

Thus in the first three matches played by Endon there were only three goals scored. This was accounted for by the rules of the Sheffield Association which allowed scrummages to take place not unlike those found in Rugby football.

Association football flourished in other forms in late times, nevertheless the sporting and venturesome spirit of the villagers, notably the Heatons, may have become more relevant if the Sheffield-style game had prevailed.

Weaving in Endon

The first reference we find of the presence of weavers in Endon is in 1656 when Thomas Clowes is shown as a weaver and was a tenant of Mr. Bellot of the Ashes.[30] White's Directory of 1834[31] shows that persons under the name of Hassell were operating as linen, tick and sacking manufacturers, and were to be found in Endon, though by mid-century they had gone. Pieces of material, believed to have been woven in Endon, are still in existence.

The papist returns of 1767 and 1781[32] made for the chapelry of Endon record that there were two men living in Endon and working as ribbon weavers. The men are not named thus making any effort to trace where they lived or where they worked as ribbon weavers impossible.

However, there are few references to weaving as an occupation and by 1851 none of the people living in the weavers' cottages are shown as weavers. Up to about 1800, however, flax was grown in Endon and the name of the Weavers' Cottages bears witness to the occupation carried on there and on the adjacent field known as 'tenters' field, an area where the finished linen would be put out to dry and to be stretched on the tenterhooks. Sunnybank as a name could have been associated with the bleaching of linen, often indicating the area facing South where the linen was put out to be whitened. By the beginning of the last century cotton replaced flax as a staple textile or fibre in the country as a whole and the large scale cotton mills, and silk mills in the case of Leek, took over. The weaving therefore in Endon was a domestic industry of a limited size and not employing many people.

There are no tithe maps for Endon in existence, but an award of rent charges was made in 1847. It reads as follows: [33]

'Know all men by those present that Joseph Townsend of Wood End in the County of Buckingham having been duly appointed and sworn an Assistant Tithe Commissioner according to the provisions of the Act for the Communication of Tithes in England and Wales, and having been also duly appointed to ascertain and award the total sum to be paid by way of Rent Charge instead of the Tithes of the Chapelry of Endon in the Parish of Leek in the County of Stafford do hereby award as follows that is to say.

Whereas I have held divers meetings near the said Chapelry touching the matter aforesaid of which meetings due notice was given for the information of the landowners and titheowners of the said Chapelry.

And whereas I had duly considered all the allegations and proofs tendered to me by all parties interested, and have myself made all enquiries touching the premised subject which appeared to me to be necessary.

And whereas I find that declarations of Merger of Tithes in the land comprised in the first schedule here to annexed have been made by the several owners thereof and duly confirmed by the Tithe Commissioners of England and Wales.

And whereas I find the estimated quantity in statute measure of all the remaining lands of the said Chapelry which are subject to payment of tithes amounts to nine hundred and ninety-two acres which are cultivated as follows:

Six hundred acres as arable land, and three hundred and ninety-two acres as meadow or pasture. The whole of which said lands are liable to payment of all manner of tithes in kind.

And whereas I have estimated the clear annual value of the said tithes in the manner directed by the said Act of Parliament and have also taken into account the rates and assessments paid in respect of such tithes during the seven years of average prescribed by the said Act.

And whereas I find that the several persons whose names are set forth in the first column of the second schedule hereto annexed are respectively owners of the tithes arising from or accruing due upon the lands specified in the said second schedule opposite to their several respective names.

Now know ye that I the said Joseph Townsend do hereby award that several annual sums specified in the fifth column of the second schedule hereby annexed by the way of Rent Charges subject to the provision of the said Act shall be paid to the several persons respectively whose names are set forth in the said second schedule. Opposite thereto and to their several heirs and assigns, or to the persons entitled in remainder or reversion after each of them respectively in lieu of the tithes to which they are severally entitled as aforesaid.

In testimony whereof I the said Joseph Townsend do hereby affix my hand this sixteenth day of December in the year one thousand eight hundred and forty-seven.

Jos. W. Townsend,
Assistant Commissioner.

First Schedule referred to in the Foregoing Award

Names of Persons Merging	Acreage A	R	P
Thomas Heaton	6	—	10
Charlotte Roden	2	—	7
Thomas Weatherby	66	2	15
Thomas Phillips	85	2	6
Charles Heaton	15	2	4
Francis Ann Ward	3	—	5
Edward Mary Challenor	21	3	12
Samuel Phillips	162	3	6
William Phillips	39	3	0
Josiah Gaunt	3	1	29
Ralf Shaw	56	—	—
Mrs. Frances Ann Ward	70	1	7
George Thompson	119	—	26
Reverend James Turner	8	—	—
William Sneyd	143	—	7
Thomas Birch and James Abbot	40	—	—
James Abbot and John Phillips	33	1	9
William Critchlow	8	1	9
Mrs. Mary Grosvenor	121	3	21
Hannah Harrison and Margaret Unwin ...	24	2	15
Earl of Macclesfield	141	3	6
Mrs. Mary Grosvenor	50	3	36
John Bennett	77	—	35
John and William Crompton	17	—	—
James Chadwick	4	—	15
Edward Chorley Esquire	15	2	11

Second Schedule referred to in the Foregoing Award

Titheowners	Landowners	Names of Estates	A	R	P	£	s	d	
Brooks, James ...	Himself	Hough Lane	5	—	—		14	—	Cancelled Sept.
Bratt, Sampson ...	„	Brown Edge	3	—	—		8	6	Merger
Basnett, William ...	„	Moss Hill	111	—	—	14	16	—	Merger
Late of Devisers ...	„	Moss Hill							
Basnett, James ...	„	Moss Hill	16	—	—		15	—	Merger
Basnett, Samuel ...	„	Endon Edge	3	—	—		9	—	Merger
Brindley, Thomas ...	„	Endon Edge	1	—	—		3	—	
Challinor, Elizabeth ...	Herself	Kids Meadow	4	—	—		12	—	Cancelled by Sept.
Clewlow, Joseph ...	Himself	Brown Edge	1	2	—		4	6	Merger
Frost, Hannah ...	Herself	Brown Edge	2	—	—		6	—	Merger
Frost, Ellen ...	„	Brown Edge	1	2	—		4	6	Merger
Gratton, Thomas ...	Himself	Endon Edge	1	—	—		3	—	Cancelled by Sept.
Goodwin, Edith ...	Herself	Harbour Meadow	5	—	—		15	—	Merger
Goodwin, Arthur ...	Himself	Water Meadow	4	2	—		13	6	Merger
Heaton, Charles (Junior) ...	„	Hough Lane	2	3	—		8	—	Merger
Hilditch, Charles ...	„	Fernyhough	74	2	—				
		Crofts Edge Wood	12	1	—	13	—	—	Merger
Hammersley, Richard ...	„	Morris House	45	—	—				
		Wood	3	—	—	7	15	—	Merger
		Brown Edge	3	2	—				
Hadfield, Alfred ...	„	Lane Ends Farm	58	2	—				
		Endon Edge	7	1	—	8	8	—	Merger
Jackson, James ...	„	Bunnells	11	—	—	1	13	—	Merger
Keates, William ...	„	Cross Edge	2	3	—	1	8	—	Merger
Lockitt, Thomas ...	„	Greenfields	12	1	—	1	17	—	Merger

Titheowners		Landowners	Names of Estates	Quantities			Rent in lieu of Tithes		
				A	R	P	£	s	d
Mountford, George	...	Himself	Brown Edge	3	2	—		10	6	Merger
Mountford, Abraham	...		Brown Edge		2	—		1	6	Merger
Mountford, Hannah	...	Herself	Brown Edge	2	3	—		8	0	Merger
Phillips, William	...	,,	Holehouse	39	3	—	6	—	—	Merger
Puddock, George	...	,,	Park Hayes	40	3	—	6	3	—	Merger
Plant, Thomas	...	,,	Park Land	6	2	—		19	6	Merger
Rowley, John	...	,,	Endon Edge	1	1	—		3	—	Cancelled
Roden, Thomas	...	,,	Hough Lane	9	3	—	1	10	—	Merger
Smith, Thomas	...	,,	Park Lane	63	—	—				
			Woods	8	2	—	10	14	—	Merger
Stonier, John	...	,,	Lady Moors	39	—	—	5	17	1	Merger
Steel, John	...	,,	Lake House	26	3	—	4	1	—	Merger
Steel, Elizabeth	...	Herself	Clay Lake	28	—	—	4	4	—	Merger
Sutton, Thomas	...	Himself	Wood	3	3	—				
			Endon	72	1	—				
			Holling Longer	22	—	—	17	5	—	Merger
			Hall Water	15	—	—				
			Jack of the Green	1	3	—				
Shaw, John	...	,,	Endon Edge	18	—	—	2	14	—	Merger
Sherratt, Hugh	...	,,	Brown Edge	2	1	—		6	—	Merger
Sparrow, John	...	,,	Knowles	91	3	—		13	6	Merger
Stannah, Josiah	...	,,	Hedge Fields	14	3	—	2	5	—	Merger
Smith, John	...	,,	Park Lane	33	1	—	4	19	—	Merger
Turner, William	...	,,	Greenfields	14	—	—	2	2	—	Merger
Tomkinson, Samuel	...	,,	Brown Edge	5	—	—		15	—	Merger
Trubshawe, Mary	...	Herself	Stockton Brook	3	2	—		10	6	Cancelled Sept.
Willatt, Samuel	...	Himself	Brown Edge	9	—	—	1	7	—	Merger
Willatt, Thomas	...	,,	Brown Edge		2	—		1	6	
Wilkinson, Elizabeth	...	Herself	Sims Hays	26	3	—	4	1	—	Merger

Know all men by these present that I George Wingrove Cooke of the Middle Temple Esquire, Barrister at Law, have been duly appointed and sworn an assistant tithe commissioner, for special purposes according to the provisions of the Act for the Commutation of Tithes in England and Wales, and have been also duly appointed to ascertain whether by reason of any manifest error of the confirmed Award for the Chapelry of Endon in the Parish of Leek in the County of Stafford is unjust and whether such error (if any) is of such a nature that the Tithe Commissioners for England and Wales would if informed thereof have declined to confirm the same and in case I should ascertain that such error as aforesaid had accrued in the said confirmed Award by way of supplement to the said confirmed Award in respect of the said error.

And whereas I have duly held meeting within the said Parish of Leek touching the matter aforesaid of which meeting due notice was given for the information of all parties interested and I then and there made enquiry and received evidence touching the said matter. And whereas I find that a manifest error of the nature aforesaid has occured in the said confirmed Award in the manner and in the respect following that is to say that by the said confirmed Award. A Rent Charge of fourteen shillings is erroneously awarded to James Brooks, a rent charge of twelve shillings to Elizabeth Challinor, a rent charge of three shillings to Thomas Gratton, a rent charge of three shillings to John Rowley, and a rent charge of ten shillings and sixpence to Mary Trubshaw in lieu of the tithes of certain land which are set forth and described in the second schedule. To the said confirmed Award annexed whereas in truth and in fact none of the persons afore mentioned are titheowners within the said Township of Endon in as much as portion of the lands in respect of the tithes whereof the said rent charges are awarded are by prescription or for other lawful cause totally exempt from the render of all tithes both great and small and the tithes of the portion of the lands in respect of which the said rent charges were so made payable were duly merged by the owners thereof previously to the making of the said original Award.

And further that the said Award erroneously omits to state that all the lands of the said Township except only those lands whereof the tithes are recited to be duly merged and those lands the tithe whereof are by the said confirmed Award commuted into Rent Charges are by prescription or for other lawful cause totally exempt from the render of all tithes both great and small.

Now know ye that I the said George Wingrove Cook do by this my separate Award by way of supplement to the said confirmed Award and in correction thereof direct order and award that the rent charges by the said confirmed award awarded to the said James Brooks, Elizabeth Challinor, Thomas Gratton, John Rowley and Mary Trubshaw and herein before specially recited shall be and the same hereby cancelled and annulled.

And I do further declare and award that all the lands of the said Township (except the lands which by the said confirmed Award are recited to have merged in them the tithes of such lands and except also the lands the tithes whereof have been commuted into Rent Charges by the said confirmed Award) as corrected by this Separate Award are by prescription or for other lawful cause exempt from the render of all tithes both great and small. In Testimony whereof I have hereunto set my hand this lawful day of July in the year of our Lord one thousand eight hundred and fifty.

Geo. Wingrove Cooke

We have seen that the system of Poor Law Relief operated from the vestry meetings at Leek Church, and the overseer at Endon, does not provide us with much documentary evidence.[33] Nevertheless a record of payments is still in existence in Endon parish chest. It has also been established that there was little connection with the earlier Poor Law workhouses except for the odd reference to Leek and Ipstones. Staffordshire did not have many workhouses in the eighteenth century and progress in the building of them was slow. During the latter part of the eighteenth century there was, in the county, a rapid rise in the poor rate and an increase in paupers and a 'general demoralisation of the working classes due to methods intended to be philanthropic but really disastrous to everyone concerned.'[34]

In 1796 an Act of Parliament abolished the workhouse test and gave authority for more outdoor relief to be granted. The records at Endon would suggest that this had been the case for some time and outdoor relief was the chief method of amelioration.

In the county of Staffordshire as a whole the revenue from Poor Law rates was as follows: 1819 — £155,309
1822 — £133,701
1825 — £107,634
1829 — £119,977
1832 — £133,971[35]

With the passing of the 1834 Amendment Act larger unions were brought into being and a stricter control on various forms of relief was made. Outdoor relief was to be discouraged. Perhaps Carlyle's description of the attitude at the time is most accurate: 'If paupers are made miserable, paupers will decline in numbers, this is a fact well-known to rat-catchers.'

The first meeting of the Guardians of Leek Union was held on 4th December 1837.[36] John Cruso junior was elected chairman and other members were Anthony Ward, Thomas Smith, William Critchlow and Thomas Carr junior. They agreed that they should meet in the Sunday School at ten o'clock on Wednesday mornings and that the clerk should receive a salary of £80. At first there were to be two districts for the admission of outdoor relief. Endon was placed in Horton district along with Rushton James, Rushton Spencer, Longsdon, Stanley, Norton, Horton Hay, Blackwood and Crowbrough.

Endon, Longsdon and Stanley during the initial stages were represented by Thomas Wooliscroft and William Beardmore. The area covered by the Union was extensive, and each of the following areas sent a representative in addition to the ones already mentioned who represented Leek town. The union area comprised of Leekfrith, Rushton, Rudyard, Tittesworth, Bradnop, Hollings Lea, Sheen, Onecote, Heaton, Horton, Horton Hay, Blackwood and Crowbrough, Norton, Quarnford, Warslow, Elkstone and Farfield Head.

On December 20th 1837, William Heath of Horton was made the Registrar of Horton district, and at the same meeting it was proposed that 'there shall be a workhouse built to contain 300 paupers at Leek upon the land belonging to Leek and Lowe on Leek moor.' Tenders were put out for a building which was opened in 1838.

This was also the occasion on which it was proposed that the meetings of the Guardians 'should be held at the Swann Inn, because the landlord had offered it for five shillings per week.' Mr. Cruso the chairman suggested the committee should offer six shillings to the school trustees, 'instead of going to a public house.'

Another meeting ordered 'that each clergyman of every parish be allowed to send tickets for medical men to attend paupers in cases of emergency.'

At the next few meetings the Registration districts were re-arranged as Leek, Leek Frith, Longnor and Norton. Endon, along with Longsdon and Stanley, was placed in the Norton district, and Mr. Charles Heaton of Endon was appointed to be registrar of the Norton district. Some idea of the relative sizes of the district is to be found in the following table of populations which was presented to the meeting:

Norton in the Moors district   ...   3,466[37]
Leek district   8,731

Norton district being less than half the size of Leek district, though much more extensive in acreage.

The records of the Leek Union are well kept. It was a period of efficiency in matters of public accounting and the workhouse took on a sinister image, being called in some areas 'the poor law bastille.' The sexes were segregated on admission and families, consequently, broken up. Some of the distress in Endon in the early nineteenth century is clearly illustrated by extracts from the union records of Endon people who applied for relief, often for 'outdoor', but frequently receiving 'indoor', or, as the records boldly state—'workhouse'. Such

186

was the fate of James Clowes, aged 14 years who was born at Cheddleton and worked at the tanyard in Endon. He was described as an orphan of tender years earning four shillings per week. His plea for charity money received the committee's reply: 'stopped or workhouse'. His brother Ralph, aged ten, also worked in the tanyard and earned two shillings and sixpence a week. He was allowed one shilling and sixpence a week from the Guardians. On May 2nd 1838 a widow, Ann Alcock, of Endon was earning one shilling and sixpence by washing (she is described as a 'washer'). The report continues 'she has four children, John aged thirteen born Wall Grange, in service, maintains himself. Harriet aged eleven born in Leek, with her uncle in service, maintains herself. Ann aged seven, born Endon, George her son, five. Allowed eight pounds of bread and two shillings.' On the same day another entry reads, 'James Berrisford, aged seven, born Brown Edge, orphan, has one sister Elizabeth aged four, orphan. Allowed five shillings.'

Jane Bloor was aged thirty-six, born Leek, Married and described as a washer. Her husband was in prison. The records of 1838 state: 'Earns one shilling per week, has five children. William aged thirteen, helper, earns three shillings and sixpence per week. Isaac, eleven, helper, earns two shillings and sixpence per week. Elizabeth, seven, helper, earns one shilling per week. Emma, three and a half, Thomas, one and a half. Total earnings eight shillings per week, allowed twenty pounds of bread.'[38]

Old age too had its problems. John Dean aged seventy-four of Endon is described as a mole catcher, very lame, earns a little. His wife, Patience, was aged seventy-three but infirm and 'earns nothing'. They were allowed eight pounds of bread and two shillings and sixpence.

A receipt book of 1842 shows that the rate for Endon was fixed at one and a half pence in the pound, thus the tanyard's owners paid one and sixpence per annum and an additional fourpence halfpenny for the land. The owner-occupier of the Plough Inn, one Thomas Hopkinson paid four shillings and fourpence halfpenny on a rateable value of thirty-five pounds. The owner-occupier of the tanyard is shown as Charles Heaton, a representative for Endon on the Poor Law Guardians at Leek. The tanyard had ceased to function as such, by this time.

However, the entries continue. One Mary Frost, aged twenty-three of Brown Edge, described as a single servant 'pregnant, being pregnant allowed two shillings at present.' Sarah Goodwin aged eight, born at Norton, is described as a bastard of tender age, 'father is gone to America—Workhouse.' Similarly William Hollinshead's claim was referred to the overseer. He was three, 'being a bastard, father pays'.

The prevalence of child labour is shown in the case of Edna Mountford, aged nine, who worked as a piecer earning two shillings per week.

Finally, there is the family of John Hargreaves who was aged fifty, was born at Bank End and lived in Endon. The report says of him and his family: 'sells sand but subject to fits and unable to work, earns two shillings per week. Mary his wife aged forty-nine has three children. Richard, aged fourteen works at coalpits, earns one shilling per day when at work. Joseph, nine, sells sand and earns two shillings per week. John, six, earns nothing. Total earnings ten shillings per week.' Hargreaves and his family were granted sixteen pounds of bread.

On January 1st 1884 and 1885, the number of people receiving relief in the Leek Poor Law Union was,

				Indoor	Outdoor[39]
1884	...	...	...	111	653
1885	...	...	...	113	636

In 1885 contracts were agreed by the Guardians as follows: 'Bread of the Best Seconds Flour, loaves of four pounds each, weight twenty-four hours after baking, to be delivered at the following places and times, in such quantities as the Guardians or their relieving officers may order. At Relief Station for Tittesworth, every Wednesday at twelve o'clock noon. At Endon, every Friday, at nine o'clock a.m.'[40]

For those in receipt of indoor relief life had its brighter side. The Leek Post and Times recorded the following event illustrating the attitudes of the times and the responses of the financially better off to say nothing of the 'English-ness' of the menu.

'Saturday, October 13th 1888, a treat to the Workhouse inmates at Leek. Through the kindness of Mr. Edwin Heaton, land surveyor of Endon, the whole of the inmates of the Leek Union Workhouse were provided on Thursday last with a substantial dinner of roast beef and plum pudding. Amongst those present were the Reverend Heaton and Mr. F. J. Heaton, sons of Mr. Edwin Heaton.

After the meal the children were regaled with fruit and adults with tobacco, snuff and beer, also a Punch and Judy show was provided.'[41]

Returning to the middle years of the ninteenth century we find that in spite of some poverty, Endon was a good place in which to live. The Registrar-General's figures for the Leek district comprising of Norton, Leek, Leek-Frith and Longnor sub-districts had a very favourable average age 'of living to death', which would suggest that this part of the moorlands had something to offer. More likely it was the absence of any great concentrations of industry and the consequential squalor following the rapid growth of the towns, which prevented Endon from having the same distressing poverty to be found in some parts of England.

References

[1] Census Returns 1851, Enumeration Sheets, Endon.

[2] See chapter VI, The People, etc.

[3] Manor of Horton Records. Deeds relating to 'The Plough Inn' and the sale of the property.

[4] See documents of the Plough Inn now held by Bass Charrington Ltd., Burton-on-Trent. We are grateful for the assistance given by this Company in connection with 'The Plough Inn'.

[5] Church Rate Endon Record Books, 1842, C.R.O., Stafford.

[6] Kelly's Directory, Endon 1892.

[7] Land Tax Canvas Book 1820, C.R.O., Stafford.

[8] Church Rate Endon Record Books 1842, C.R.O., Stafford.

[9] Church Rate Endon Record Books 1854, C.R.O. Stafford.

[10] Annual Reports, Endon Friendly Society and press cuttings, reports of parades, etc.

[11] 'The Mount' so it is claimed was once known as 'The White Cock Pheasant', see chapter 9.

[12] Cary, J.: 'Roads' 1808.

[13] Paterson, Daniel: 'Roads of England and Wales', 1811.

[14] Leek Parish Records, the parish chest, Leek Parish Church.

[15] Leek Poor Law Union (Guardians) Minute Books 1838, C.R.O., Stafford. d/699/AG/1838.

[16] Stafford Assizes 1832-45 Records, C.R.O., Stafford.

[17] These extracts are intended to show the severity of the sentences passed. Few Endon people appear to have been involved.

[18] Leek Post and Times 1885.

[19] Leek Post and Times—letter to the editor 1885.

[20] Leek Post and Times, November 1885.

[21] Endon Parochial School, Log Books 1885.

[22] Endon Friendly Society Records 1828. very few of these records are available.

[23] Church Rate, Endon Record Book 1845, C.R.O., Stafford.

[24] Church Rate, Endon Record Book 1854, C.R.O., Stafford.

[25] Documents related to the property 'The Plough Inn', Bass Charrington Ltd., Burton-on-Trent.

[26] Endon Friendly Society, Club Card, Rules and Regulations.

[27] Chairman's Report, Endon Friendly Society 1873 (see Staffordshire Advertiser).

[28] Chairman's Report, Endon Friendly Society 1873 (see Staffordshire Advertiser).

[29] Endon Friendly Society, Club Card, Rules and Regulations.

[30] Leek Parish Records, Parish Registers, baptisms 1656.

[31] White's Directory Staffordshire 1834.

[32] House of Lords Record Office, Papist Returns 1767, 1781.

[33] See first and second Schedule. Separate Award, Staffordshire, this chapter, Tithe Redemption Office, London.

[34] *V.C.H*: 'Poor Law in Staffordshire', Vol. 1, p. 296.

[35] *V.C.H.*: 'Poor Law in Staffordshire', Vol. 1, p. 299.

[36] Leek Poor Law Union (Guardians) Minute Books 1837, C.R.O., Stafford, D/699/AG/1837.

[37] Leek Poor Law Union (Guardians) Minute Book 1838, C.R.O. Stafford, D/699/AC/1838.

[38] Leek Poor Law Union (Guardians) Relief Book 1838, D/699/AG/1838.

[39] Leek Post and Times, January 1885.

[40] Leek Poor Law Union (Guardians) Minutes. See local newspapers for the period advertising for tenders, D/699/AG 1837-1930.

[41] Leek Post and Times, October 1888.

Chapter XI

EDUCATION

'There is a public school chiefly maintained by contributions of the Parish. English, Latin and Writing are taught to 35 scholars. They are instructed in the principles of the Christian religion.'
report by Rev. Enoch Tompkinson (Articles of Enquiry) 1751

E ndon was not however among the first places to have an endowed school. At Leek 'The Grammar School' was founded under the Road's charity in 1712 and since Endon was in Leek parish at that time, it is likely that some Endon boys found their way to the school.[1] In 1750 a school and a master's house were built by the free-holders of Endon, on land left by Mr. John Wedgwood and in 1797 a Thomas Harding added a quarter of an acre to the site. This was used as a garden. Two other bequests in 1781 and 1786 providing for the education of six poor children were made by Thomas and William Sherratt who held an estate in Park Lane. The endowment worth one hundred and ten pounds gave an interest of four pounds ten shillings for the schoolmaster. By 1860 a further four pounds ten shillings was received from the Endon turnpike tollgate receipts (or interests) for two free boys to be educated at the school. The donor of this last endowment is not known. In 1751 the school housed some thirty-five pupils in what the incumbent at the time described as, 'a public school chiefly maintained by contributions of the parish.' English, Latin and writing were taught and the children were 'instruct-ed in the principles of the Christian religion.' So it would seem that in a community of sixty-five families, the school had made a good start with thirty-five pupils on the roll.[2]

The master of the Leek Sunday School between 1787 and 1791 was one John Jones of Kiln Lane, Leek, described as the father of fourteen children, appointed at a vestry meeting in Leek parish church to be the master of Endon Free School.[3] This was on the 23rd of May 1791, but by 1792 Mr. Jones had left Endon for Chester where he became involved in the work of the Methodist new connection group there. John Salt, the curate in 1830, was also the school master, and he reported that the endowed school received seven to eight pounds per annum from interest charged on lands which it owned. He remained as schoolmaster for some considerable time, at least until 1851 when the census returns for that year show him as still following the occupation of schoolmaster.[4] At this time he was aged fifty-five years and his wife was fifty. He lived in the Endon Free Schoolhouse with his wife and their three children: Henry aged fourteen, Charles ten and John seven, all of whom are shown as scholars. John Salt himself was born in Kidderminster, Worcestershire. The rest of his family were born in Leek parish, which of course could have meant Endon at that time.

In the middle of the nineteenth century some thirty-two per cent. of the population were aged five to fifteen years. This would account for some one hundred and eighty-eight children who were engaged in varying occupations. Some sixty-nine, however, are shown as scholars, and seventy-two were not employed. We know that some children went to school, but others sought employment. Of the children under fourteen the numbers indicated are shown as following these occupations:

Boys		Girls	
Farm labourers	3	House servant	7
Farm servant	2	Laundress	1
Butcher apprentice	1	Apprentice	1

These are few compared with the non-employed who are not shown as scholars: thirty-three boys and thirty-nine girls. This compares favourably with other rural areas, but in those towns affected by the industrial growth of the nineteenth century there would be quite a different picture. Taking the total number of children under fourteen and over twelve months as eighty-three boys and seventy-three girls, a grand total of one hundred and fifty-six children, the teaching resources of Endon would have been stretched to the limit if all children had gone to school. The one schoolmaster at the Free School could not have managed even if joined by the two teachers from the private boarding school, which had twelve pupils aged between five and fourteen. In 1833 the charity commissioners reported that in Endon chapelry and the townships of Longsdon and Stanley (population 1,003) there were 'Seven Daily Schools wherein are 102 males

Endon School at a time when the roadway on Endon Bank could be used as a playground.

Brown Edge School.
1920

The Edwardian Garden Party held in the field behind Hallwater House
with Hallwater Farm House in centre background.

Soldiers and sailor staging a recruiting campaign outside 'The Plough' during
the First World War (1914-1918).

Endon Band.

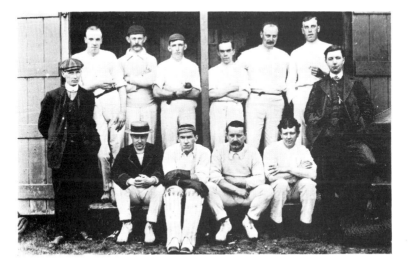

Endon Cricket Club, early 1900's.

Outside 'The Black Horse', looking towards Leek, after the floods of 1927.

A scene in the village after the floods of 1927.

and 56 females: one of these schools is endowed for the instruction of six males: with this exception, all the children are instructed at the expense of their parents. Two Sunday schools, supported by voluntary contributions, are attended by 122 males and 94 females.'⁵

Concerning the 'dwelling house and schoolroom at Endon built in 1759' a new scheme was drawn up by the County Court held at Leek on 18th May 1855. It was an attempt to provide new regulations for the charity which supported the Endon Parochial School as it was now to be called. On the first of June 1855 the trustees were summoned to hear details of the new regulations at the Red Lion Inn at Leek. On the 15th of June they met. Those in attendance were the Reverend Daniel Turner, John Cross, William Orford, Samuel Young, Charles Heaton, junior and James Yates. The scheme was finally approved on 20th July 1855. The school house and master's house were to be maintained by the Trustees. The school was to be 'open to the children of all resident inhabitants of the township or chapelry of Endon between the ages of six and sixteen years who shall apply at the school for admission.'⁶ School pence charges ranging from twopence to eightpence per week were approved and the trustees were to receive income from the original endowments. Records showing the state of the school under the new scheme are few and it would seem that a decline had set in. The new headmaster's report in 1871 suggested that there were only dame and private schools for the children, whom he regarded as backward.⁷ Other sources suggest there had been a shortage of funds. However, the 1870 Education Act gave the denominations six months in which to bring their schools up to standard.

In 1871 a 'Return relating to elementary education (civil parishes)' shows Endon chapelry, Longsdon and Stanley with a population of 1,300 and a rateable value of £9,678.⁸ In operation, before the Act of 1870 there were:

Private School	1
Adventure Schools	2

The report continues that two schools were in the course of being supplied and that the amount of accommodation which existed 'or is being provided at the rate of 10 square feet per child' was:

Public Schools (elementary)	163
Private Schools	32
Adventure Schools	46

The schools functioning prior to the opening of the public elementary school on 9th October 1871 were:

Church of England or National School Society   1

British and Foreign School Society   ... —

Wesleyan School Society 1

Of no religious body   1

The dame schools which existed during this century and which a headmaster some years later was to regard with some distaste were carried on by Miss Heaton at Brown Edge, Mrs. Critchlow in Endon village, and Mrs. Bowden at Plough Bank.

In 1880 Kelly's Directory records a private school run by Mrs. Elizabeth Jane Bailey and in 1892 there is one run by Miss Charlotte Critchlow.

Following the 1870 Education Act, which to some extent set up free elementary education for all who wished to take advantage of it, the school re-opened as a public elementary school and it occupied the small plot of land below the church, now used as a car park. The dimensions were:

Main room	33′ × 15′ × 13′
Class room	22′ × 17′ × 13′
Infants room	22′ × 15′ × 13′[9]

The area of ground was one thousand, two hundred and sixty square yards, of which the playground occupied eight hundred and sixty square yards.

This building occupied the site of the old Free School, which by this time had disappeared from the educational scene. A list of benefactions written at the time recites how the bequests made by John Smith, Thomas Sherratt and William Sherratt 'should pay the schoolmaster . . . for the instruction of as many children as they could agree for', but adds in brackets, 'This has *not* been paid since (space) up to this January 1871.' Other evidence would suggest that the payments ceased about 1867.

The 'new' school still known as Endon Parochial was opened for scholars on the 9th October 1871, but not without some persuasive action by the Reverend James Badnall and the schoolmaster, who together toured the village recruiting children for the opening. The interest shown in parochial schools was not only a matter for the Church. Under the 1879 Act, ad hoc school boards could be set up, usually at a higher rate cost to the parishioners, causing some individual ratepayers to complain. Endon never had a Board School, but the effects of opening a parochial school at Bagnall in 1874 caused the headmaster to report a falling off in numbers of children at Endon because 'they were living under the influence of the School Board of that District.' The Board concerned was the Stoke School Board which covered a vast area, including Bagnall. The school at Bagnall was opened and was dedicated by the Reverend Stammer, Archdeacon of Stoke.

School fees were to be paid, generally at one penny per week if the children used a slate. If the school provided paper then the fees were two pence per week. At Stanley, the long building which is now part of the Mission bears the initials T.E.H.C., A.D. 1812. It formed part of the farm of Mr. Thomas Edward Hope Cooper, and was used originally as a barn. It was converted into a school and the village schoolmistress was Miss Emma Lucas. In October 1875, she married the headmaster of Endon Parochial School, Mr. John Chadwick.

The early log books of Endon School start in October 1871, and the first entry appears as follows:

'The above school was opened on Monday the 9th of October 1871 under the charge of Mr. John Chadwick late assistant master of the Blue Coat School, Walsall.

The number at the opening was good, but this may be accounted for in part from the fact that the Reverend James Badnall, Vicar, accompanied by the Master, previous to the opening, visited a number of the parents in the parish. There is every prospect of this being a good school.

October 13, 1871   *Signed* Thomas Heaton
                                                              Hon. Sec.'

Mr. John Chadwick followed with his first report:

'I the undersigned commenced duties in the above school on Monday, 9th October 1871, when I admitted forty children which I considered good and which may be accounted for from the reason stated above (report by Thomas Heaton).

The admission did not occupy very long, as I had previously obtained particulars in many cases from the parents. The classifying of course is a longer task. The children are in a very backward state as they have only been able to attend dame schools. Three boys who had been to a commercial school were tolerably well up. Previous to the opening I drew up a timetable in lead pencil, leaving it thus for a few days in order to see how it would act. The Reverend James Badnall, Vicar, very kindly assisted in the scripture lesson. The sewing has been voluntarily undertaken by the two ladies, Mrs. Badnall and Mrs. Smith.

Signed John Chadwick

13th October 1871"

The school in 1871 was much affected by the local events, thus one reads of attendance being adversely affected by Endon Wakes and on another occasion the children were given a holiday because the schoolroom was to be used for the Harvest Festival Tea. In March 1872, several children were absent 'for agricultural purposes', whilst during the last week in May the attendance was 'very low indeed' because many children were taking part in the traditional welldressing celebrations.

On August 2nd of that year, the children returned 'rather wild' after the summer break. The attendance was low because some children were 'helping with the harvest, much of which still remains to be gathered.'

In February 1873 the headmaster gave a holiday on arrival at school when he found only one child present. 'The state of the weather was extremely severe', says the head. The school bell had its place in village life. The head entered in his log book, 'The bell has been re-hung in the bell tower after being out of order for six months, and thus a great deal of late coming will be doubtless avoided.'

The 1880s were most marked for the series of epidemics which swept the area. March 3rd 1882, the head reported, 'Re-opened the school after being closed (by Medical Authority) for a period of five weeks on account of a local epidemic of scarlet fever.' Even as late as March 24th, he reported that 'Attendance still poor owing to many children still away with the Fever.' April 21st saw yet another entry relating to the same outbreak. It read, 'There has been another outbreak of scarlet fever in the village this week.'

Two years later, in April 1884, the school was faced with another outbreak. This time it was measles, and in 1889 measles had reached epidemic proportions when the head logged, 'The school was closed by order of the Sanitary Authority because of a serious epidemic of measles, seventy per cent. of the children were away.'

In spite of this the children found time to sing. A list of the songs taught in 1882 includes:

Now is the month of Maying
The Violet
Murmur gentle lyre
Farmer John
O come, come away
The old house by the Lindens
Christmas Song, and
God save the Queen.

On matters educational, the local attendance committee discussed the 'injurious effect of the dame schools in the neighbourhood,' but the attendance officer said he was 'powerless to act in the matter.'

With the passing of the 1880 Education Act and the introduction of compulsory education, an effort was made to reduce the stressful situation which had developed as a result of payment results. H.M.I. were warned against hurried annual examination, and a new system of grading was introduced giving greater power to inspectors to grade schools, as 'Fair, good or excellent'. The merit grant depended upon the classification awarded and the over-pressure increased. In Endon School, the consequences of such a system were to be seen. They are contained in a report in the Leek Post and Times of June 6th 1885 under the heading of 'Over-pressure':

'We regret to state that Mr. Spencer Stevenson, schoolmaster of Endon has lost his reason, presumably from over-pressure consequent upon preparation for the forthcoming examination. We trust the terrible visitation will prove but a temporary affliction.'

Happily it did and Mr. Stevenson continued at the school until December 1896, thus completing a service of twenty-one years at Endon School. Payments to schools made as a result of examination (payment by results) were abolished in 1895.

On the 18th of January 1922 the following entry appeared. 'today completes the twenty-fifth year of service of the headteacher, Mr. T. Coleman.' This entry was made by the head himself, and suggests that he joined the school as headteacher in 1897. Mr. J. Coleman was father of the railway engineer, T. F. Coleman, whose successful career with 'The Knotty' and at Derby is described elsewhere in this book.

197

On October 26th the school closed until November 1st, but not before a presentation was made to Mr. Coleman from the scholars in the presence of the managers and parents. After the break the new headmaster, Mr. Edward Baker, began his career at Endon.

The earliest part of 1922, however, was not without incident. On the day he recorded his twenty-five years in the school, Mr. Coleman also said that there were only nineteen children present, that the ink was frozen in the pots and that it was impossible for the children to use their pens because they were never warm. In January 1924 the new head was also recording severe weather 'with many children sick with chickenpox.' He states, 'this morning I spent three-quarters of an hour stoving the school on account of sickness', presumably of the caretaker. Undeterred by it all he continues, 'Hymns and prayers were taken in the schoolyard at 9.02 a.m.'

Shrove Tuesday, February 28th 1922 seems to have been a big day. It is recorded that there was a 'whole holiday for Princess Mary's wedding day.' The arrival of a piano at the school on the 18th November caused the head to state that it 'had been obtained on the results of social work and events in the parish room by the Ladies' Working Party and the Girls' Friendly Society.'

Mr. Baker's period as headmaster came to a tragic end as a result of an accident in which he was knocked down by a motor cycle on the 11th June 1928. He sustained injuries from which he died.

The new headmaster was Mr. A. Evans, of Brown Edge and it was soon apparent to him that the buildings were too small for a village steadily increasing in size. A modern senior school was opened near the main Leek to Stoke roadway in 1939.

After the passing of the 1944 Education Act, this became the Endon secondary school, and it received children between the ages of 11-16.

The old parochial school was replaced in 1963 by a modern structure to be known as Endon St. Luke's Church of England Primary School. It cost £35,000 and had accommodation for one hundred and twenty children. The first headmaster was Mr. R. E. Biddulph. Endon Hall School was opened as a county primary in 1969, with Mr. F. Ballington as headmaster. He had previously been at Bagnall school which about this time was burned down and the headmaster and his pupils were accommodated at Endon Hall school.

The fate of the old building was sealed when it became apparent that the foundations were moving slowly and were unsafe. It was decided to demolish it in 1964, but ownership of the building had passed to the County Council, and the Endon Parochial Church Council was invited to purchase it back. A report of April 8th 1965 reads, 'One shilling buys a village school. Endon's old village school next to the parish church has been sold, for the price of one shilling.'⁰ The General Education Sub-committee reported that following a decision last October to ask the Department of Education and Science for advice as to the proceeds of the sale of the former school, the Department had stated that the premises were "in such a plight" that it was necessary to pull them down.

It was found that the cost of doing this would exceed the value of the site.

Endon Parochial Church Council, however, preferred to take over, and it was thought the best method of enabling them to do so was to convey the place to them for one shilling. The sub-committee reported that the local Education Authority was therefore now entitled to receive the sum of one shilling and that perhaps it might be desirable from an accountancy point of view that it should be received.

If so it would be credited to the same account as the proceeds of other sales. The sub-committee therefore recommended to Thursday's meeting that the County Council should accept the shilling from Endon Parochial Church Council "being the proceeds of the sale of the old school buildings".'

Connections between Endon and Leek have remained in education since the founding of Leek Grammar School in 1712. Children have attended schools there throughout the period. However, as we have seen elsewhere in this work, some attended the endowed school at Newcastle, and others turned to the developing centres of education in the pottery towns in more recent times.

Perhaps the best way to conclude this account of education in Endon is to quote the report in religious instruction at Endon school mixed department almost fifty years ago, on 6th July 1926:

'I am very glad to have made personal acquaintaince with this school and to have seen for myself the excellent work that is going on there.

The teaching is sound and thorough, the interest, responsiveness and behaviour of the scholars are splendid. A first rate school.

(Signed) Ernest Deacon
                Organising Diocesan Inspector for
                the Stoke Archdeaconry.'

Headmaster/Headmistresses at Endon Parochial School between 1871 and 1974

John Chadwick	1 October 1871—December 1875
Spencer Stevenson	10 December 1875—December 1896
J. H. Coleman	18 January 1897—31 October 1922
E. Baker	1 November 1922—11 June 1928
A. Evans	11 June 1928—26 February 1937
Miss D. V. Williams	1 March 1937—31 August 1941
Mrs. Anne Latham	10 November 1941—31 August 1947
Mrs. M. A. Ashton (temporary)	9 September 1947—31 December 1947
Miss G. Pointon	6 January 1948—31 December 1949
Mr. C. Williams	10 January 1950—April 1952
Mr. R. E. Biddulph	April 1952—

Endon Secondary School was opened on April 17th, 1939 with 242 children but with official accommodation for 360. The title Endon Secondary School was adopted in 1963. Headteachers since its opening are:

Mr. G.E.Y.Ingley, B.Sc.	17 April 1939—31 August 1947
Mr. S.Edwards	11 September 1947—31 August 1963
Mr. J. W. Hawley, B.A.	1 September 1963—31 August 1970
Mr. P. Durber, B.Sc.	1 September 1970—

St. Anne's Church of England Schools

A tythe map of Norton-in-the-Moors for the late 1830s suggests that there was a school in operation in the village of Brown Edge at that time. It was situated near to Little Stone House Farm, and was probably the place where the early Church of England services were held before St. Anne's Church was built in 1844. In 1851 Sarah Beech was living at the school and is shown as a schoolteacher in the census returns of that year. The school had been formally opened a few years before at a cost of £450 and under endowments made by Hugh Henshall Williamson of Knypersley, the children were to be educated according to the tenets of the Church of England. Later more land was purchased and an Infants School, together with a cottage for the schoolmistress, was purchased by the same Mr. Williamson. A system of payment by results was introduced in 1862 and log books were required to be kept. However, at Brown Edge no such books are available until 1870, the date of the famous 'compulsory' education act, when Mr. and Mrs. John Jones were at school. They remained until 1872 when they were succeeded by Mr. and Mrs. W. F. Pollard who arrived in April. By June the new man could not agree with the vicar about the school pence paid by the children and in spite of a visit to Robert Heath at Greenway Bank, he was obliged to resign before the end of the summer. In September, Mr. F. R. Wilkinson took over the school which had one hundred children on roll, and a staff of two, Miss Hannah Mollart, pupil teacher, and John Phillips, the monitor. During the winter the poor attendance at the school was caused by a heavy fall of snow in December. In January 1873 the school pence was raised from two to three pence, and several parents refused to pay. An inspector's visit showed that the children were backward in reading, spelling and arithmetic 'but order is good and the present master is working hard.'[11] The experiment of opening the school in the evening was not a success since only two boys turned up, but sucess of another kind was rewarded. When Robert Heath was elected Member of Parliament for Stoke-on-Trent, the master took the school children to Greenway Bank to congratulate the new M.P. on his election. The visits to Greenway Bank became regular affairs, often the children were accompanied by the Brown Edge Band.

In 1875 the headmaster recorded that 'several large boys presented themselves at school because they were out of work as a result of the miners' strike', but the report of that year shows that the school was not as efficient as it was a year ago. School pence was a problem. Because of the poor state of work at the colleries, where some men were only working two days per week, it was difficult for families to pay the money required for schooling. Another indication of the poverty at this time is shown in an entry where the head states that he received two weeks' supply of chalk sufficient to cover the period of the vicar's holiday. The masters' salaries at this time were £72 per year. By 1876 the school received new desks and reference is made to a School Attendance Officer, the first. Digging potatoes, 'souling', dancing at the Endon well-dressing, Burslem Wakes, scarlet fever and measles were occasions for absence from school. Under the new head, discipline steadily improved and he tells how the boy he had had to cane two weeks previously had now become one of his most obedient boys.

By September 1886, the average attendance at the school was one hundred and ninety-nine, and the children 'pay their school pence, but very indifferently.' In 1892, when the attendance had risen to two hundred and twenty-eight, a shed was erected where 'the girls could wash their hands, a much-needed addition.' 1894 saw a smallpox outbreak at Ridgway and pupils from that area were told not to attend school. At the turn of the century Robert Heath, a school manager, moved to Biddulph Grange, and a presentation was made to him, and at the same time an inspector complained in his report that there was no supply of water on the premises, either for lavatories or for drinking purposes. In 1901 a heavy snow fall caused the school to be closed, and in 1902 three children of one family returned to school after an absence of eight months, necessitated by diptheria. Combined with nature walks to Rudyard and Mow Cop, the school celebrated the Coronation of Edward VII and the good attendance of the two hundred and sixty-three children at the school earned them a half-holiday.

The school was by this time overcrowed and the headmaster was driven to state 'Teaching at all times is difficult on account of the size of the classes and the crowded state of desks.' He also complained about lavatories and the lack of a heating system, especially in cold weather. Extensions were completed in 1909, and by 1911 the composition of the school was as follows:

Mr. William Jones
Mrs. Jones

Miss Knowles	Class I	accommodating	95	children
Mr. Walter Jones	Class II	,,	58	,,
Miss Pickford	Class III	,,	38	,,
Mrs. Johnson	Class IV	,,	46	,,
Miss Procter	Class V	,,	45	,,

In July 1911, the school was closed for five weeks by order of the sanitary inspector because of the poor state of the closets, but afterwards the building was said to be much improved apart from the heating system. The school depended entirely on open fires, so that all the rooms were unevenly heated, while the main room fifty feet long was dependent on one open fire situated at one end of the room. The other end of the room opened on to a long and draughty corridor. So the school continued with improvements in the fabric, catering for the children of Brown Edge until 1939. In this year the school became a county primary school and the senior children went to the modern school at Endon.

Headmasters at St. Anne's Large School

George Holloway	1845—1860
John Jones	1860—27 March 1872
W. F. Pollard	28 March 1872—September 1872
F. R. Wilkinson	30 September 1872—June 1874
William Bott	June 1874—March 1876
Thomas Roscoe	April 1876—15 December 1879
W. R. Warren	5 January 1880—1 April 1880
William Jones	19 April 1880—31 March 1920
Walter J. Jones	2 April 1920—18 December 1938
R. Jennings	28 March 1939—24 July 1944
Charles Eric Fisher	1 May 1945—April 1968
P. B. Owen	1968—September 1971
John Ellis	31 September 1971—

References

[1] Griffith, G.: 'The Free School and Endowments of Staffordshire', 1860, p. 538.

[2] Articles of Enquiry, Rev. E. Tompkinson 1751 (Endon), Joint Record Office, Lichfield (1636-1756), B/V/3.

[3] Leek Parish Records, Vestry Minutes.

[4] Enumeration Sheets, Census Return 1851, Endon.

[5] Charity Commissioners Report 1833. Endon Chapelry and the townships of Longsdon and Stanley, C.R.O., Stafford.

[6] Endowed School, printed report, Vol. XIII, p. 395.

[7] Endon Parochial School Log Books, 1871.

[8] Return relating to Elementary Education (civil parishes) 1871, C.R.O., Stafford.

[9] Endon Parochial School Log Books 1871.

[10] The Evening Sentinel, April 8, 1965.

[11] St. Anne's, Brown Edge, Church of England Schools Log Books.

Chapter XII

WELL-DRESSING

---

*'They have also a custom in this county . . . of adorning their wells
with boughs and flowers: this it seems they do too at all gospel places
whether wells, trees or hills: which being now observed only for
decency and custom sake is innocent enough . . . it was usual to pay
this respect to such wells as were eminent for cureing distempers, on
the saints day whose name the well bore, diverting themselves with
cakes and ale, and a little music and dancing, which, whilst within
these bounds was also innocent recreation.'*

Robert Plot, ch. 8, para 89[1], 1686
The Natural History of Staffordshire.

So reads an account of well-dressing in Staffordshire in the seventeenth century. But well-dressing was a commonplace old English custom practised more widely than it is today. Little documentary or literary evidence is available on well-dressing, but the
delights of decorating a well and enjoying the accompanying dances
and celebrations have been handed from generation to generation,
particularly in Endon. To some of the villagers it is the continuation
of an ancient rite which is lost in mystical and biblical connection. To
others it is a delightful activity adopted in the early and mid-nineteenth century by several local gentlemen who took advantage of the
occasion when Mr. Thomas Heaton arranged for a new stone structure
to be built at a point in the centre of the village. This was more convenient than the natural site of the spring in the field above. Some
effort has been made here to present both the traditional view which
to some extent is confirmed by Plot, and the more utilitarian view that
the event was one which grew up in more recent times. To both,
however, the most significant thing is the date, May 29th, Oak Apple
Day. This date was celebrated in many villages in Staffordshire after
the escape of King Charles II by hiding in an oak tree.

The date also has some significance in that it is the date on which
the monachy was restored in England in 1660. To come nearer home

and perhaps to account for Endon's part in the celebrations on this date, a terrier of the early eighteenth century awards a noble of 6/8d (six shillings and eightpence) to the minister to preach a sermon on Oak Apple Day. It has been the usual practice for the well-dressing celebrations to begin with a service in St. Luke's Parish Church at which, particularly in the last century, a sermon was expected, and delivered.

The connection between the Oak Apple Day celebrations in the restoration of the monarchy, the preaching of a sermon, the bequeathing of money for payment for doing so, and the date of the present day well-dressing must be accepted. Whether it is connected with the ancient traditions, however, is open to conjecture. It seems a far cry from the claim that 'water is the oldest and most widely diffused of the symbols of creative power known to mankind', or that 'it has received the homage of philosophers and poets' to the one positive fact we do know, that in 1845 a stone monument was erected by Mr. Thomas Heaton a local landowner, at a spot below a point in the field where villagers used to collect water. The modernists' view is that this was built to make water collection easier. Water from the spring was piped to the trough. Villagers were so delighted with the extra facility that it was decided, spontaneously, to celebrate the event. The story is recounted by Mr. Alfred Williamson,[2] the great-grandson of the blacksmith at the time, Thomas Walker, telling how Philip Rogers, shoemaker (cord wainer), Joshua Stubbs, carpenter, and Thomas Gratton the tailor, along with Walker procured 'homemade pikelets soaked in butter, bread and butter, cured ham and other good things; a cup of tea with cream if desired and rum to celebrate the first "dressing".' He also recalls that 'much merry making followed.' Earlier in the day, May 29th, Mr. Philip Rogers, the cordwainer and several other villagers dressed the well with oakleaves, boughs and flowers. This annual dressing of the superstructure of the trough and the attendant celebrations continued so that in 1853 the Staffordshire Advertiser could describe how 'the whole party returned to the well . . . and the company partook of the tea and plum cake.'

However, after the church service the following year, the party returned to the well and then to a field close by, which had been prepared with terraces suitable for dancing.

On this occasion the Staffordshire Advertiser reported the events as follows:

'The 29th May falling this year on a Sunday, this annual festivity which, with every succeeding year becomes increasingly interesting and attracts an augmented number of visitors was held on Monday afternoon 30 May.

The well was very tastefully decorated with flowers in which were executed "Glory to God in the Highest" and "Thanks to the Donor" with "V.R." the Crown, and "The Staffordshire Knot". Over the decorated well floated the flags of all nations and upon several buildings near were hoisted streamers of different colours gaily floating in the breeze.

Soon after 2.00 p.m. a procession was formed and headed by the village band, climbed the hill to the church where prayers were read and the appropriate sermon delivered by the Reverend Daniel Turner.

The procession was reformed and returned to the well where a hymn was sung by the assembly, who then adjourned to a field close by of Mr. Charles Heaton and partook of an excellent tea served in a marquee obtained for the occasion.

Afterwards the village band took their station at the head of a part of the field which had been levelled for the purpose by Thomas Heaton and the first country dance was led by Mr. Thomas Heaton and Mrs. Turner the lady of the incumbent.

The dancing was kept up with both spirit and order until past nine o'clock in the evening.

The children in the afternoon under the leadership of the Parish Clerk enjoyed games of football and prison bars, running and bag races.

Before the gathering dispersed some rounds of lusty cheers were given for Mr. Thomas Heaton, The Ladies, The Committee (Messrs. Hand, Clementson and Walker) and their lady assistants. Also to Mr. Richard Heaton and the "Strangers" and finally to our next merry meeting.

There were a goodly number of visitors from the Potteries and Leek, and the assembly on the whole not less than 400 persons.'

About this time decoration of the well with boughs and leaves was discontinued and flower petals were set in clay on a wooden frame to make a design which was changed annually. The originator of the idea of floral decoration is generally believed to be Mr. Hand, the village policeman, and was probably copied from other well-dressing festivals, possibly in Derbyshire. William Hand continued the work of decorating the well and in 1870 was awarded a testimonial for his services.

When the Reverend James Badnall became vicar of Endon in 1865 he quickly entered into the well-dressing activities and introduced the notion of a May Queen and her attendants. The Queen has variously been carried in a chair, on the back of a pony, in a carriage and pair (1904-1941) and since then in a motor car. The Queen was, and still is, entertained by twelve girls who dance round the Maypole wearing hats, white frocks with frills and sashes, six of the girls wearing their sashes in the boys' fashion.

In 1868 it was decided that there should be some control of this increasingly popular event, and a trust was formed so that the proceeds could be put to use in the village.

Deeds were drawn up and the following were elected as trustees:

Thomas Heaton, Gentleman of Endon
Rev. James Badnall, Vicar of St. Luke's, Endon
Robert Cleminson, Land Agent of Endon
Rev. Joseph Dodd of Hampton Poyle, Oxford
George Foster, Commission Agent of Endon
James Hall, Tanner of Endon
Richard Heaton, Gentleman of Endon
Thomas Hulme, Gentleman of Endon
William Orford, Landowner of Manchester
Joseph Pinder, Earthenware Manufacturer of Endon
Thomas Smith, Yeoman of Endon
Benjamin Yardley, Yeoman of Stanley.

The trustees were also responsible for the protection of the water which was so precious to the people of the village, and the document 'allows the inhabitants of the village of Endon aforesaid and neighbourhood the free uninterrupted use of the said well but only for their own private and individual use and subject thereto Unto Trust that the said Trustees on the 29th May in every year continue to allow the said Well to be decorated or dressed in decoration in the accustom ways and observance.' The beneficiaries of the money raised were to be the 'Sunday Schools of the Established Church, The Wesleyan Chapel and the Purchase and Distribution of Bread among the poor on the 21st December to take place in the vestry.' Some of the proceeds were

ENDON
WELL-DRESSING

FESTIVAL (75th Anniversary).

This Popular and Well-known VILLAGE 'ESTIVAL will this year be celebrated on

SATURDAY & MONDAY,
MAY 29th and 31st, 1920.

The first day's proceedings will commence with

A Thanksgiving Service with Address in the Parish Church at 2-15 p.m.

AFTER DIVINE SERVICE THE

Leek National Reserve Band will head the Procession to the Village Well,

WHICH WILL BE FLORALLY DECORATED FROM DESIGNS BY L. & H. GOFF.

THE MAYPOLE DANCE

WILL BE CARRIED OUT UNDER THE DIRECTION OF Mr. T. H. COLEMAN.

THE QUEEN OF THE MAY (Miss Annie Roddis Platt)

(Attended by her Maids of Honour will be Crowned in the Well-Dressing Field at 3-30 p.m. and the MAY DANCE will immediately follow. The Dance will be repeated at 6-40, and on Monday at 4 p.m. and 6-40 p.m.

OPEN SPORTS

WILL BE CARRIED OUT EACH DAY.   NO ENTRANCE FEES   Programmes on application after May 10th

THE BAND WILL PLAY SELECTIONS AND FOR

DANCING .. on .. Both Days

Admission to the Ground: Adults 1/-, 3d. Tax; Children 6d. 2d. Tax.

NO PASS-OUT CHECKS GIVEN AFTER 7 p.m

TEA and other REFRESHMENTS at Reasonable Charges.   NO HAWKERS ALLOWED ON THE GROUND   NOTE. The Well will be covered Sunday, May 30th

Trains and Buses at frequent intervals.   See Time Tables.

Rev. J. S. MORRIS, Chairman of the Committee.   W. OWEN, Vice-Chairman.
T. H. COLEMAN, Secretary.

Well-Dressing Poster, 1920.

A typical modern 'dressing' designed by Mr. Percy Williamson and prepared by a team of some six villagers. Note the girth of the tree in the background and compare with the illustration showing Wesley Place.

Maypole Dancing, 1910.

also 'for the general use and benefit of the Free Grammar School at Endon.' To show their concern for the well-being of the public image of Endon, the trustees accepted the following responsibility, 'And it is hereby declared that the said Trustees shall as far as they can discountenance all excessive drinking and immorality in connection with the dressing of the said Well, and any Gala of Festivities thereto it being the wish of Thomas Heaton in the Grant intended to be hereby made by him to provide innocent recreation and enjoyment for the inhabitants of the village of Endon without giving encouragement to any act of intemperance or vice.'[4]

By 1872 the event was held in such high esteem by the residents of North Staffordshire, that the Staffordshire Advertiser should carry the following report:

Endon Well-dressing, May 29th, 1872

'On Wednesday this popular and interesting fete—the twenty-eighth of its kind—took place, but its success, so far as the enjoyment of visitors was concerned, was greatly marred by the very wet weather which prevailed. In the morning there were some faint hopes that the clouds, which rolled heavily about, and which portended pluvial discomforts to pleasurists, would clear away, and that a bright and pleasant afternoon similar to that of Tuesday, would follow. Hundreds were therefore allured to Endon by the announced attractions of the day, and at one o'clock, the time the proceedings were announced to commence, a goodly company had assembled. The train from Leek was filled, and the afternoon train from Stoke—and which had a double complement of carriages—was filled, despite the fact that rain had already poured down, and the prospects of the day as to the weather were anything but hopeful. It took nearly an hour to get from Hanley to Endon, perhaps because the train was so heavily freighted. The arrangements for the fete were, as usual, directed by the Reverend James Badnall, vicar, and were admirable in character, the entertainments being varied to suit all tastes. As usual prior to the al fresco enjoyments of the day, there was a service at Endon Church. The service was plain, short and enjoyable. The building was nicely decorated; if flowers were less profuse than in some former years, there was better taste shown in the arrangements. The choicest bit of adornment was the rear of the communion table, where in a bedding of moss were some beautiful fuschia, lily and pansy blooms, and springing up from their midst were three vases of rich conservatory flowers. In a groundwork of moss appeared the words, formed with flowers, "With thee is the well of life". Within the altar rails was a festooning formed of the passion flower. The pulpit was clothed with a floral panelling, the lectern was neatly enwreathed with ferns and flowers, and the font was chapleted with a few choice flowers with fern droopings and flower garlanding down to the base. The window sills bore a deep bedding of moss, brightened with flowers. At the service the church was crowded. Prayers and the lessons were read by the Reverend J. Badnall, and the sermon was preached by the Reverend J. T. Jeffcock, Vicar of Wolstanton. His text was 26th chapter of Genesis, 19th verse: "And Isaac's servants digged in the valley and found there a well of springing water." The sermon was very appropriate, and in some allusions to the festal character of the day, the preacher spoke of the necessity for, and advantages of recreation, when it was of the right kind. He liked the idea of having a religious service to precede the festivities of the day, and concluded with some practical applications arising out of the text. At the close of the service a procession was formed in the following order: the village band, banner of the diocese; Endon, Stanley and Longsdon Church Sunday School scholars; the Churchwardens, the Vicar and Preacher of the day; Endon, Stanley and Longsdon Church Choirs; the Committee, Parishioners, and Visitors. The company marched to the village fountain, where a hymn was sung. The decorations at the fountain were ornate; a screen formed of flowers, the daisy-bud and May flower blooms forming the chief ground, rose up to a considerable height, the whole forming a complete embossment of flowers. Interworked were the royal arms of England, Staffordshire knots, etc. In the centre were the words "The water saw thee, O God". Another sentence, worked in with pretty effect was, "He only is my rock". The lower well was also decorated, the devices being neat and effective. Worked in flowers were the words "Seek ye after God". In the gala field there were attractions of the usual kind, dancing on the terraces being the chief enjoyment. For those who wanted something more sensational there was an exhibition, said to contain the correct portraits of Mr. and Mrs. Horry. The pleasant old English custom of dancing round the Maypole was revived, and excited much interest. A pole was erected in one of the terraces; it was crowned with a garland of oak leaves, evergreens and flowers. A dozen girls dressed in white, with coloured sashes, and wearing hats, uniformly decked with a wreath of flowers, each took hold of one of the red or green ribbons which hung from the pole, and a pretty dance was gone through, under the direction of the Rev. James Badnall. Miss Lily Tennant was the May Queen. After the dances, several melodies were sung. The general amusements were then engaged in, and were kept up, notwithstanding the rain which began to prove very troublesome. A good tea was provided at ninepence each, and there were other refreshments obtainable. Although the day was so inauspicious, the attendance was considered larger than last year. The collection at the church was in aid of the Endon augmentation fund, and the proceeds from the fete go in the main towards the new schools, a surplus being reserved to purchase bread and coals for distribution amongst the poor of the parish at Christmas.'[5]

The expenditure of 1872 is shown in the following statement produced by the Committee:

ENDON WELL-DRESSING 1872

    Attendance: 2,271
    Taking: £56.15.6d.

    Some payments made:

Hire of four (4) policemen and fares from Leek ...	£1	2	0d
Hire of Endon Brass Band	£4	0	0d
Advertising—Staffs. Sentinel		13	0d
Leek Times		10	9d
Workmen's wages at 3/- a day	£7	8	9d
Purchase of 106 x 2½'' land drain, pipes and a new gate		3	5d
Best Beer for Committee and Workman at 2/- gall.	£3	11	0d
Tea for village children		10	6d[6]

On June 6th 1889 the Leek Post and Times carried the following report,

'The well-dressing celebrated its forty-fourth anniversary this year. It is an imitation of that at Tissington which is held on the same day and is the oldest known. The first celebration was held nearly fifty years ago at the village smithy when the late Mr. Baddeley and Mr. Walker acted Secretary and Treasurer. The feast was free to the old villagers and 'pikelets' were figured in the menu.'

Besides Mr. W. Hand, many eminent artists have designed and helped to decorate the well including Mr. LeRoy a pottery artist in 1880, and Mr. William Herbert Foster. Others were local villagers such as Mr. J. Thorley, Mr. Chas. Stubbs, Mr. James Hall, Mrs. Horry and Mr. E. A. Bagley. During the thirty-five years up to 1970 Mr. Percy Williamson, a farmer of Endon, was responsible for the dressing, which earned him the respect of many thousands of people who came each year to see the well he had designed and decorated.

In the year 1876 the P.O. Directory said of Endon, 'Every 29th of May (Restoration Day) a curious custom is carried on in this parish of "Dressing the Well" with flowers and flags, it is observed as a holiday, a service is held in church, and strangers from a distance come in large numbers.'

Kelly's directory of 1880 referred to the old English custom of dancing round the Maypole and the fact that the proceeds of the festival were devoted to the school fund, and the supplying of bread and coal to the poor.

In 1892 Kelly's directory described it as 'an ancient local custom'. However, there is little documentary evidence of the custom before 1845 though experts in well-dressing folk-lore are quick to point out that this is a common feature in well-dressing circles.

Down to the present the tradition continues as witnessed by an account dated May 1973 in the Leek Post and Times and headed, 'The most spectacular Endon Well-dressing in living memory.

The festivities got off to a good start last Wednesday evening when members of the Well-dressing Committee gathered round the well in Victorian and Edwardian costume, and then paraded to the Black Horse Hotel for an evening in the style of "The good old days".[7]

A village poet, however, sees the event differently and has recorded his impressions of the occasion in the following lines:

May, merry May, Darling of the year,
Kissed by the sunshine, dispelling dull care,
Thy blossoms adorn the hedgerow and tree,
And the lark to the Heavens sends its song winging free.

Sweet babbling brook that crosses the lane,
Fed by the Well, and swollen with rain,
Hurrying along without worry or care,
Not stopping to notice the Village, so fair.

The Well hard by, with flora adorned,
Fashioned by the Muse in His name that's mourned,
Giving thanks for His mercies and bounteous Grace
And lovingly spelt on the mossy-surface.

The trees on the hill side the Church so serene,
And from the Holy bower comes the sweet Village Queen
Attended by maidens all blushing and gay,
And dancing with joy on this merry May-day.

Endon, dear Village, rest contented and sure,
Thy ceremony sweet, for e'er will endure;
As long as thy children to their God remain true,
And let not false pleasure in their hearts imbue.

Reginald Twemlow.[8]

In recent years it has become clear that the Endon-style festival was originated by local village leaders, many acting in the belief that they were reviving an old custom. Its popularity has been helped by the proximity of the Pottery towns and the convenience of the railway. Today the motor car brings the visitors who never fail to admire the earthy cultural heritage of the Endon Well-dressing.

However, not all the sources of water supply received the same adulation as the trough and its superstructure. Some pumps were situated in remote farm yards, others were at odd places in the village. The Parish Council met on January 2nd 1912 and discussed the following point on their agenda: 'With reference to an interview with Mr. Adams, who declined to allow access to the source of the stream supplying the well opposite the Black Horse in the village unless the council could show him they had a right.'[9]

On February 14th of the same year the clerk reported to the Parish Council 'that he considered Mr. George Adams could not object to the Council repairing the supply to the well near the Black Horse.' On May 9th 1913 the Leek Rural District decided to put the well in order and to pay Mr. Adams the sum of one pound for trespass.

Since then the constitutional function of the parish pump has declined and there is no need for villagers to carry buckets of water into their homes. Today a well-organised piped system feeds the village and few people would consider a thanksgiving service for the supply of water appropriate. However, the traditional ceremony at the well continues, perhaps subconsciously allowing people in a modern village to recognise the privations of the past and nostalgically associate themselves with a national heritage from which they have been irreparably separated.

References

[1] Plot, Robert: 'The Natural History of Staffordshire', Chapter 8, para 89, 1686.

[2] Nettel, R.: 'An Englishman Makes Music', contains a detailed account by Alfred Williamson related to the well-dressing at Endon.

[3] Staffordshire Advertiser, June 1853. This is one of the earliest recorded accounts of the events at a well-dressing.

[4] Trustees agreement drawn up to regularise the responsibilities of the Trustees of the Endon Well-dressing—document in the possession of the Endon Well-dressing Committee.

[5] Staffordshire Advertiser, June 1872.

[6] Trustees' Minutes and Balance Sheet 1872. Endon Well-dressing Committee.

[7] Leek Post and Times, May 1973, Leek Office.

[8] Reginald Twemlow the retired village constable was also responsible for the tribute to Mr. Percy Williamson.

[9] Endon Parish Council Minutes, January 1912.

Chapter XIII

ENDON AND ITS NEIGHBOUR BROWN EDGE

E ndon is a small village situated on the side of a broad valley which drains into the river Churnet near Leek. Rising high behind the village is a ridge which has from time to time acted as a barrier to communication, and at others provided the village with a link to the West. On the ridge is situated Brown Edge, a small compact hamlet which owes its existence as the base for a community to the development of coalmining in the area. The village runs North to South adjacent to the old turnpike road, the highest point being nine hundred and twenty feet above sea level. The land on the West side of the village slopes gently down to the head waters of the river Trent, and is good agricultural land on which a number of older farms have survived. The land on the East side slopes down to the Endon valley. Many of the farms date from about 1600 AD, and bear such names as Judge-field, Tongue Lane, Stone House, Woodhouse, Fold Farm, Bank End, Annat's Farm, Morris House and Fernyhough. But from all accounts the higher land along the ridgeway was for centuries waste land. Thus the early community was situated at a watershed. Some parts were in Endon parish and others were in Norton-in-the-Moors.

In 1755 there were twenty-eight copyholders in the parish of Norton, and the following relate to Brown Edge:

Judgefield tenement	...	...	...	8/1
Tongue tenement	...	...	...	10/2
Stone House Farm	...	...	...	0/7
Bank End Farm	...	...	...	11/0
Singleton House Farm		...	...	12/10[1]

One of the best descriptions is to be found in White's Directory of Staffordshire for 1818, which describes the parish of Norton-in-the-Moors as cold and hilly.[2] In 1761 the population of Norton Parish was three hundred and twenty-nine, and included Smallthorne, Milton, Bemersley, and the hamlets of Baddeley Edge and Brown Edge. The description continues: 'the last two being commons on which several cottages had been built.' By 1828 the part of the village in Leek parish housed the following:

Joseph Mountford (Butcher)
Enoch Mountford (Tailor)
Richard Lowe (Blacksmith)
George Mountford (Labourer)
Nathan Frost (Labourer)

The early days of the hamlet were marked particularly by the absence of inns and beerhouses. In 1834 none are shown.[3]

The population grew when the small coal mines were worked at Ridgway and Norton, and more cottages were built on waste lands belonging to Lord Norton, often without permission. The lands had earlier belonged to Sir William Bowyer of Knypersley Hall, whose eldest daughter married and assumed the name of Bowyer Adderley and this family through C. B. Adderley became the principal owners of land in Brown Edge. Joseph Chadwick, a blacksmith, lived in a cottage behind the 'Lump of Coal Inn', but his smithy was situated on the turnpike road where the present day 'Roe Buck' public house stands.[4] Sampson Bratt moved from a cottage now the newsagents shop to a plot of land in Breach Road where he built a house, a shop and a bakehouse. At the Lane Ends part of the village, the Charlesworth families were well established as nailmakers. At this time the newly developing hamlet received a good deal of patronage and support from the local landowners who were also industrialists. The Adderleys have been mentioned already. Another benefactor was Mr. Hugh Henshall Williamson who lived at Greenway Bank Hall, Knypersley. His mother, Ann Brindley, widow of Brindley the Canal Builder married Robert Williamson an earthenware manufacturer in 1775.[5]

Of the five hundred and ninety-eight people in Brown Edge in 1851 some four hundred and thirty-one were living in that part of the village in Norton parish and one hundred and sixty-seven occupied some forty cottages in the area of the chapelry in Endon.[6]

In some respects the divided nature of the community in Brown Edge makes a thorough examination of the history almost impossible in a work which is primarily about Endon. Equal attention would of necessity have had to be paid to the records at Norton. This has not been possible. However, in order to make a comparison possible, some further details of Brown Edge in the nineteenth century help to show the contrast between the two communities, Endon and Brown Edge.

In 1851 the 'Holly Bush' was classified as a tavern, Joseph Bullock was the licensee there and John Dawson kept 'The Lump of Coal'. He was permitted to brew and sell beer, but Eliza Simcock at the 'Foaming Quart' could only sell beer. This was also the position of Richard Sheldon.[7]

The census of 1881 showed that since 1871[8] the population had increased by two hundred and twenty-seven to one thousand and six. Some idea of village life can be imagined when we consider that the nearest transport was at Stockton Brook Station or at Endon Station. The nearest shopping centre was at Burslem, some four miles away. There was no piped water supply to the village, most of the cottages having to 'fetch' a water supply from the well or from springs. Every cottage had a large water butt to collect the rain water. During the summer it was common for some of the wells to go dry and it became a familiar sight to see a barrel mounted on a platform between two wheels being pulled away from one of the springs still functioning.

The sewage system was of the most primitive. Waste water from the sink frequently ran down the open fields and 'night soil' was collected by a local farmer under contract from the parish council. Scarlet Fever, diptheria, measles, typhoid fever, and occasionally small-pox were diagnosed among the children, as instanced by the closures made at the school on account of an epidemic of one kind or another.

In 1894 local government reorganisation took place. The Norton-in-the-Moors parish council was to have fifteen members, seven from Norton, five from Milton and three representing Brown Edge. Mr. William Jones the headmaster of St. Anne's School was the clerk. The Leek Board of Guardians gave way to the Leek Rural District Council, a newly constituted body made up of representatives elected from each of the parishes in the area. This included Endon as well as Brown Edge.[9]

So the villagers moved into the twentieth century, virile, active, independent in attitude, but taking their pleasures seriously. Brown Edge was a village of contrasts, some drinking and brawling at the week-ends, others attending chapel, or church, on Sunday followed by a family 'get together' in the evening.

Shopkeepers:

Mrs. Sarah Berrisford in Sandy Lane

Mrs. Mary Simcock in Sandy Lane (also uncertified midwife)

Mr. Nathan Gibson at Hill Top

Mr. Joseph Bratt, Post Office in Breach Road, Sub-Postmaster also Road Surveyor

Mr. Sampson Bratt, Butcher in Sandy Lane

Mr. Thomas Sheldon, Butcher in Sandy Lane, next to 'Lump of Coal' Inn

Coal Dealers:

Mrs. Mary Simcock in Sandy Lane

Mr. William Wiltshaw in Sandy Lane

Coal Carters:

Mr. Henry Sherratt, St. Anne's Vale—conveying workmen's concessionary coal from the colliery to Brown Edge by horse and cart.

Mr. William Simcock, Sandy Lane

Clog Maker:

Mr. Daniel Holdcroft, Lane Ends, also boot and shoe repairer

Chips and Fish Fryer:

Mr. Daniel Tomkinson, Hough Hill

Builder:

Messrs. Simcock and Brooks, School Bank

Blacksmiths:

Mr. Ben Chadwick, Sandy Lane

Mr. Samuel Turner, Hill Top

Headmaster of St. Anne's 'Big' School:

Mr. William Jones, also Clerk to the Norton Parish Council

Mistress of St. Anne's Infants School:

Miss Alcock

Farmers:

Annats House Farm	Mrs. Finney
Ball Lane Farm	Mr. Hugh Carp
Bank End Farm	Mr. Arthur Goodwin
Fold Farm, Woodhouse Lane	Mr. Levi Heath
Woodhouse Lane Farm	Mr. Samuel Heath
Old Woodhouse Lane Farm	Mr. John Forrester

Singlet House Farm	Mr. William Bratt
Upper Stone House Farm	Mr. John Hodkinson
Lower Stone House Farm	Mr. Roland Shirley
Little Stone House Farm	Mr. Robert Lomas
Tongue Lane Farm	Mr. Jabez Heath
Judgefield Lane Farm	Mr. John Holdcroft
Knypersley Mill Farm	Mr. Daniel Lees, also miller
Lion's Paw Farm	Mr. George Lovatt
Brown Edge Farm	Mr. William Willshaw
Burnfields Farm	Mr. Thompson
Steign Fields Farm	Miss Hodkinson
Morris House Farm	Mr. Ainsworth
Broad Lane Farm	Mr. Dutton
Clay Lake Farm	Mr. Thomas Sheldon
Breach Farm	Mr. Alfred Bowyer
Fernyhough Farm	Mr. George Goodwin

Population of the village: 1090

Residences:

Pool Fields, Sandy Lane	Mrs. Heaton
Rock Cottage, off Breach Road	Mr. John Slater
Willfield House Willfield Lane	Mr. George Phillips
The Fenns, Moss Hill	Mrs. Sarah Homer

Parish Clerk:
Mr. James Basnett

Village Policeman:
Police Constable Lycett

Horticulture:
Scarlett Brothers, Sandy Lane
Mr. Leonard Bourne, Bank End

Tinster's Wood Isolation Hospital:
Matron Mrs. Mountford

Boarding School:
Miss Mary and Kate Heaton at Breach Road, Sandy Lane

Doctors:
Doctor Leys of Norton Lane Surgery, Norton
Doctor Aspinall of Ford Green House, Norton

Places of Worship:
 St. Anne's Church   Vicar Rev. W. G. Young
 Wesleyan Methodists, Sandy Lane Steward Mr. James Pointon
 Primitive Methodists, Chapel Lane Steward Mr. James Simcock
 Free Missioners on Hill Top Steward Mr. John Charlesworth

Public Houses:
 Holly Bush in High Lane   Mr. Francis Knowles
 New Inn in Sandy Lane   Mr. Enoch Pickford
 Lump of Coal in Sandy Lane Mr. Richard Sheldon
 Roebuck Inn in Sandy Lane Mr. William Lambsdale
 Foaming Quart Inn, Hough Hill Mrs. Charlotte Goodwin
 Colliers Arms on Hill Top   Mr. Daniel Holdcroft
 Rose and Crown on Hill Top Mr. John Sherratt

Brass Bands in Brown Edge

 The first record of a brass band in the village was in 1870, when the Brown Edge Brass Band played at Endon on the occasion of the local Friendly Society's Feast Day. It was again mentioned in 1874 when Mr. Robert Heath of Greenway Bank Hall, a school manager at St. Anne's Church invited the teachers and scholars from the two schools to his home, where he provided a tea and treat for them, and the Brown Edge Brass Band was in attendance.

 The Band played regularly for the Endon Friendly Society and for the Endon well-dressing ceremony during the latter part of the nineteenth century. The members of the band were mostly coal miners. In 1905 it is recorded that the band gave a series of concerts in the recently-erected Young Men's Christian Association hut on School Bank under their conductor Mr. Samuel Knight. Their headquarters were in a room over a stable at the bottom of Hough Hill, but later they moved to a large practice room adjoining the Roebuck public house. This room was originally built as a workshop for Mr. Charles Frost, a local builder and licensee of the nearby New Inn public house.

 By 1920 the majority of the bandsmen were elderly with a few young members and contained four brothers named Turner, four brothers named Dawson, three of the Knight family, three members named Sherratt, two members named Homer, and several members of the Heath and Pointon families.

 At this time there were two brass bands in the village, this one and a smaller band connected to the Primitive Methodist Chapel, which held practice meetings in a cottage in St. Anne's Vale.

In 1930 the village band decided to find new headquarters away from licensed premises, and at this time the Norton Silver Band who had their headquarters in an ex-Army hut in the village of Norton disbanded, and their headquarters put up for sale. The hut was purchased by the Brown Edge band and was erected on a plot of land in High Lane, near to the Sytch, which had been leased to them by Mr. Sampson Bratt. Some of the members of the former Norton Silver band joined the band at Brown Edge and the rejuvenated band was in great demand during the summer months with engagements nearly every Saturday afternoon. On Christmas and Boxing Day mornings, the band used to tour the village playing carols and hymn tunes, and collecting funds for the band.

After the war interest in the band was low, and gradually it ceased to function. In 1947 the wooden band room was sold and the assets of the band were distributed amongst the remaining members.

Until the coming of the railway, there was no post office in Endon, and letters were directed through Leek. However by 1876 the village boasted a post office superintendent by no less a person than Noah Baddeley. The letters through Stoke-on-Trent arrived at his office at 5-00 a.m. and were delivered to the houses in the district at 7-00 a.m. The last dispatched letters were taken out at 8-40 in the evening. In 1880 the pillar box on the highway near the Wesleyan Chapel was cleared at 8-45 p.m. This evening mail was collected by the mail van drawn by two horses en route from Leek to Stoke-on-Trent.

For these years the nearest telegraph office was at Leek but in 1890 telegrams could be sent from Milton. Noah Baddeley was also well known as the secretary to the well-dressing committee and as a bootmaker. When he died in 1915 at the age of eighty-one, it was said of him that 'almost to the last he retained all his old activity, even receiving the early morning mails as they arrived at his office.'

So the century came to its last decade with the Reverend James Badnall living in Lane End House, the Heaton family established and listed among the private residents. Perhaps one of the most significant developments among this class of people was the tendency to style their new homes as villas. Or were they following a style already established at Heaton villas? Thus we have Lancaster Villa, Eagle Villas, Platts Villas, Lincoln Villa, Fair View Villas, to say nothing of the residence of Mr. Samuel Thomas Timmis which was called Beauvale. However, Moss Cottage, Hallwater House and Sutton House remained, but surrounded by the new property built by people from the pottery towns, adding new surnames to the lists which had existed since the Middle Ages. Surely such names as Tennant, Watkin, Powell, Pinder and Grimwade were new to Endon. Perhaps this was the real golden age for Endon Village. A quiet rural village dominated by the agricultural community, yet tolerating a few townsfolk who could afford a somewhat better place. Accessibility was easy, yet not too convenient, and one could go readily to Leek or Hanley on a visit to town. Not all would find life easy, especially if they happened to be mill girls catching one of the early trains to Leek for a long day in one of the mills.

But the twentieth century had more in store. More houses, and more easily accessible routes to bring new residents and possibly an atmosphere of the pottery towns, in social terms at least. The railway declined and the roadway became wider. The canal was closed.

About 1914 the Potteries Electric Traction Company and a proprietor named Charles Knight ran buses from Hanley via Cobridge to Endon and Leek. This was followed by more intense activity in the 1920s when Henry Harding commenced a private service from Stockton Brook Station to Hanley via Abbey Hulton. The real challenge to the railways had begun. Sport was not far away from the thoughts of Endonians, the village having a soccer team which played on the fields now occupied by the new St. Luke's primary school. The cricket team played in Station Road before moving to a field near the Black Horse Hotel and finally to Stockton Brook. The pigeon fanciers of Brown Edge were to be seen at the Endon post office on Saturday afternoons during the summer having the time of arrival of their birds confirmed by the post office clock, which presumably satisfied everybody's requirements as a reliable time-piece. For many years during the 1920s the landlord at The Plough was Mr. Henry Brown, a dog breeder and judge of wire haired fox terriers. In the 1930s horse racing was promoted, from time to time in the Endon Valley between the village and Denford, but because it was low-lying the course suffered from floods after heavy rain. The prospect was abandoned. Considerable local attention was directed to this problem of flooding, especially in 1927 when headlines hit the Staffordshire Sentinel on Tuesday, July 12th: 'Havoc by storm and flood', 'Railway track washed away', 'Devastation at Endon and Stockton Brook', 'Worst in living memory'.

The newspaper continued 'Havoc has been caused in North Stafford-shire by two violent thunderstorms on Monday afternoon and evening. The first storm was the worst for many years; indeed, it is stated that there has been no local storm comparable in its destructive effects for the past eighty years.

Owing to the overflowing of the Pool at Stanley, and the consequent bursting of the banks of another pool at a lower level, devastation of an extraordinary scale was wrought in that area. A section of the permanent way on the Leek Branch of the L.M. & S. Railway was washed away for a distance of 200 yards, and train services on that line are suspended indefinitely.

From other parts of the district come reports of flooded railway tracks, roads transformed into rushing rivers several feet deep, and families washed out of their homes.

Houses were struck by lightning, and a number of fires caused.'

As with the Civil War and the Jacobite Rising, the ravages of war in 1914 and 1939 may have left the physical appearance of Endon outwardly unscathed, but the two wars left their marks in personal grief and sorrow. Men from the village went away and never came back and a memorial was erected to help later generations remember their sacrifice. The tablet bears the following names:

The Roll of Honour of the Men and Women of Endon with Stanley Parish who gave their lives in the two World Wars.

1914-1918

Pte James H. Harding	Pte. James Frost
2nd Lieut. Homer J. Harding	2nd Lieut. Arthur Green
Sapper Levi Harding	Pte. Thomas Scott
1st Lieut. Ernest Hulme	Capt. A. T. Scrivener
Gunner Reginald Oulsam	Pte. William A. Shardlow
Pte. James A. Bailey	Pte. Joseph Sheldon
Pte. Alfred Columbell	Pte. John Simcock
Sgt. Frank Ford	

1939-1945

Pte. Cyril Bailey	Pte. Robert Hann
Sapper Fred Berrisford	Signalman Anthony G. Johnson
Nurse Joan Coulter ,	Sapper Kenneth Mee
Q.A.I.M.N. S/R.	L/Cpl. Walter S. Stubbs
Guardsman Joseph Hancock	L.A.C. Arthur Titley
Guardsman William Hancock	Pte. William Watson

As if to show that the war was over and that the village should get down to its parish pump business after hostilities elsewhere had ceased, a parish meeting was called for November 5th, 1946 in the then Senior School, to discuss the 'Adoption of the Lighting and Watching Act'. Mr. G. W. Robson presided over a large assembly which was to discuss the placing of forty-five lamps throughout the district. Poles had already been placed in position and it was estimated that the expenditure involved would be covered at the cost of a sevenpenny rate. After a considerable discussion the resolution was rejected. Again in 1951 'It was resolved by the parish council that the West Midlands Electricity Board be requested to afford figures, on the basis of the scheme submitted to them, some few years back.' Again there was strong feeling that the introduction of street lighting would detract from the rural and remote image of the village, and that illumination was not wanted. Endon was not to be an extension of any large town. But the battle was lost and the streets were lit up in 1960.

Other development proposals have caused heartaches among the villagers, notably the large scale developments of housing on Endon Bank and, one which perhaps affects a wider public view, the route of the new highway through the valley. Whatever the outcome of these developments it would be more than tragic if villages like Endon were to lose their connection with an age we have almost lost. It has been voiced by many people closely connected with the work of U.N.E.S.C.O. that among the older nations in all five continents, the country whose people are most separated and detached from its early folk-lore, customs and heritage is England. This may have been caused by the early upheavals in the period of the Industrial Revolution, but it is perhaps as well that some people are determined, as they are in Endon, to maintain a village of a character which they regard as essentially English. It is to be hoped that the members of the newly created Staffordshire Moorlands District Council are sympathetic with these ideals.

References

[1] List of copyholders, Norton parish 1755. Records of the Old Nortonian Society 1952, p. 189.

[2] General and Commercial Directory of Staffordshire, 1818.

[3] White's Directory 1834.

[4] Norton Parish Tithe Map 1843, J.R.O., Lichfield.

[5] Ward, John: 'The History of the Borough of Stoke-on-Trent, 1843, pp. 175-177.

[6] Enumeration Sheet, Census Return 1851, Endon.

[7] White's Directory 1851. Also see Enumeration Sheets 1851, Census Endon.

[8] Census Return 1881.

[9] Records of the Old Nortonian Society, 1952. Leek Rural District Council.

Abbreviations

H.C.S.	Historical Collections of Staffordshire.
N.S.J.F.S.	North Staffordshire Journal of Field Studies.
T.N.S.F.C.	Transactions North Staffordshire Field Club.
V.C.H.	Victoria County History.

The Well   Endon

THE OLD ROAD TO ENDON - 1994 REPRINT

ADDENDA

Page 50   Hill Top Mission was sold by the Diocese of Lichfield. It is now a private house, although a part of the field nearest to Brown Edge was retained, perhaps to build a small mission at some future date.

Page 103 A number of documents relating to Lawn (or Laund) have come to light. These are at the moment in the possession of C.G.Perkin.

Page 104-5 The grave of John Daniel and his sister was demolished when the house Tall Ashes was built for Mr. Lidyard.

Page 177-8 The original hand written rules of Endon Friendly Society, dated 1820, with signatures and names of officers and members are at the moment in the possession of C.G.Perkin, along with the final receipts and records of the winding-up of the Society in 1913 - 1914, with the amounts received by each member.

Facsimile Edition printed by Heathland Printers, Leek, Staffordshire.

226